ACCLAIM FOR THE PAST WORKS OF CHARLES MARTIN

"Beautiful writing . . . offers hope and redemption without too-neat resolution."

—*Publishers Weekly* review of *Maggie*

"How is Charles Martin able to take mere words and breathe such vibrant life into them? Each character [in *Maggie*] is drawn with an artist's attention to detail, beauty and purpose. Readers won't want the story to end because that means leaving these lovable people who have become so much more than just a name in a book."

—inthelibraryreviews.net

". . . charming characters and twists that keep the pages turning."

—*Southern Living* regarding *When Crickets Cry*
Southern Living Book-of-the-Month selection, April 2006

"[*The Dead Don't Dance* is] an absorbing read for fans of faith-based fiction . . . [with] delightfully quirky characters . . . [who] are ingeniously imaginative creations."

—*Publishers Weekly*

"[In *When Crickets Cry*,] Martin has created highly developed characters, lifelike dialogue, and a well-crafted story."

—Christian Book Previews.com

"Martin spins an engaging story about healing and the triumph of love . . . Filled with delightful local color."

—*Publishers Weekly* regarding *Wrapped in Rain*

"[O]ne of the best books I've been asked to review, and certainly the best one this year!"

—bestfiction.tripod.com regarding *When Crickets Cry*

Maggie

A NOVEL

CHARLES MARTIN

THOMAS NELSON
Since 1798

NASHVILLE   DALLAS   MEXICO CITY   RIO DE JANEIRO

Published in Nashville, Tennessee by Thomas Nelson. Thomas Nelson is a registered trademark of Thomas Nelson, Inc.

Thomas Nelson, Inc. titles may be purchased in bulk for educational, business, fund-raising, or sales promotional use. For information, please e-mail SpecialMarkets@ThomasNelson.com.

Scripture quotations are from the New King James Version®, © 1979, 1980, 1982 by Thomas Nelson, Inc., Publishers.

Publisher's Note: This novel is a work of fiction. Names, characters, places, and incidents are either products of the author's imagination or used fictitiously. All characters are fictional, and any similarity to people living or dead is purely coincidental.

Library of Congress Cataloging-in-Publication Data

Martin, Charles, 1969–
  Maggie / Charles Martin.
    p. cm.
  ISBN 10: 1-59554-055-5 (pbk.)
  ISBN 13: 978-1-59554-055-3 (pbk.)
  1. South Carolina—Fiction. I. Title.
  PS3613.A7778M34 2006

                                        2006004522

Printed in the United States of America
HB 05.19.2020

FOR CHRISTY
—*who stood beside me and believed.*

chapter one

SOMETIME BEFORE DAYLIGHT, I HEARD IT. INCHES
from my face, it sounded like a mouse sliding a saltine across a
wooden floor. Seconds later, it sounded like the horn section of
a symphony, tuning up. Then like cat purring lazily in the sun.
And finally, like a woman who'd been in a coma for several
months and was regaining the muscle tone she'd lost in her
throat.

It was one of my favorite sounds—the sound of sweet
dreams, the sound of contentedness, the sound of my wife
next to me—the sound of Maggie sleeping. At that moment,
she was sacked out and snoring like a sailor. I lay with my eyes
closed, playing possum, listening and smiling because she'd
die if she knew. *"I don't snore!"* Unconsciously, I had paced my
breathing with hers, making sure to inhale deeply enough and

to exhale slowly enough.

Moonlight filled our bedroom with a hazy grayish-blue, telling me the moon was high, full, and shining like a Milky Way spotlight on Maggie. I watched her, lingered there, and milked the Milky Way. Most nights she flopped around like a fish tossed up on the beach; then, on into morning, she'd settle down a bit and start spreading out horizontally. Now she lay sprawled across the bed like a snow angel, hogging all corners as if she'd grown accustomed to having the bed to herself. My left cheek barely hung on the edge of the mattress, and not a single square inch of sheet covered me, but I could not have cared less. If I ever do, somebody ought to beat me into next week. Her feet told me she was wearing socks, her neck told me she was wearing Eternity, and her arms told me she was wearing me.

All the world was right.

Around four in the morning, Maggie flung herself sideways, stretched like Blue, and then reencircled me like an octopus. When she settled, her hair draped across my chest like tentacles, mingling into me. Maggie's hair had grown well past her shoulders. Long and shiny, it was made for shampoo commercials. Mine, because of the coming summer heat and what would be long hours atop the tractor, was cropped relatively close, exposing my neck to the sun, dust, and dirt. When Maggie cut it, she had nodded in approval, reminding me that my grandfather would have nodded too.

She tucked her nose up close to mine, where her breath filled my lungs either before or after mine had filled hers. Her chest rose and fell in an easy rhythm, and her skin was warm. Making sure she could not be uprooted, she hooked her right leg around mine like a boat anchor, stretched her right arm across me like a bowline, and then drove her right hand into the mattress like a tent peg.

Reluctantly I untangled myself and slid out from beneath the pegs. I pulled the covers back over her bare shoulders, tucked the hair behind her ear, and walked to the kitchen to put on the percolator. Blue followed, stretched, and stood at the screen door, his nose pressed against the latch. He knew how to flip it open, but with Maggie around he'd grown lazy and now waited on me with an air of expectation.

I looked at him, and his ears dropped. I pointed toward the bedroom. "Hey, pal, *she* was in the coma. Not you. Let your own self out."

Blue whined, nosed up the latch, and disappeared off the porch.

While the percolator coughed and sputtered—the sweet sounds of my addiction—I stepped out onto the porch under a clear sky and onto the stage of my life. Judging from the thick black figures silhouetted against the dawning skyline, several turkeys roosted in the trees that lined the river and towered above our son's grave. I couldn't see it, but unless something really bad had happened to the world, the river flowed silently beyond those trees, filling the earth—or at least most of South Carolina, and me—with life.

Before me spread the rows of corn, silent sentinels, six feet tall and swaying in rhythmic, military unison under the quiet whisper of the spring breeze. As my eyes adjusted, ten thousand shades of black reflected off the cornstalks like slender hands waving toward heaven. Papa once told me that farmers are the choir conductors for heaven. It took me a few years and several hundred hours atop the tractor to understand what he meant.

From my perch on the porch, I could almost read the brass plaque that squatted below the roses—my testament to

Maggie's "Yard of the Year." I stared and shook my head because I was smiling at a post-coma memory. Something that, at one time, I wasn't sure I'd have again.

The evidence that Maggie was alive, breathing, and back home spread around our house like an English garden. Camellias, roses, gardenias, wisteria, iris, anthurium, agapanthus, and even orchids bloomed in every patch of earth not covered by grass, porch, stepping-stone, or house.

I sniffed the air and walked to the side of the porch, looking over the tips of the cotton rows that had come up thick and bulbous. It was only May; it'd be late June before we saw any blooms. And, like everything in life, that depended on the rain. Waist-high now, they would be the last plants to show their color. And I'm not talking about the cotton; I'm talking about the little white flower that precedes the cotton, telling all the word that the white gold is coming, spring is over, summer has arrived, and the hard work is about to start. Judging by the buds, we were still a couple of weeks off.

I jumped, grabbed the porch rafter, and stood hanging and swaying from the truss. I looked at the cotton primed to erupt and paint the world with white flowers, and I marveled at the life I lived. Each day of my existence amazed me. I pulled up a couple of times, remembered that I wasn't as young as I'd once been, hopped down, skirted around the roses, and then stepped into the cotton—walking up one row and down another. The bolls slapped my thighs while the sandy dirt sifted up through my toes, reminding me of Charleston and our month at the beach. I looked up, closed my eyes—the stars still shining in my mind—stretched my hands across the heavens, and filled my chest with the night—yawning in his pasture was a farmer's delight.

Between the buds, the many and various flowers lighting up

the house, and the smile that spread daily across Maggie's face, I noticed someone unusual, an old invisible friend, as I walked around my house. He had moved out just after delivery, but once he heard she'd come home, he did too. He had returned slowly—a flash here, a sound there. He'd been back a week when I finally cornered him in the barn. When I asked him to stay, he moved his things into the space above the ceiling fan and made his bed on the rafters.

I tried to make him feel welcome, because he brought with him the smell of gardenias and magnolia blooms, hot baths, cool sweat, and gut-busting laughter. He routinely tap-danced on the roof, sang in the rain, listened to Dean Martin and Frank Sinatra all hours of the night, and laughed for little to no reason. Each day, he'd flutter down off the rafters, or the ceiling fan where he enjoyed multiple revolutions, and light on Maggie's shoulder. Pretty soon, he went wherever she did. And that was good.

I walked back to the house, pressed my nose against the window, and gazed at Maggie sprawled across the bed just a few feet away. Her eyes were moving back and forth behind her lids, and her right index finger looked like it was writing in cursive.

Yes, life had thrown us a curve, but nothing short of death would dim her desire to have a child. You could tell it in the way she had repainted the nursery, the way she ran her fingers along the teeth marks on the railing of our secondhand crib, and the way she tapped me on the shoulder in the middle of the night when her clock told her it was time.

I suppose she was like most women. Maggie dreamed of the delivery, of the excitement of getting to the hospital on time, of timing the contractions, of her pushing and me cradling her head and helping her count. Of looking down across her swollen tummy at the doctor's face as he waited for our child's head to appear through the canal. Despite the pain, the sweat, and the blood, she dreamed of hearing his or her first cry, of being handed our child with the umbilical cord still attached, of watching me cut the cord, and then, finally, of pressing him to her pounding chest and feeling him breathe, suckle, and pull at her with tiny, wrinkled, God-fashioned fingers. She dreamed of watching his eyes open and being the first person he saw. She dreamed of needing, being needed, and giving unselfishly—something she was good at.

But I knew that she, my simple complexity, and the dream didn't end there. She dreamed of pulling that wet, gooey, covered-in-white-paste kid—who no doubt looked a lot like me—off her sweating, flushed chest and of passing him to me—of extending him across space and time and placing him in my shaking arms. She dreamed of watching my face light up as I cradled the son or daughter we'd made—of giving me that part of herself, a second time.

For me, the desire for a child had grown over time. Maggie had planted the seed, watered it, and then waited. I first recognized it as my own desire, distinct from Maggie's, some twenty months ago. It was the moment I placed my son's casket in the dirt down by the river beneath the oak. It was a strange and new feeling. Something unexpected. I didn't know what to do with it.

Yes, I felt guilty—what parent wouldn't—but I also knew I wanted to try again. I wanted to be a dad, and I wanted Maggie to be a mom. I wanted us to share the ups, the downs, the hard times, and the great times. I wanted to build a fort with our son or daughter, play catch, go to the beach and dig in the sand, laugh, wrestle, go fishing, teach him how to whistle, how to drive a tractor, and yes, I wanted to walk her down the aisle.

I cracked open the screen door and crept inside. I tiptoed

down the hallway, making the floors creak, sat in my chair, pulled the door shut, and picked up my pencil. The single lightbulb fell out of the seams in the tongue-and-groove pine ceiling, dangling from a fraying cord a foot above my head.

My writing closet was exactly four inches wider than I on each side, and if I scooted my chair up to the bottom shelf, the door just shut behind me. I fell into my writing position, resting my head on my left hand and holding the pencil in my right.

Since Maggie woke up, I . . .

Wait. Stop.

Saying *Since Maggie woke up* amazes me still. Every time I say it, I think the clouds should part, a huge brass horn should descend, and God should give me five minutes to blow at the top of my lungs for all the world to hear before I shout, *"Hey, World! Maggie woke up!"*

Before me sat a three-hundred-page dilemma. Maggie had asked me to tell my story, and I had. From the night our son had died on August 15 to the moment she woke up on New Year's Day—some seventeen months ago. My sweaty palms rested on the pages as the two sides of me waged war. I stared at the words and knew the pictures I'd painted would reopen wounds that had not yet begun to heal. I also knew that opening those wounds would increase the sense of responsibility that she had yet to express but that was written all over her face every time we failed to talk about it.

On the other hand, I had never lied to Maggie about anything, and before me sat two versions.

Hers was the watered-down, G-rated version, which told enough of the story to satisfy her desire to know, and yet protected her from the R-rated version with all the ugly parts left in. The one on the right was the real story, the one I had written for myself—the director's take that would cut her to the core because it contained all my doubts and fears. I had written it because something deep inside me demanded that I rid my soul of the secrets that I kept there—those conversations with myself that I never voiced.

The discrepancies were simple: While I told her about the delivery and about our son's never crying a peep, I didn't mention her own screaming or my being crumpled in the corner covered in blood while the doctors worked to repair the damage to her body. While I told her about the funeral and Amos singing and the sun shining, I didn't tell her that I held the casket between my knees after we'd picked him up at the morgue, or that I buried the teddy bear with him, or that I had wished every day between then and the time she woke up and even some days since that Amos had just lowered my son down on top of me and covered us both.

While I did tell her about the fire I set in our dead cornfield, I did not explain the scar on my arm or how it got there. While I told her about watching movies with Bryce to pass the time, I did not tell her that there were nights I could not drive home afterward. And though I told her how I pulled Amos and Amanda out of the ditch that slippery, snowy night, I didn't say that I stood in the ice and snow and screamed at God, shaking my fist at heaven and daring Him to strike me down. Or that, when He didn't, I wished He had.

In Maggie's version, I told her about being in the hospital, how I had sat with her and talked with her. I told her that on most nights, when the halls were quiet, I'd rub her legs to keep the circulation going. I didn't mention that while the therapist had said ten minutes was all that was needed, I often massaged for hours. And I did not tell her that when Amanda came daily to change her gown, I helped so I could see my wife, touch her skin, and feel her warmth. I did not tell her how I bathed her, put socks on her feet when they were cold, held her hand beneath the sheets. I did not tell her that I slid my chair close to the bed and whispered in her ear, "Please come back to me."

And I didn't tell her that finally, for one reason or another, I had come to the place that, even if she never woke up, I could have lived without her—and now that memory, that ability to be alone, was maybe the greatest betrayal of all. I stared at my work and remembered something my grandfather said one night, "There's just one problem with pulling the wool over someone's eyes. And it surfaces whenever they take it off."

While I collected my nerve, both manuscripts had sat collecting dust. I had finished a week ago, but it had taken that long to muster enough gumption to do what I was about to do.

I pushed back from the desk, stacked the pages, and wrapped my version in a plastic grocery store bag. I knelt on the floor, opened my pocketknife, and pried up the single board that hid the cash box where Papa used to hide Nanny's jewelry when they went on vacation. It was about a foot square and locked relatively watertight. I lifted out the box, dusted it off, and flicked the lock. Inside I kept our birth certificates, the deed to the house, and a few other keepsakes. I laid the manuscript in the box, locked the lid, and slid the entire thing back into its safe place.

I licked my fingers so the bulb wouldn't burn me and twisted it off, listening to the sizzle of spit on lightbulb. I walked into our bedroom and leaned against the door frame, watching my wife sleep wrinkle-free and without torment.

I tiptoed across the floor and gently pushed her Audrey Hepburn hair out of her Bette Davis eyes. I knelt next to the bed and watched her. If she had any idea I was there, she didn't show it.

I whispered, "Maggie," and waited. No response. I whispered

again. Finally I touched her cheek and said, "Honey?" She swatted my hand like a mosquito and flopped to the other side of the bed as if the bugs weren't biting over there.

And then I did something I'd never done before. I lied to Maggie. I laid her version on her bedside table, set a cup of coffee down on top, and crept out. Once an early riser, Maggie had awakened from the coma and found her internal clock reset. Now she was happy to sleep till ten thirty. Knowing that, I was pretty much assured that the coffee would be good and cold by then—just the way she liked it.

I slipped on my jeans and hat, made sure my writing closet was locked, and stepped into my boots. Then I hopped onto my tractor and dropped the harrow into the ground—something I'd seen my grandfather do five hundred times.

With a slight breeze cooling my face, I turned around in my seat, saw the deep cuts in the soil, and remembered something else Papa once told me. He had his pocketknife in one hand, scraping the fingernails of the other.

"Funny thing about farming . . ." He'd pointed out across the field with the tip of his knife. "To grow anything new, you've got to cut the soil and get rid of what remains of the old. I imagine if the earth could speak, it would tell us that it doesn't like that too much." He shrugged. "But life is like that. The past fertilizes the future." He snapped his knife closed, slid it into his front pocket, and stared at me with no expression. "Problem is, we have a tendency to forget that."

chapter two

WHEN MAGGIE OPENED HER EYES THAT NEW YEAR'S
Day some seventeen months ago, I felt like I could see again.
The fog lifted off my soul, and for the first time since our son
had died and she had gone to sleep—some four months, sixteen days, eighteen hours, and nineteen minutes earlier—I
took a breath deep enough to fill both my lungs.

I knelt and placed her hand in mine, and the tears and
tremors I'd been holding back bubbled up and out. In truth,
I cried like a baby. She did too. A long time passed, but neither of us spoke. At least not with words. Besides, just what
would I say? Where would I begin?

Finally she managed a hoarse whisper. "Missed you."

It took me a second. "Me too."

She swallowed and tilted her head. "How long?"

I shrugged and swallowed hard again, wanting to break it to her gently. "Couple of months." She patted the bed, then shook her head, the tears spilling down the lines of her nose. "I knew when you were here. Each time. I tried to wake up, but . . ."

She ran her fingers across the scar on my arm, a puzzled look appeared on her face, and she started to speak again.

I stopped her. "Shhh . . ." I placed my finger to her lips, and she reached for me.

But before I could hold her and let her hold me, I had to tell her. She had to know. "Honey . . . he didn't . . . I mean . . ."

She nodded. "I know." The lines around her eyes slanted downward, the need showing. "Where?"

I nodded out the hospital window in the general direction of our farm. "Down by the river." I bit my lip, trying to gauge her response. "Amos and I . . . we . . ."

She reached again, and this time I let her pull me toward her, her breath washing my face, her eyes searching mine. Her mind was working hard to get the words out of her mouth. "You forgive me?"

I shook my head. "Maggs . . . there's nothing to forgive."

She placed her hand behind my head, pressed my forehead to hers, and I knew that we were still "us."

Two weeks later, they told me I could take her home. Word spread, and even staff members who weren't scheduled to work packed the hallways to see her off and wish us well. Their faces and eyes suggested both a homecoming and a sending off. I'd have taken either one.

I pulled the truck around in front of the hospital, pushed the wheelchair into her hospital room, and for the first time since she woke up, wore something other than running shoes to the hospital. Maggie took one look at my feet and said, "Nice boots." She never did miss much.

"Blue picked them out."

She sat in the chair. "How's Pinky like them?"

"'Bout the same."

To much applause and too many cameras, I wheeled her out of the hospital and up to the side of an orange truck she'd never seen. She eyed the truck, then me, but didn't say a word until we drove off. She looked from hood ornament to tailgate and said, "Where'd you get this . . . thing?"

"Jake's."

She put her feet up on the dashboard, looked again at mine, and then leaned back against the headrest. "You mean . . ." She paused for effect. "Jake's Jalopy?"

I nodded.

She shook her head and reached for my hand. "I really am married to the Marlboro man."

I tried not to take my eyes off the road and not to smile. I almost managed.

My friend Amos, in his sergeant's stripes and black SWAT T-shirt, escorted us home in his Crown Vic—lights flashing, siren blaring. We ran all three stoplights between there and here. When we passed over Johnson's Ferry and by Pastor John's church, I didn't say a word. Maggs and I had a lot of talking to do, but neither of these was the place to begin. We came into the drive, and I circled the house around back.

Maggie put her hand on mine and nodded toward the big oak down at the river.

That'd be a good place to start.

I parked the truck in the shade and helped her out, and she stood next to the grave, propped between me on one side and her cane on the other. She knelt on the grave and kissed the stone-cold face of her son. Maggie's tears trickled off her face and filled the carved granite letters. When they mixed with the dust and dirt on the grave, she dipped the tip of her finger on the drops and traced the shape of a heart like she would on a fogged-up bathroom window. I think she'd wanted to do that for a long time.

We walked into the house and by the nursery door, where she just leaned against the frame and looked inside. She stood there a long time, then wandered through the rest of the house, saw my drum on the mantel, read some of the letters from my students. Then she walked to the barn, sat down in the middle of Pinky's stall, and laughed for an hour while Pinky and twelve little pigs all vied for a scratch between the ears. It was glorious, smelly fun.

It didn't take me long to figure out that we were two people on two totally different schedules. She was used to sleeping twenty-four hours a day, and I had grown used to sleeping only three to four hours a night. I also found that she wanted to be near me, my hand on hers, hers on mine, asleep on my chest, whatever—she didn't let me out of her sight. And that was just fine with me.

MAGGIE HAD CREATED QUITE A STIR IN THE MEDIA WORLD. I held the reporters at bay, but sometime in the first week of February they found us. Tucked away in our seclusion and protective bubble, the media attention became pretty intense. Everybody wanted Maggie's story. Finally I called in Mr. Clean, aka Amos, and we brought all the reporters onto the back porch and gave a group interview that lasted about three hours.

Blue lay instinctively at Maggie's feet and bared his teeth while Amos controlled the crowd and questions. When Maggie got tired, I gave him the nod, and he started ushering people and cameras off the porch. Given the size of Amos's biceps and the way his shirt looked shrink-wrapped around his torso, nobody argued. That night we watched ourselves on the six o'clock news, and that weekend we watched an hour-long special in Amos's den along with Amanda—his wife—and Li'l Dylan, who had taken a liking to sitting in my lap.

The next morning, I left Maggie sleeping and drove up the road to the long-since-closed drive-in movie theater that was now home to our reclusive, multimillionaire neighbor, Bryce. I hadn't seen him for about a month, but that wasn't unusual. Bryce didn't keep time like everybody else.

Finding no sign of him, I picked up a paper in Walterboro, filled up the tank, and drove home. When I saw our picture on the front page of the lifestyle section, I shoved the paper below the seat and figured we'd had about enough of our own story. Maybe Maggie could use a few days at the ocean.

We drove to Charleston, where I rented a house on the water for a week. When the owner saw Maggie, his bottom jaw dropped. In a European accent I couldn't place, he said, "Momma, come quick."

An older, baggy woman came to the door, wrapped in a shawl and loose-fitting slippers. Her eyes grew wide, and she said, "Oh my, it's . . . Miracle Maggie."

That was the first time we'd heard anyone call her that.

The people were so blown away by Maggie's story that they gave us the top-floor suite for free. Every morning when we woke, the owner would cook us eggs, toast, jam, and strong coffee. We stretched a week into a month, and between midnight walks on the beach and that woman's cooking, Maggie found her sea legs. By the time we left, her cane was collecting dust in the corner.

Our second week there, we went to a famous seafood restaurant not too far from the water. For decades all kinds of famous people had frequented the place, and when they did, the owner nailed a bronze tag at the seat to let later patrons know who had sat there before them. He put me in Pat Conroy's seat.

Just before we left, the owner approached us, held up a shiny bronze tag, and asked, "Do you mind?"

I smiled and shook my head, and we watched as he nailed MAGGIE STYLES into place. Eyeing his handiwork, he brushed it off, turned, and said, "Please come back."

We walked home through the historic district, returning to our room about midnight. Maggie propped one foot up on the sink and began painting her toenails.

I picked up a magazine. "You know, I'm pretty good at that."

She eyed her pinky toe. "Uh-huh."

I stepped out onto the balcony, reading by flashlight when something metal clamored into the sink, followed by a single scream. I poked my head in and found her leaning in close to the mirror, studying the top of her head. She frowned and dug through her hair with the tips of her fingers like a mother monkey with her young. Then she stopped dead, pulled apart her hair like a curtain, and looked at me. "Is that what I think it is?"

"What?"

She rolled her eyes upward. "That!"

I stepped toward the sink and looked at Maggie's hair under the light. "Ahhh . . ." I fingered out the single gray hair and plucked it.

"Ouch!" she said, eyes narrowing. I held up the hair and was about to say something cute, but she held up a finger and said, "Not one word, Dylan Styles."

Yes, ma'am.

For two more weeks, we strolled the streets, rode in horse-drawn carriages, and somewhere in there began swaying to the same rhythm. Somewhere in there, we started walking in sync.

WHEN WE GOT HOME FROM THE OCEAN IN THE FIRST WEEK of March, we walked down to our son's grave site, and there we heard the pipes. Bryce appeared, decked out in full military regalia, and stood blowing till his face looked like a spark plug. Maggie walked over and kissed him on the cheek, and with tear stained freckles, he faded away down the riverside.

We walked back to the house, and parked in the drive sat a brand-new red Massey Ferguson tractor. We walked around it like it was a snake, then decided it wouldn't bite us, and better yet nobody would accuse us of stealing it. Somebody had tied a case's worth of empty Old Milwaukee cans to the back and hung a sign from the rear of the seat that read JUST WOKE UP. On the front, an airbrushed sign read MAGGIE LOVES DYLAN. Corny, yes, but who am I to change Bryce? We spent most of the next day on that tractor, and Maggie drove the entire time.

Life in Digger had returned to some sort of normalcy. That is, if anything in Digger was ever normal. Love had returned. Smiles cracked the faces of once-cold hearts. And me? I could smell gardenias even when they weren't blooming, and seldom a day passed that I didn't walk to the river and palm the acorns and dirt off my son's tombstone.

chapter three

By mid-March, much of Maggie's strength had returned. As had her green thumb. Propped up on the front porch swing, she spent an entire morning sketching an aerial view of the house and designing the yard layout. The next morning, with plan in hand, she tugged on my arm, batted those trademark eyes, and said, "I'd like to buy a few plants for the yard."

She flashed her design, and I knew instinctively that the next step in this parade would be an expensive one. I also knew occupying her hands would free up her mind, giving her time to work through two hurdles we had yet to address. The first was children, and whether or not we could ever have one of our own. The second was trying to explain to Maggie what I'd done for four and a half months while she lay sleeping.

I looked at the yard, where I'd let weeds take over, then back at Maggie. "A *few* plants?"

She arched her eyebrows and said with a sneaky smile, "Well, maybe more than a few."

She pulled on a tank top, stepped into an old pair of bib overalls, laced up her running shoes, and stuffed her hair under a baseball cap. When Blue and I got in the truck, she was unconsciously tapping her foot and making notes on her list.

We reached the nursery and grabbed two flatbed carts and the assistance of a young guy with a "Can I help you?" look pasted across his face. Midway through the first greenhouse, I had serious déjà vu. Toward the end of the aisle, I figured it out. The wholesale baby outlet. Although this little trip promised to cost even more. And just as I had in the baby store, somewhere down the second aisle I quit counting and just said, "Honey, I think whatever that is looks great, and we probably need a couple of those."

She rolled her eyes, stuck her pencil up into her baseball cap, and put her hand on her hip. "You're not helping me."

To say she was task-oriented would be an understatement. Chances were good that if she kept at this current pace, we'd be putting plants in the ground by flashlight. And I didn't care. My grandfather had lived by a pretty simple philosophy that made good sense to me—*Happy wife, happy life.*

Sweat had begun to bead on her top lip, and an *I'm thinking* wrinkle had creased the skin between her eyes. The ripple effects of the coma had been many, but it had done little to dampen her intensity.

I prodded her. "No, seriously, we probably need a few more of those."

She pointed a crooked, double-jointed finger in my face and said, "You want to end up on the couch?"

"Only if you're there."

She turned and kept counting flowers. "Don't get your hopes up."

"Yeah." I spread out my arms and yawned. "That whole snow-angel thing probably wouldn't work too well on the couch."

She cracked a smirk, picked up a handful of dirt from a nearby pot, and threw it at me.

Unfazed, our young assistant smiled and held up every plant like a true professional. With each one, Maggie stuffed her pencil behind her ear and weighed the look of the plant, the color, the size, and the cost. Several times she put back a perfectly good plant because the price was too high.

I picked up on her process and sensed her growing disappointment at the expense. I could see the high prices were quickly diminishing her idea of what our yard would look like. She had come in here thinking Martha Stewart's garden and was walking out thinking Charlie Brown's Christmas tree. So I backtracked to pick up what she'd passed over. When I reappeared, she looked at me and whispered, "Dylan, we can't afford all that."

I looked at the cart. "You're right, but I'm married to a woman who spends twenty dollars on a Christmas tree and a hundred and fifty on lights."

Our assistant laughed and then, seeing we needed a minute alone, excused himself and disappeared toward a huge greenhouse at the back of the property.

"Maggs," I whispered, "I don't care what they cost, because—"

I looked at her. She had regained some of the muscle she'd lost in the hospital, and the chiseled tone in her face and jaw had returned. Her overalls were faded and baggy, but they couldn't hide her strong shoulders, lean arms, the way the sweat beaded on her temples and just in front of her ears, and the penetrating depth of her eyes. Maggie was still that complexity that found meaning and expression between extremes, and all that beauty was just starting to bubble back up to the surface. Like the flowers she tended, my wife was full of buds and on the verge of exploding with color.

"But, Dylan . . ."

Blue circled around us, wagging his tail.

"It's all right. Really."

"But how?"

"'Cause at the end of the day"—I held up my hands, dirty and green from loading pots—"we're living . . . and life is thick."

Our assistant returned, leading an older man who wore a straw hat with a hole in the brim. "This is Mr. Wilson, my boss."

The man extended his hand. "Merle, all my customers call me Merle."

Maggie turned, tried to wipe her eyes without being seen, and stood behind me.

"Hello, sir. I'm Dylan, and this is my wife, Ma—"

"I know who you are. I seen the papers." He smiled and blinked several times, then pointed around the nursery. "Anything you want, at my cost. And if you'd like, come with me."

He led us to an enormous greenhouse out back where it looked as though he did his own seeding and potting. The place was overgrown with mature plants. "This is where I bring some of my best customers and those folks who really know and love plants."

Maggie stepped inside, eyed the rows of his well-kept secret, and sucked in a breath of air large enough for a woman three times her size. When her head and shoulders slowly lifted, it looked as if someone had shoved an air hose into her spine and filled her up.

I extended my hand. "Thank you, sir."

He nodded and stepped backward out the door. "Jes' holler, if'n you need anything."

We filled six carts that would later require four trips in my truck to haul it all back to the house. Eventually, Merle just let me borrow his mulch trailer, which on the last trip I had them fill with about eight cubic yards of potting soil and mulch. I returned the trailer, then found him at the register so I could pay our bill.

While he totaled it, I noticed a pink orchid stretched out across the counter. "How much for the orchid?"

He smiled, cleared out the calculator, spat a stream of dark juice into a can behind him, and said, "Follow me." We walked around the back of the property, and he led me into a humid greenhouse filled entirely with orchids. "These are my favorites," he said. "I don't usually let customers in here, but . . . again, at my cost—whatever you want."

There must have been two hundred plants. As Merle explained the story behind several of them and told how to care for them, I made mental notes. When he finished, I bought fourteen. He totaled my order and laughed like a man who knew the pleasure of dirt beneath his fingernails. He followed me home in his van so the wind wouldn't damage the orchid buds, which were just days from opening.

I thanked him again, carried the orchids into the house, and then found Maggie out between the house and the barn surrounded by her plants. She was holding a watering hose set on high, and the spray spread out into a wide fan that was doing a pretty good job of soaking everything we'd just bought. I tipped back my hat and sat on the front porch steps, trying to estimate the number of planting hours I had coming.

She clamped the hose off and said, "Honey, how much did all this cost?"

I smiled and stuffed the receipt back into my pocket. "Let's just say we won't be going back to New York City anytime soon."

Her jaw dropped. "That much?" Then she smiled, looked at her plants, and said, "Well, this is better than *Riverdance.*"

I scratched Blue's head and laughed. "Honey, you're weird."

She nodded, and then a sneaky look stole into her eyes. I tried to jump out of reach, but I slipped on the steps, tripped over Blue, and landed on the grass face-first. Maggie unclamped the hose and doused me in about three gallons of well water. By the time I wrestled myself free of Blue and out of the stream, Maggie was on top of me and showering my head with her fire hose. I grabbed her by the pant leg and wrestled the hose free.

When she realized she was about to get a taste of her own medicine, she howled, "Dylan Styles! I do not want to get wet!" But it was too late, and she didn't really mean it anyway. I held her by the bibs and poured ten seconds' worth of egg-smelling water down the back of her bibs. She squealed at the feel of cold water that had come up from almost six hundred feet below-ground and was now spilling out the bottoms of her pant legs.

It took us the entire next day just to set the plants where she wanted them, and another three to get them in the ground. The day after we finished, I drove to the hardware store and had a bronze plaque made that read YARD OF THE YEAR.

chapter four

AFTER TWO DAYS IN LABOR AND ONLY MOMENTS before delivering our son, Maggie's cheeks had become flushed as she lay in bed. She'd clenched my hand, watching the contractions under the haze of the epidural, and I watched her. I remember thinking that there in that place, draped in sweat, exhaustion, and the giddiness of expectation, Maggie had never seemed more alive.

Moments later she opened her soul and pushed for what seemed like hours. Physically spent, defying what I thought were the laws of physics, she did what only she could do, and then, as if his universe somehow collided with ours, he appeared. The doctor caught him, there was a gush of liquid, and the doctor never even hesitated. He rushed him to the table, spread him like a lab experiment, and started to work.

That's when the smile left Maggie's face. Blazing only seconds before, it drained out of her like light from a candle that
had burned out its own wick. It dimmed, sputtered, and
snuffed itself out. Only the trail of smoke and the threat of hot
wax remained.

Maggie had never held him. She had never held her own
son. Wide-eyed yet afraid to breathe, she'd watched as they
failed to revive him. Then she watched as they pulled the
sheet over his scrunched, blue head and recorded the time.
That was one of the last images she'd seen before she went to
sleep. The other was my face. When she woke up, he'd been
in the ground for months.

For Maggie, the desire to have a child was like that. It was
like breathing. It was as hardwired into her DNA as the sound
of her voice, the look in her eyes, and the touch of her skin.
Take it out and you might as well take the Maggie out of
Maggie. But it was that very desire that had put her in the
coma in the first place. I wondered how she'd see it from the
other side, but if anything, it seemed that the coma had made
the desire that much stronger. If I'd thought she was on a mission the last time, I had another thing coming.

Toward the end of March—having conquered the weeds—
we returned to the hospital for her first female checkup.

Dr. Frank Palmer was a good man. Midforties, father of several kids himself, he was always running between soccer, basket-
ball, or baseball games. His wife and his kids were his life. I
liked him and admired him for the way he went about his doc-
toring. Let's face it, people's privates are private for a reason,
but he spent his entire day invading other people's privacy.
Somehow he managed to do it with class and respect for his
patients. He treated Maggie like a niece or a cousin whom he
was both comfortable with and protective of.

Following her exam, Dr. Frank pulled me aside while Maggie
was getting dressed. He raised his eyebrows and lowered his
voice. "You might want to exercise some caution for a while in
what you two do together."

"Like?"

"Don't watch too many Hallmark movies, don't go to a baby
store anytime soon, try to keep her away from anything that
involves needing Kleenex, and—most importantly—try to
keep her thoughts on the future, not the past."

I looked down the hall. "But I don't understand. She's not
responsible."

He nodded. "We know that, but her emotions don't, and
until they level out, no power on earth can reason with them."

Dr. Frank referred us to a reproductive specialist whom he'd
heard was setting the world on fire. With referral in hand, we
drove to Charleston and saw a female doctor with more degrees
on the wall than anyone I'd ever met. Between medical school
and residency, she'd been in training for twenty years. And
judging from all the plaques and signed pictures of famous
people, I knew we'd come to the right place.

Her nurses ushered us into the examination room, which
was nice as examination rooms go. In fact, it was the nicest
one I'd ever been in. Of course, it had the cold, hard examination table with the stirrups tucked up along the sides, but it
also had some artwork on the walls, a few comfortable chairs,
and even a couch along one wall, suggesting that they had
worked to put their patients at ease.

As I was studying the room, a petite nurse with a ponytail so
tight it was pulling back her eyes set a small plastic cup on the
table next to me and said, "We'll need a sample." She pointed
over her shoulder at the small sliding door that led from this
room into what must have been a lab or something, and said,

"Just slide it through there when you're done." Then, as if she'd just asked me to record the time of day, she walked out and pulled the door shut behind her.

I eyed the cup. *Why would a fertility doctor need a urine sample from me? What good would that do them?* Confused and bewildered, I turned to Maggie, who, unable to hold it any longer, began laughing like a hyena. That was about the time I understood what the nurse meant when she said *sample.*

I looked around the room again and got a whole new understanding of the décor. I shook my head. "Is she serious?"

Maggie was laughing so hard she couldn't talk.

I pointed at the cup. "I'm not doing that."

Evidently Maggie had assumed I knew that when a couple visited a fertility doctor for help, the first test they performed was a sperm count. She slid the lock on the door, turned off the light, and sat down next to me. Swinging both her legs across mine, she hung her arms around my neck and pressed her forehead against mine.

"Hey, forget them. It's just me, and we can do this together. We're good at this."

I looked around, wiped the sweat off my face, and nodded. Sunlight broke through the cracks in the blinds and lit the dust particles that were floating through the air, settling on Maggie's skin as she changed out of her clothes. She slipped into a pink, flowery gown and then tiptoed across the room barefooted, took me by the hand, and led me back across the room to what I understood was the husband's couch. With my heart pounding inside my chest, the growing fear that someone was about to walk in that door, and my embarrassment evident, my wife did the one thing she alone could do. She made me forget about everyone but her, and she loved me.

A few minutes later, Maggie slid the sample into the lab and unlocked the door. I guess that sent a signal to the nurse, because she appeared pretty quickly after that. Maggie sat on the end of the table, knees together, her legs bouncing slightly on her toes. The nurse laid Maggie back on the table and prepped the equipment for the doctor, who walked in a few minutes later.

She was older, maybe midfifties, and looked serious. She extended her hand to me, then to Maggie. "Hi, I'm Dr. Madison."

She slid her hands into rubber gloves and, with little introduction, began a less-than-tender probing of Maggie's insides. When finished, she quickly inserted cameras into and over Maggie's tummy, taking pictures and studying the screen above her. Despite her limited bedside manner, I did not for a minute doubt her ability. She knew what she was doing and didn't have to prove anything to anyone. For that I was grateful.

Twenty minutes later, feeling a bit like two cattle in a stockyard, we followed the doctor into her office, where she sat across from us searching for an entry point into her results. After fifteen minutes of explanations and diagrams that I didn't really understand, I raised my hand and said, "Pardon me, ma'am, but what does all this mean?"

I could tell she was trying, but even Dr. Frank will tell you that medical school does not teach you how to deliver bad news. She closed her clipboard, took a deep breath, and let it out slowly. "I don't believe you'll ever—absent a miracle—have more children of your own."

She looked out the window, then back at us. "Sometimes I love my job. I really do. And sometimes, like today, I hate it, because despite all that I know and everything I've studied, modern medicine has its limitations."

Maggie swallowed, then asked, "What are my chances?"

Dr. Madison tossed her head slightly side to side. "One in several hundred thousand."

Shaking, Maggie stood, collected her purse, and waited for me to open the door.

Dr. Madison met us at the door and shook my hand. She looked at Maggie, who didn't look up. "I hope you beat the odds."

AS THAT MAY MELTED INTO JUNE, MAGGIE BOUGHT EVERY pregnancy book that Barnes & Noble offered or could order. Hoping to find something the doctors might have missed, one shred of hope, one single ray of light, she read everything she could get her hands on. Few of our activities or conversations weren't preoccupied with getting pregnant. Which was fine with me, but as the months ticked by, it took its toll on Maggie.

Each month, the start of her cycle was the hardest to take. And because cycles are just that, cyclical, I often knew it was coming. She'd return from the bathroom, retreat into the kitchen, pretend she was fretting over dinner, and try to hide the depression that crippled her face.

I'd order pizza, then take her by the waist and lead her into the den and onto the worn magnolia planks, where we'd imitate Nanny and Papa. Most nights, we'd dance into the morning. Our life felt like a school dance where the DJ kept starting and stopping the music without warning.

Some dances need to finish.

Then came August 15. His first birthday. We walked down to the graveside, Maggie carrying flowers. She knelt on the slab, wiped away the leaves and dirt, and kissed it. She placed the flowers on the grove, brushed her palm across his name, and painted our son's stone with her tears. Then, her lips just inches from his name, she whispered words that only a mother can.

She stood and slid her arm beneath mine, and we took a walk by the river. That's when she surprised me. She tugged on my arm and whispered, "Maybe . . . maybe we could . . . adopt."

I studied her face, her lips, the tilt of her head, and it didn't take a genius to see: just saying the word was painful. I'd thought of it months before, actually, but hadn't wanted to bring it up for fear of hurting her feelings.

But as I saw it, the hard part for us was actually making a baby, not wanting one or knowing what to do with it once we got it. So looking at the situation objectively, I thought adoption might be a good way to go. The more I thought about it, the more I liked the idea. Besides, how hard could it be? It certainly couldn't be any worse than what we were currently up against.

Or so I thought.

chapter five

CLASSES AT DIGGER JUNIOR COLLEGE STARTED THE
first week in September, bringing me seventy-five new oppor-
tunities. After a week of learning their names and adjusting
my seating charts, I drove with Maggie to the only adoption
agency listed in the Charleston phone book. The receptionist filled us in on the general stuff, then handed us a three-
inch stack of papers and said, "Fill these out and get them
back to us."

Doing so took us a little more than a month. They wanted
to know about our family, like, starting at Ellis Island, about
any family diseases and addictions, about our relationship,
our medical histories, how much money we made and how we
spent it. Since we didn't feel we had anything to hide, we
answered honestly. Maybe that was our mistake.

The written interview felt more invasive than Dr. Madison—but we didn't know what rigorous was until they called us in two weeks later for a follow-up interview.

The receptionist sat us down in front of two psychologists, Mr. Sawyer and Ms. Tungston, a man and a woman who looked like they had done this sort of thing before. They were looking at duplicate copies of our notebook of answers and, without much introduction, began firing questions. To say they were impersonal, sterile, and detached would be too kind.

Mr. Sawyer went first. Without looking up from his notebook, he pointed his pen at me and said, "How much money do you make?"

That struck me as an odd way to start, but okay, I could roll with the punches. "Well, sir," I said, waving my hand at the notebook in front of him, "I make $27,000 a year teaching and almost another twenty between my farming and the crop and pine-straw leases we have with—"

"So . . ." He studied his notes. "What do you think you'll make this year?"

"Well, sir, I'll make pretty close to, if not more than, what we've written there." I looked at Maggie and then back at him. "I think what you see there is a worst-case scenario based on—"

He shook his head. "Please understand, your income methods are rather unconventional and not too predictable by today's standards." He pointed to Ms. Tungston, then back to himself. "We, as a committee, want to avoid placing a child into a poverty situation."

We seemed to have a disconnect. I shook my head and almost spoke up when Maggie placed a restraining hand on my thigh.

"Sir, Dylan's a hard worker. You can look at him and tell that." She put her hand on my neck. "See, his neck's even red."

Neither smiled. Mr. Sawyer took off his glasses. "Just curious, how does a farmer end up with a Ph.D.?"

"My grandfather taught me to farm long before I took an interest in school." I shrugged. "Just something I wanted to do, sir."

Seeing an entry, Ms. Tungston turned her attention to Maggs. She tapped her notebook with her index finger. "Last year you spent four months in a coma after delivering a stillborn child?"

Maggie nodded and gulped. "He would have been a year old in August." She put her arm around me. "We named him after . . ."

Ms. Tungston returned to her notes. "Did the doctors ever determine a cause?"

Maggie shook her head. "No."

"Was your coma related to the pregnancy?"

I spoke up. "Ma'am, the delivery was pretty rough, and, well, Maggie . . . hemorrhaged pretty badly, and . . ."

The woman paused, and her voice softened. "We often encounter mothers who have lost a child." She waved around the room. "That's how they end up here. Dealing with that takes time." She looked at me and back to Maggs. "Have you two dealt with this issue in your life?"

Maggie sat up straight. "Ma'am, if you're talking about the loss of my son, and four months of my, our, life, I'm working on it." She held my hand, her knuckles turning white. "We're working on it. Every day. But some hurts need more than just Band-Aids."

Lord, I love my wife.

Maggie's eyes had begun to water. Deep down I was starting to get pretty angry, but I knew that anything even vaguely resembling a temper would kill our chances altogether. I bit my tongue and tried to smile. Maybe this was all part of the game, and they were just trying to see what we were made of.

Mr. Sawyer continued. "As for transportation, we place a premium on safety. I see that you drive a truck?" His heavy eyebrows bobbed above his glasses and said more than his mouth.

Thinking we could use a little levity in the conversation, I said, "Yep. And if that breaks, we own a pretty good tractor."

No one seemed to get the joke.

"You realize that federal law mandates that you cannot put a child-restraint seat in the front seat of a truck?"

I hadn't thought about it, but I was quick on my feet. "Sir, that's no problem. I know this guy in Digger, and he can get us pretty much whatever you think we should have." I threw it back at him. "What would you prefer?"

He didn't like my asking the question, but he tossed out an answer. "We approve of the safety ratings on most major minivans."

I nodded and said nothing as I felt the water rising around my neck.

Then they threw in the bomb.

He scanned his notebook with incredulity. "You understand that this process can be rather expensive?"

I nodded assuringly, hoping that he wasn't about to say what I hoped he wouldn't.

"Given your financials, are you sure that you can come up with the $38,000 down payment en route to the almost $45,000 you will need to complete the adoption process?"

I knew these numbers and had given them considerable thought, but, like many things lately, I'd kept them from Maggie. She had enough to worry about. She looked at me in disbelief as I spoke quickly and with confidence.

"I've already obtained approval for a loan that exceeds that amount. Won't be a problem."

He looked as though he half-believed me. "From a reputable lending institution?"

I knew this lingo. "A+."

He made a note and said, "And you can fax me that approval form . . ."

I nodded and waited for the next question, though in my mind I had yet to answer his last. This was not going as I'd planned.

He lowered his eyes. "What's your collateral?"

"The farm."

"And if you default, what happens to that child's home?"

"Sir, I've never defaulted on anything, and I don't intend to now." I paused and stuck out my hand. "I give you my word."

Evidently he didn't place the same value on my word that Maggs or Amos or my grandfather or I did.

I continued, "We only have one credit card; other than some plants, its balance is nearly zero. And our monthly payment on the truck is less than $300." I pointed proudly at the truck in the parking lot outside the window.

Mr. Sawyer's eyes followed my finger. "You're making payments on that vehicle?"

"Yes, sir, it says so . . ." I tried to point to the financial tab of his notebook, but he waved me off.

"Never mind."

I admit, prior to walking in there, I had visions of Little Orphan Annies bottled up in run-down shanties with cranky Miss Hannigans browbeating them while they waited to be rescued by another Daddy Warbucks. But halfway through this interview, I thought, *If this is what it takes to adopt a child, then you can just keep Annie and her little dog too.*

It's a good thing he couldn't hear me.

Abruptly, they both stood. He pointed at me, and she pointed at Maggs. Both said, "Follow me."

Maggie gripped my hand, and I could see the doubt growing. I whispered, "Hey, no big deal. Forget her. Just answer like you're talking to me, and we'll be fine."

She smiled, or tried to, and we went behind separate doors. Thirty minutes later we emerged from our respective rooms, and I could tell by the look on her face that her interrogation hadn't gone much better than mine.

We drove home in relative silence. Maggie chewed on a fingernail and pulled her knees up to her chest. I stared out the window and wrestled with how and where to get the money.

THE NEXT MORNING I LEFT MAGGS A NOTE THAT READ "Back before lunch." I drove to Jake's and pulled into the gate, and he walked out of the trailer, smiling. I could tell by the look on his face that he was already thinking about his steak dinner.

I hopped out of the truck, shook his hand, and skipped the small talk. Walking quickly, I led him down the row of six minivans. "Jake, I need one of these."

His roadside marquee, lit with dozens of tiny lightbulbs, towered above us. JAKE'S JALOPY flashed intermittently with FREE FINANCING and NO MONEY DOWN.

Jake smiled and tried to slow down the conversation. He laughed and leaned back, sticking out his growing belly, and said, "Needing to upgrade to the old family car, eh?" He had changed the picture of his family just below the flashing sign. They had added another child, and everyone's face was a little plumper. Business was good.

"Jake," I said, eyeing the options, "think of this more as a lateral move. I need to trade my truck for one of these."

"Well, let's see." He pulled a three-by-five-inch card from his shirt pocket and began scanning the years, models, and prices.

I knew that he knew all those by heart, so I stepped closer, placed the card back in his pocket, and said, "My wife needs a car to take our child to and from school, the grocery store, and wherever else he or she needs to go. What can I get for my truck?"

Jake bit his lip, eyed the truck, then eyed his vans. Then he looked back to the truck. "Looks like you've taken pretty good care of it, but the depreciation on something like that is—"

"Jake," I said, lifting a hand, "at last count I've sent seventeen people down here to buy a car from you."

"You have?"

I began rattling off the names. His eyes grew bigger.

"Guess you have." He walked up to a white Honda minivan that was about five years old. He kicked the tire. "This one was owned by a woman who didn't never go nowhere. It's only got 40,000 miles on it, got meticulous service records, ain't never been wrecked, comes with a factory extended warranty and the highest safety rating in the industry." He looked at me. "For you—your truck plus $5,000."

I shook my head. "Jake, you don't understand. Think"—I cut the air with my hand moving side to side—"horizontal." I stuffed my hands in my pockets and let out a deep breath. "Adoption ain't cheap."

He stepped back. "You guys adopting? I thought Maggie was pregnant."

"Jake, that didn't work out like we'd planned. Work with me here."

"Your truck plus $3,000." He was getting closer.

"My truck plus $1,500."

"Two thousand."

I stuck out my hand. "Deal, but I don't want it on paper. I want you to take my word for it, and on paper I want it to look like I traded my truck for this thing."

His face grew contorted. "I don't understand. You want me to take your word?"

I nodded and led him to the trailer. "I want you to trust me to drive out of here in your van with nothing but a promise that I'll bring you $2,000 cash within the week."

Jake looked at me like I'd lost my mind.

I sat back, crossed my arms, and nodded. "Deal?"

Jake let out an exasperated, disbelieving breath. "I appreciate what you've done for me, man, but I can't—"

"Jake," I said, "I need a favor. And yes, I will bring you cash on the barrelhead before the end of the week."

He looked at me, raised both eyebrows, and held out his hand, palm up. I was talking his language, and I knew now that we had gotten through all the baloney.

"You'll put it in my hand."

I tapped his palm with my index finger and then curled his fingers into a fist. "Right there."

Ten minutes later, I cranked the engine in the white minivan. The corner of my rearview mirror told me it was seventy-seven degrees, which was not unusual for South Carolina in November. God didn't usually turn on the AC till January. I waved my hand back and forth across the vent. *Maybe the soccer-mom mobile isn't that bad after all.*

I drove out of Jake's lot, looked in the rearview mirror, and saw my truck parked in the lot, waiting on the next buyer. I shook my head and spat out the window. *No one on the planet will ever love that truck as much as I did.*

I fastened my seat belt, adjusted the air vent, and concluded—AC or not—that Honda couldn't hold a candle to either my old '72 C-10 or the '76 Ford I was now leaving behind. But if it would help Maggie and me qualify in the eyes of the adoption committee, I'd drive a horse and buggy.

From Jake's I drove straight to the office of John Cagle-stock. His secretary, Lorraine, stepped from behind her desk to greet me. "Hi, Dylan. You don't usually just show up without calling. Everything okay?"

"I just wondered if I might have a word with John."

She waved me to a nearby chair. "Let me check." She walked into his office and then out again ten seconds later, followed by John.

"Hey, Dylan, come on in." He shut the door behind me, and we sat at the small conference table across from his desk. I had come to John with my hat in my hand, and he sensed it. He also knew that as the guy who overlooked Bryce McGregor's affairs, I knew exactly how much money John and his firm had made off Bryce. And it was millions. So, while I needed John, John also needed me. I was banking on this.

John also knew I'd never ask him or Bryce for anything that wasn't really important, so if I was here, looking as though I needed a favor, well . . . he could read the writing on the wall.

I cut to the chase. "John, Maggie and I are trying to adopt a child."

He nodded, wrapped his glasses behind his ears, and settled them on his nose.

"I need $38,000 as a down payment, $45,000 total, plus I need another $2,000 to pay off the minivan I just bought. I wondered if you could . . ."

John didn't even blink. He touched the phone next to him. "Lorraine, please bring me my checkbook. Personal."

Two seconds later, she appeared in his office and laid the checkbook on the table. Ignoring my protests, he opened the book, scribbled, signed, and then tore out a check, made out to me, for $40,000.

I shook my head. "John, I can't. That's not why I came here. I need a cosigner at the . . ."

John punched the button again and said, "Lorraine, get me Richard at American National."

Two minutes later our phone beeped, and Lorraine interrupted. "Sir, I'm putting him through now."

John put him on speakerphone. "Richard, how are you?"

"Good, John. How're things?"

"Listen, Richard, I need a favor."

"Anything."

John looked at me, then at the phone. "A good friend of mine is going to come see you about a loan. He doesn't have much to show, but he's good for it, and I'll guarantee it."

"You want your name on the paper?"

"Yes, and he needs the money pretty quickly."

"As in, how quickly?"

John looked at me, and I shrugged.

"How about an hour? He's trying to adopt a child and needs to show that he's good for it."

This sounded like something John had done before, and it sounded like Richard, whoever he was, was in a position to make it happen.

"I'll have the paperwork ready when he gets here. How much?"

John spoke without blinking. "Extend the line to fifty. He probably won't use it, but I want him to have some room."

Richard murmured, "Uh-huh," and I could hear him scribbling near the phone.

John continued, "Thanks, Richard. If you'll courier me my end, we'll take care of it this afternoon."

"Will do."

John punched the speakerphone button and hung up. He looked at me, and I wanted to kiss him.

I stood up and shook his hand. "Thanks, John."

He extended his personal check a last time. "I'm happy to loan it to you myself."

I patted him on the shoulder and turned toward the door. "Thanks, John. You've done enough already. We're grateful." I took a step back and whispered, "Oh, and, John?"

He raised his chin.

"I need this to be between us."

He nodded and drew a horizontal line through the air with both of his hands like an umpire calling a runner safe at home plate. "Whatever you wish."

I drove out of the lot, made one quick stop at the Baby Superstore, and then drove to American National, where Richard, the bank president, met me at the door. I signed several pieces of paper, and within three minutes he handed me a checkbook for my own line of credit. The entire transaction didn't take five minutes.

I thanked him, left the bank, and then drove an hour back to Charleston, where I walked into the adoption agency and handed the receptionist a check for $38,000. She eyed it and quietly disappeared.

When Mr. Sawyer, the male member of the inquisition committee, appeared from his office wearing a rather confused look, he held the check out in front of him as if it were hot.

He was about to say something when I pointed toward the door. "Sir, if you would just follow me."

I led him out the front door and clicked the unlock button

on my key fob twice just to make sure he heard the chirp. I opened both side doors, cranked the engine, turned the AC on "snow," and pointed at the brand-spanking-new baby seat buckled in tight and proper in the backseat.

He looked at the check, then the van, and then back to the check. "I will say I am very impressed, Dr. Styles, but . . ." His face turned cold again. "I've got to be honest with you. We were more than a bit concerned about your wife's answers during her individual interview."

I turned off the car and followed him back inside. "Sir?"

He wiped the beading sweat off his head. "Have you ever considered getting Maggie professional help?"

"Sir?"

He looked at me. "A psychologist."

"You sure we're talking about the same woman?"

Once again, my attempt at humor had little effect.

He lowered his voice and eyes. "A stillbirth can be one of the most difficult hurdles a woman ever faces. Your wife might need professional help to deal appropriately with the trauma of the past."

The sound of my breath exiting me was like the sound of a helium balloon that had been untied. "Sir, I just don't understand." Maybe it was the deer-in-the-headlights stare that convinced him I was serious.

He loosened his tie and squinted through the glare of the window. "Dr. Styles . . ."

"Dylan, please."

"Dylan, in our experience, the loss of a child isn't something a woman simply 'gets over.' It takes awhile. Many think that adopting will fill the empty place that remains." He squinted again and tossed his head slightly. "Our work with several thousand mothers over more than two decades leads us to this conclusion."

I stared at him, trying to make sense out of what he was saying.

He tried to help. "Dylan, mourning"—he let the word roll off his tongue and hang there for emphasis—"is healthy. It is something that needs to take place."

"Sir, I don't mean any disrespect, but I think that's what we've been doing."

He nodded as if I'd just proved his point. "You might let that run its course and then come back and see us."

"Sir, you'll not find a home with more love than ours." I was losing, and I knew it. "Or a mother with more love than Maggie. Sir, I know."

He nodded, "If you wish to withdraw your application, you could return in, say, six months and reapply." He paused. "The committee would look favorably upon this."

"Sir, I just don't think I can walk into my house right now and tell my wife that I've withdrawn our application. In football terms, that's called 'piling on.'"

He extended his hand. "I understand. We'll be in touch."

I followed him to the door. "Sir, do you know when that might be?"

He stood in the doorway to his office and grabbed a handful of yellow slips that noted his missed phone calls. He riffled through them, registering a few, then considered me again. "The committee has not completed its evaluation, but when we do, we'll notify you in writing."

Knowing that answer would not satisfy Maggie, I tried to ask respectfully. I took a slight step forward and half whispered, "Is that two weeks or two months?"

He placed a hand on the doorknob and lowered his voice. "Months."

He shut the door, and I walked out past the receptionist. I didn't feel like being friendly, but I said, "Ma'am," anyway.

She looked over her shoulder and whispered, "Sometimes it can take a year or more."

I walked out and, not being too experienced with the key fob, pressed the wrong button, setting off the Honda's alarm. It honked, flashed, and woke up everyone for four square blocks. The only benefit was seeing Mr. Sawyer glance out his window. At least he knew the minivan came well equipped.

I arrived home shortly after lunch. Maggie was sitting on the porch with a bowl of pole beans between her legs. She had tied a bandanna underneath her hair at the base of her neck. Scarlett O'Hara had nothing on my wife.

Maggie saw the van, then me driving it, and jumped off the steps. "Something wrong with the truck?"

I opened the door and left the car running. "Not that I know of."

She put her hands on her hips. The wrinkle appeared between her eyes, and her lips tightened. She went from restful to ballistic in less than a second. She almost shouted, "You traded your truck!?"

I backed up. This was not what I'd expected. "Yeah, honey. We need to show an appropriate vehicle to the adoption agency, and—"

Her eyes narrowed. "Forget them. You loved that truck."

"You're right, I did, but—"

"Don't 'but' me. We can't let those people run our lives. They don't know us. They can't even begin to understand what we've got."

The wind had picked up the ends of her scarf and was blowing them around the sides of her face, tickling her cheeks. Her face was flushed and sweaty.

I shrugged. "Maggs, there will always be other trucks." Deep down, I knew this was not true.

She looked inside the Honda, sat on the seat, ran her fingers through the ice-cold AC, smiled, raised her eyebrows, saw the baby seat buckled in the back, and said, "And to think I was just starting to like that orange . . . thing."

We drove around for an hour, letting her get used to the steering with no play, the quiet accelerator, the lumbar support, the seat heater, the surround sound, the side mirrors with turn-signal flashers, and the leather seats. By the time we turned back into the drive, I think she'd all but forgotten my truck.

THAT NIGHT, AMOS SAW THE WHITE VAN AND DROVE IN TO check on us. He rolled down his window and took off his sunglasses. "Got visitors?"

Maggie clutched her stomach and doubled over, laughing.

He looked at me. "What'd I say?"

I shook my head. "No visitors." I kicked at the dirt and lowered my voice. "It's . . . ummm . . . Maggie's new car."

Amos looked around. "Where's your—?" Then it hit him. He smiled, covered his mouth, and then burst out laughing.

"It's not funny," I said.

As he pulled out of the drive, he was still laughing.

The following week I started getting itchy to hear from the agency. I watched the mail. Then I thought about the possibility of that letter not saying what I hoped. I'd never been very good at getting the mail on a regular basis, but starting that night, I made a point of getting to the mailbox before Maggs. Every day.

chapter six

I COULDN'T HAVE BEEN MORE THAN TWELVE THE DAY
I came home from school with my hands stuffed in my pockets and tried to tell Papa why the underside of my eye was
black and puffy. No, I had not thrown the first punch, but that
didn't mean I wasn't guilty. The shiner proved that. I sat on
the front porch and struggled with my story while Papa
cleaned his fingernails.

He knelt down and stuck his face about two inches from
mine. "'Almost true' ain't true," he said.

"Well . . ."

He held up a finger and led me around back to his work-
shop in the barn, where he picked up a six-foot bricklayer's
level and held it up for me to see the bubble. He leveled it,
centering the bubble, then lifted one end just slightly, sending

the bubble off plumb. He raised his eyebrows. "It either is, or it isn't."

EVER SINCE WE'D FINISHED UP WITH THE ADOPTION COM-mittee, I'd been trying to tell Maggie more about my four and a half months alone. But every time I tried, I got tongue-tied and twisted, adding more confusion than resolution. So one cold January day—nearly a year to the day that I'd brought her home—Maggs finally just put her finger to my lips and said, "Shhh." She took me by the hand, led me to the linen closet, and opened the door.

There I found three empty shelves—the bottom of which was desk-high—a rickety chair not any wider than my butt, ten yellow pads, and a coffee cup filled with No. 2 pencils.

She sat me in the chair and said, "Just write it."

I looked at the blank page. "But I don't even know where to start."

She shrugged. "Start with us."

I scratched my head, and she shut the door behind me. I sat there for a long time trying to find an entry. Just how do you tell a story like that? I mean, seriously, where should I start? Despite her tough exterior, Maggie's insides were eggshell frag-ile. Should I tell her everything? Let her know the depth of my thinking? Every event? The extent of my loneliness? How far back down into that pit should I lead her? Should I tell her there were times when I looked up and saw no light at all?

Maggs was walking a narrow ridge as it was—it wouldn't take much to push her off either side. Her emotional ups and downs had been difficult to anticipate or gauge. Dr. Frank said this was "to be expected," and I should just act as if nothing were out of line. I told him it was kind of like riding Space

Mountain at Disney World—a roller coaster that ran along a track at breakneck speed in pitch-black darkness. Not even the driver knew when the turns or flips were coming. Maggie couldn't quite seem to get her emotions in check, and when she did express them, she couldn't control them. She'd cry at the drop of a hat and laugh when things weren't funny, and once she started crying, it took her awhile to stop.

If I told her the whole truth about the four months she spent asleep in that hospital bed, I ran the very real risk of making her feel responsible. And with all the pregnancy and adoption stuff running through her head, no amount of explaining would change that. So I looked at the blank page in my new "office" and wondered if it wouldn't be better for selected scenes in the director's cut to end up on the editing room floor. So I closed the door behind me and began writing half the truth, excusing it by saying I loved her.

I hadn't done much writing since grad school, so it took me awhile to remember how. As a teacher, I had always told my students that when you face a blank page, the hardest part is getting started. So to help yourself out, write the word *The* and you're on your way.

I took my own advice, and once I did, things I'd forgotten returned. *Some things are so simple.* I think that's partly the reason Maggie sent me in there. Yes, she wanted the story, but she knew me well enough to hold off in the hearing of it until she was certain that I'd emptied myself of it—proving that therapy comes in many forms. Maggie still knows a lot that I don't.

Every morning I wrote for an hour. Memories surfaced and flashed before my mind's eye—the hospital, tear stained nights, never-ending days, loneliness so deep I thought I would drown—and maybe sometimes I wanted to. I flung open the doors of my mind, dug them out of their holes where I'd hidden them from Maggie, and pretty soon ten pads turned into twenty, and all the beauty and wonder—and yes, even ugliness—of my life stared back at me. The mirror told no lies.

Spring arrived, I turned in my grades, and I could tell she was getting antsy about the amount of time I'd been spending in the closet. When she saw me installing a lock on the closet door, she looked at me as though I'd lost my mind. She put her hands on her hips and said, "Dylan Styles! What are you doing?"

"Making sure you're not tempted."

"Tempted to do what?"

"Read my book."

"But you're writing it for me."

"Right, but I know you. And the thought of those pages just sitting in there waiting to be read is more than your sneaky little fingers can stand." I waved the brass key in my hand, then hung it around my neck and smiled.

She huffed and shook her head. "I can't believe you'd accuse me of trying to read something before you gave it to me."

I smiled and slipped on my John Deere baseball cap. "Believe it."

"Couldn't I just read a chapter or something?"

I pulled the cap down to shade my eyes. "Nope."

She threw a couch pillow at me. "I don't like you anymore."

I walked out, laughing, and let the screen door slam behind me.

She bounced another pillow off the doorjamb and yelled, "You're on the couch!"

"Maybe," I said over my shoulder, "but I'm taking my book with me."

Later that night, I came home and found her trying to pick the lock. "Hi there," I said, waving the key.

She jumped and dropped the screwdriver. "Dang you, Dylan Styles!"

Remember that *Waltons* episode about the house fire, in which John Boy had to choose between rescuing his family and rescuing his notebooks? I remember watching him stand helplessly as the flames climbed out of his attic window, and how much emotional strength it took him to rewrite his novel in the following months. The fear of his fiery loss made an imprint on me. I didn't want a house fire to wreck several months' worth of effort. So I double-checked the lockbox, making sure it was watertight, and the "safe" in my house was just that.

IT HAD BEEN ELEVEN HOURS SINCE I LEFT MAGGIE THE counterfeit. Sitting on that tractor for the better part of a day while she stowed away in the house, reading, gave me plenty of time to regret my decision. I pulled the tractor out of gear and rolled to a stop. I pulled off my hat, wiped my brow, and studied the storm clouds as they thundered in the distance.

In my mind's eye, I imagined giving both copies to my grandfather. Palms up, he walked into the kitchen where the light was brighter and hefted each like Lady Justice—balancing the scales. Feeling the difference, he squinted an eye and asked me why I had not centered the bubble.

chapter seven

THE AFTERNOON SUN BORED INTO MY BACK, REMIND-
ing me that not even Hades was hotter than South Carolina
between May and the better part of September. It was as if God
held a magnifying glass as big as the state in between us and
the sun, cooking us from the inside out.

The mixture of sun and heat can do crazy things to a man, especially when he's sitting atop a tractor. Gives a man a lot of time to
reflect. Rambling along the rows, dust and diesel fumes rising up
all around me, I often thought about the slaves and how they
managed. I don't think you can farm in South Carolina and not
wrestle with that; it is what it is. Most of the irrigation ditches that
drain the low country were hand-dug by black men and their sons.

I have never been able to settle that in my mind. Where in
history did one man convince himself that he could buy

another? I understand the spoils of war and taking a man's house after you've fairly whipped him on the field of battle, but men aren't made to own one another. I don't care if I owned all the tea in China; I could no more "own" Amos than I could walk to the moon. I'd die for him, but if you tried to sell him to me or anyone else, I'd probably shoot you.

One day when I was a boy—maybe in first or second grade—I got home from school and ran out to the field to climb up on the tractor with my grandfather. He was drilling seed into the ground, his hat tilted back, straw stuck between his teeth, and pretty soon he began showing me the ditches that the slaves had dug. They're hard to miss; you could drive a Buick down them.

Whenever Papa spoke of slavery, his top lip grew tense and he shook his head, as if something disgusted him. I asked him why somebody didn't just buy up all the slaves and set them free. He stopped the tractor, cut the engine, sat me up on the wheel well, and pushed back my ball cap. He said, "D.S., a long time ago, a man did just that. He gave all He had, bought up all the slaves, and set them all free."

That didn't make sense, so I asked, "Then how come there were still slaves?"

He leaned over the side of the tractor, spat through his teeth, and switched the straw to the other side. He looked a long way across the pasture—well beyond where it ended. "That is a question I have given much thought to. And"—he smiled—"when I get to heaven, that's one of the first questions I intend to ask Him."

Whenever I think about the slaves, or the Holocaust, or Columbine, or Amanda being tied to a tree, or my son behind me buried beneath a stone slab, I know that Satan is alive and well on planet Earth. And whenever I hear my wife's voice, feel her touch, listen to her breathe, or feel her skin on mine, I know that God is too.

While the wound on my forearm had healed long ago, the reminder it left was mounded like a Band-Aid stuck between my skin and muscle. Sometimes at night I would wake to Maggie's fingers unconsciously tracing the outline while she slept.

A lot of people have asked Maggie if she could hear us— could hear me—those many months that she was in her coma. I've never needed to ask that. Of course she could. Love has its own communication—one you can't prove in a court-room, in a lab experiment, or on a doctor's chart. It's the language of the heart, and while it has never been transcribed, has no alphabet, and can't be heard or spoken by voice, it is used by every human on the planet. It is written on our souls, scripted by the finger of God, and we can hear, understand, and speak it with perfection long before we open our eyes for the first time.

A tickling breeze ushered itself upriver, bringing with it some early wood ducks and a few welcome clouds, turning the unbearable afternoon sun into the bearable evening sun. The breeze swirled about me and cooled my neck, which had once again turned red, etched with the charcoal lines of dust and dirt packed into the crevices of my sun-spotted skin. The clouds rolled in, stalled overhead, graciously protecting me from the magnifying glass, and slowly squeezed out several large drops. Big as acorns, they splattered on the dusty soil, sizzled on the muffler, trickled between my shoulder blades, and ran down the lush green leaves of the cornstalks spiral-ing above my head. Those few drops were usually the early warning system that God was about to spray hell with ice water. Within moments, I couldn't see twenty feet in front of my face.

I pulled off my cap, faced up, let the cool and delicious downpour drench me, and drank what I could. I had not seen or heard from Maggie all day. Normally, she'd have found me by now. But given the little gift I'd left on her bedside table, I didn't expect to see her till along toward dark.

It was hard to hear over the thunderous clap of drops on leaves, but toward home, I heard a screen door slam, followed by the hollow pounding of bare feet on the back porch and then screaming. Not scared screaming, but "Where are you?" screaming. I stood up on the tractor seat, looked out over the corn, and saw Maggie, wearing a T-shirt and cotton underwear, standing on the back porch, shielding her face from the rain with what looked like a stack of papers. She jumped off the back porch and started crashing through my neatly laid and quickly growing stalks.

When she appeared in the clearing, her hair was stuck to her face and her T-shirt and underwear were soaked clean through. The sides of her arms and long, thin legs were red where the cornstalks had slapped her, and the shirt stuck to her stomach. Her face was puffy, eyes red. And by the looks of her, she'd not been out of the house—or bed—all day. In her right arm, she clutched what remained of my manuscript. The rest of it had scattered like bread crumbs between us and the front door.

I stepped off the tractor and held my hat in my hand. Judging by her half-naked run across the pasture, my story had spurred something inside Maggie. I just couldn't tell how deep, or whether it was joy or anger. Both emotions are fueled by the same fire, and Maggie's face told me hers was raging. Then there was the deeper question: Could she spot the counterfeit without ever having seen the real thing?

She stood there, rain dripping off the ends of her hair, the lobes of her ears, the tips of her fingers, and cascading through the goose bumps on her thighs and calves. Her bare feet were caked with sand and mud, and so help me, with God as my witness and probably the cause, a Maggie-sized hole broke in the clouds and let through one ray of sun that, like a heaven-sized flashlight, lit the rain droplets on her skin like ten million diamonds.

Lord, I love my wife.

She walked up and leaned against me, her head to my chest. Then she dropped the pages in her hand, threw both arms around me, gripped me like a vise, and clung there while the sobs exited her chest. We stood there a long time. I wanted to tell her I had lied to her, but given the opportunity, I would do it again, so I said nothing. She wiped her face, brushed the hair out of my eyes, and tried her best to smile. She swallowed, fought for words, and then kissed me—her wet face pressed hard to mine. Finally she drew back and nodded. That was all she needed to say.

Since she'd been home, parts of Maggie's soul—down where her love lives—had been tied up in knots. Waking up from the coma didn't untie them; it just helped expose them to the daylight. We'd spent the last several months trying to get at each one. Sometimes we had to back up and start over, only to back up and start over again. But when you're untangling the rope that holds your anchor, you take all the time you need.

There in the cornfield, draped in rain, tears, tenderness, and uncertainty, her eyes told me that many of those knots had loosened. I'd like to think my story did that, but I imagine that was only part of it. The bigger part was the miracle that is Maggie.

That night we sat in the tub, floating in bubbles and laughter, soaking until our fingers grew white and prunelike while

reading her favorite parts. Finally she just shook her head and
slid up next to me. We sat there a long time, long enough for
the water to get cold.

Awhile later, she stepped out, toweled off, took me by the
hand, and led me across the room, where she hung her arms
about my neck. I don't how long we swayed atop those magnolia planks, but somewhere in that dance, we lost track of
time. Later, soaked in a sweet South Carolina sweat, she pressed
her chest and forehead to mine and managed, "Thank you . . .
for waiting for me."

I locked my hands behind her waist and tried to smile. "I'd
do it again."

Outside, the ancient gnarled oaks, covered in Spanish moss
and crawling with red bugs and resurrection fern, stood like
silent sentinels guarding us from the world that began just
beyond the edge of my tractor rows. The quilted patchwork of
South Carolina that had sewn itself into the fabric of us, with
soybean and watermelon, corn and kudzu, cotton and
tobacco, hay bales and barbed wire, old tractors and hand-dug
ditches, rivers and moonlight, sweat, blood, tears, tombstones,
and worn magnolia floors, rose up out of the dirt and covered
us like dew before the dawn. And where God had once doused
us with the other end of the rainbow, now He painted us in
starlight and all the wonder of the Milky Way.

EVIDENTLY MAGGIE'S EMOTIONS WERE IN TUNE WITH HER
clock.

Early in June—six weeks later—I hopped off my tractor and
walked up the steps, smelling worse than any man should but
led by the smell of pot roast and the promise of gravy and a
stack of biscuits. Maggie met me at the door in a turquoise-

colored sundress held up behind her neck with a single spaghetti strap. She led me to the kitchen, where the table was covered in a white tablecloth, candles, my grandmother's silver, and a small package—about the size of a Cross pen box set—tied with a bow.

I looked at the table, sniffed my yellowing shirt, and said, "I'm not sure we can live with me right now."

She pointed at the seat and half closed one eye. "If you don't open that box in the next sixty seconds, I'm going to blow a gasket." She pulled my chair out, sat beside me, and set the small box in front of me. In the background, Celine Dion and Frank Sinatra were singing "I've Got the World on a String."

Maggie was one big fidget. She pushed her hair behind her ears, crossed her legs, uncrossed them, crossed them back, and then crossed her arms. I studied the box, then untied the bow and lifted the lid. Inside sat four small, familiar white sticks with four unmistakable pink lines—all pointing directly at me. They were lined up in a row and dated—one for each of the last four weeks.

I'll never understand how she kept it a secret.

I held the four sticks, their meaning slowly registering somewhere back in my mind and then hitting me like a lightning bolt to the brain. I looked at Maggie, then at her tummy and our child growing inside and nearly six weeks old. I hit my knees, stuck my ear to Maggie's stomach, pressed in, and listened, wondering if he was a boy or she was a girl.

I've never been a fearful man. That does not mean I've never known fear; God knows I have. There's no S pinned on my chest. I just mean it's not something that stays with me all day perched atop my shoulder and whispering in my ear. In the months after Maggie woke up, I wrestled—even battled—with a long litany of *what ifs* that scared me. But her waking every morning had put that whisper to rest.

But the moment I leaned in and listened, tasting the trickle of hope and wondering at the unfathomable enormity once again, that whisper echoed. It smelled like the air behind a trash truck, the soil in Pinky's stall, or the floor of the delivery room. Its breath alone could gag a maggot.

Whereas *hope* had returned only after I'd cornered him in the barn and extended an invitation, *what if* reached up out of the floorboards, threw his bags on the couch, and made himself at home without so much as a peep. And unlike *hope*, who was tidy and neat, *what if* was a slob, seldom cleaning up after himself, and made it his point to throw remnants of his life in every nook and cranny of the house. Polar opposites, *hope* never raised his voice, while *what if* never lowered his. Not compatible roommates, they charged the air with a tension that even Blue picked up on.

That night as we lay in bed and Maggie twirled her finger through both of my chest hairs, I closed my eyes and saw the giant patchwork that had enveloped us. Once perfect and without blemish, it had begun to fray along the edges.

Within weeks, it would be coming apart at the seams.

chapter eight

DAYLIGHT FOUND ME AT THE KITCHEN TABLE NURSING some Maxwell House, reading the paper, and trying to erase the constipated look off my face. My snow angel was still zonked out with Blue, and if the last couple of months were any indication, she'd miss breakfast and brunch entirely. Don't get me wrong; every moment Maggie slept meant energy stored in reserve, so on the one hand, I was grateful. On the other, we used to eat eggs, grits, and toast off the same plate.

Since Maggie could spot a fake—especially in me—a mile away, I was trying to find a legitimate reason to get out of the house before she woke up. The moment she walked into this kitchen, she was going to take one look at my twisted face and say, "You want to talk about it?"

After sitting a long while at the breakfast table, skimming both the business and metro sections of the Charleston paper, I was no closer to knowing how to answer. In fact, my mind was swimming in questions. All I knew was that the most precious person in my life, who thought I actually had something to do with hanging the moon, who—maybe more than anything in life—wanted to be the mother of my children, was wrestling with stuff way down deep in her soul and needed me more than ever.

I was right back where we started—I couldn't protect her, nor could I wave a magic wand and make life all better. And though her doctors had not mentioned it, *what if* had echoed back into my head. I might have been staring at the newspaper, but the headline my mind read was WHAT IF SHE HEM-ORRHAGES AGAIN? I stared at the columns and knew one thing for sure: there was no easy way around. Like it or not, we were going to have to live through this.

My skin was crawling, my heart was racing, I'm sure my blood pressure was elevated, and I had no defense. I needed some time alone.

The phone rang, bringing me my chance.

"Dylan, good morning. How are things?" It was Caglestock. "I'm calling about Bryce," he continued.

Usually that meant a stock transaction, but his tone of voice told me he hadn't called to talk about money. "We've had no contact with him in over a month. Neither have the couriers we've sent for signatures. You mind checking on him?"

"No worries. I'll phone you as soon as I know something."

I scrambled some more eggs, browned a few pieces of toast, and then slopped that, along with a spoonful of cheese grits, onto a plate that I covered with foil and placed in the oven. I left a note on the kitchen table, grabbed the keys and my FM scanner, and headed out.

The scanner was a small black digital radio, covered in buttons and a single antenna, which Mr. Carter—Amos's dad and chief of the Digger Volunteer Fire Department— gave to all department volunteers. Not much happened from Charleston to Walterboro and surrounding parts that I didn't know about.

The DVFD No. 1 is Mr. Carter's baby. He put it together from nothing. He even petitioned the state for a grant that built us our own firehouse and got us a couple of trucks and all kinds of gear. We handle mostly local calls, and in truth, we're support personnel for the guys who really know what they're doing.

They don't let me drive the truck yet, and I haven't saved anybody's life, but I do have my own suit, complete with helmet, boots, ax, and air tank. I've used the Jaws of Life twice, though only in drills, and they let me blow the horn whenever we're racing through traffic. That might be my favorite part. Amos says I'm the most obnoxious horn blower he's ever heard, but he can't complain because people get out of our way. Every time I put on my suit and go running out the door to meet the rest of the team, Maggie takes one look at me and falls on the floor, laughing.

To keep us up on the latest information and techniques, and give us an excuse to practice or drive the truck, Mr. Carter holds weekly safety meetings where we learn stuff we've never even thought about. He travels all around the state getting trained and certified, then brings all that back to us.

I slid the scanner into my pocket and whistled softly for Blue, who did not appear. I walked around the house and looked through our bedroom window and saw him cuddled up at Maggie's feet. When I motioned for him to load up, he laid his head back down and covered his nose with his paw.

I could hear Pinky snorting and kicking her stall in the barn, mad that I hadn't appeared earlier. I stepped into the stall, spread a bucket of corn, and offered to give her a scratch. She ignored me and crapped on my boot.

"Hey," I said, tossing her a kernel of corn and shrugging my shoulders, "I thought we had an agreement."

Pinky grunted, buried her nose in the dirt, and then flicked a shovel's worth of mud and manure high into the air, where it umbrellaed about me.

"Thanks," I said. "Love you too." I hung up the bucket, pulled the gate behind me, and showed my heels to Pinky.

As I backed up the van, the flash of the screen door caught my eye. Maggie came stumbling over the threshold, her hair sticking up and eyes half closed, wrapping my pajama shirt around her. She jogged down the porch steps and stepped up to the window. "You okay?"

I nodded.

"You sure?"

I lied again.

She narrowed her eyes and folded her arms. "You've been kind of quiet since last night."

I shrugged and stumbled for words.

She put a hand on my shoulder and then ran her fingers through the back of my hair. "Hey . . . it's just me. I know you." She grabbed my hand and laid it flat across her tummy. "We're doing this together, same as last time. I'll be the mommy; you be the daddy. Right?" She smiled and shrugged. "All except the little hitch in the delivery."

I am such a pile of crap. How does a woman like that love a man like me? I cussed myself and nodded. "Coffee's probably cold by now."

She tugged on my sleeve, pulling me closer. "Are you listening to me?" Her lips were warm and wet. "Dylan Styles, I'm not talking about coffee. I'm talking 'bout us. All three of us."

"Maggs." I took off my cap and made a pitiful stab at the truth. "I lost you once. I don't want to . . ."

She smirked. "Well, we should have thought about that"— she pointed to the window of our bedroom—"in there."

"I know, but . . ."

She held her finger to my lips and said, "Shhh . . ." Her eyes filled around the edges, and she shook her head. Evidently *what if* had been whispering in her ear too. And here I was worried about me. I really am a pile of crap.

The tears broke, and I opened the door and stepped out, wrapping her tight. "I don't know how you do it."

She whispered, "Because you love me—and because you're there when I wake up."

"Honey, I'll always be there when you wake up."

"You weren't this morning."

I laughed. "Well, I do like to get up before lunch."

She hit me in the chest. "That's not funny. I just need more rest than I used to."

We swayed a moment more.

"Caglestock called, said Bryce has been AWOL for a month."

Maggie wiped her tears and looked concerned. "You think he's okay?"

"Don't know, but I'm going to find out. I left you some breakfast in the oven."

"Doesn't taste as good when you're not there."

"Tell me about it."

chapter nine

I IDLED THE VAN DOWN THE DRIVEWAY, STOPPED AT the mailbox, and then sat in the front seat flipping through the bills. Before me lay Amos and Amanda's house, where the front yard was strewn with kids' toys. Despite their best attempts to tidy up, the front yard looked as if it were hit daily by the same tornado. A red wagon, a tricycle, a small playhouse turned on its side, a sandbox missing most of the sand, a football, a kickball, and other odds and ends painted the picture that the proud grandparents had gone a bit overboard. Every time I mentioned to Amos that his front yard looked like trailer trash, he just shook his head and said, "In-laws. What can you do?"

"Evidently," I said, "you spread it all across the front yard, letting them know how thankful you are."

While Maggie and I had been connecting the straight-edged pieces of our puzzle, Amos had too. He had been promoted to sergeant and given command of a SWAT team that roamed all over South Carolina, focusing on narcotics. They gave him a new truck, new uniform, new pistol, and a new schedule. Thinking he needed a bit more change in his life, he'd married Amanda Lovett last June 25—Li'l Dylan's six-month birthday. Pastor John, buttons busting, performed his daughter's wedding ceremony before a standing-room-only congregation. I stood next to Amos, holding the rings, and looked out across the congregation—which looked a lot like a hat convention.

At Amanda's request, the reception took place on the riverbank—beneath the oaks. Knowing it'd be the last time they got to cook for Amos, the church ladies let out all the stops. From greens to chicken to roast to mashed potatoes to sweet potato pie to you-name-it, they covered us up in some of the best cooking I'd ever seen.

We ate until we couldn't see straight, then danced a little—something Amos has never been too fond of or good at—and then Amos and Amanda drove to the Outer Banks, where Amos said he intended to work on his tan. While Grandma Carter bounced Li'l Dylan on her knee, Amos and Amanda spent a few days at the beach. When they returned, Amanda moved in and quickly got rid of any remnants of Amos's bachelor days. Within a week, it looked as if he were the newcomer, not her.

A week or so after they returned, I was helping him take out the trash, and he held up a picture of Ted Williams. "How do you throw out a picture of the greatest hitter ever to play baseball?" He shook his head and pitched it into the trash can. "It just makes no sense to me whatsoever."

Having been through this very same gleaning with Maggie, I put my arm around him and smiled knowingly. "Brother, therein lies the secret."

"What?"

"*Your* favorites. Not *hers.*"

He nodded and said, "Yeah, I'm beginning to see that."

"Remember," I said, pointing toward the front door, "this is her house now. You're just lucky she lets you sleep here."

Six months later, there had come a single-pause-double-knock at our kitchen door—Amos's signature. The porch lightbulb was burned out, but when I opened the door and let my eyes adjust, Amos stood there giddy-faced and breathing heavily, as if he'd been running. The cold air turned his breath to smoke. Maggie flipped a switch, and the kitchen light bent around the corner, lighting his straight teeth and the whites of his eyes.

"D.S.! D.S.!" He was so excited he could barely speak. "D.S.! D.S.!"

"You already said that."

He jumped up and down as though he were skipping rope to an erratic rhythm. "Li'l Dylan's gonna get a brother."

My head was swirling with our own adoption process, and I didn't catch on too fast. I scratched my head, maybe even feeling a bit jealous. "You guys adopting?"

He shook his head and skipped faster, as if the person swinging the rope not only had doubled the pace but now was swinging two ropes. "No, dummy." He poked himself in the chest. "'Manda's pregnant."

I looked behind him and saw Amanda standing there with Li'l Dylan on her hip and a huge smile spread across her face. Maggie pushed me out of the way, gave Amos a huge kiss on the forehead, and dragged Amanda into the house, where they sat talking till long after Li'l Dylan's bedtime.

Amos and I sat on the front porch in the swing, and while Li'l Dylan curled up in my lap and napped, we sipped Coca-Cola and laughed at the changes in our lives. Close to midnight, Amos brushed Li'l Dylan's brown cheek and smiled. "He's gonna be a big brother."

NOW I SAT IN THE VAN, STUDYING THE YARD, AND FOUND myself lost in what-might-have-been dreams—a bad way to start the day. Minutes later, Amos turned into his drive in his black, state-issued Chevrolet 2500HD pickup. It was one of those "undercover" cars that comes complete with black windows and driver's-side spotlight telling everybody and their brother that the driver is a cop. He hopped out, waved, and started walking across his lawn toward the front door. Amanda opened the front door, and Li'l Dylan came crawling out, making a beeline for his daddy's black-booted feet.

I honked, pulled out of the drive, and tried not to remember that I was driving a minivan with a five-star crash test rating. I watched through my rearview mirror as the Carolina Cruncher, Mr.-Clean-turned-Mr.-SWAT, dressed in black fatigues and black T-shirt and carrying a SIG Sauer P226 in a hip holster, knelt down, picked up his son, and seamlessly transitioned into Mr. Daddy. I've seen a lot of beautiful things in my life, but that is one of the more beautiful.

I RATTLED THE CHAIN AT THE GATE THAT LED UP THE LONG drive to Bryce's drive-in. The chain and lock had been replaced and were, by any standard, huge. It looked as though he were protecting Fort Knox. I shrugged, pulled up the fence as usual, crawled under, and made my way toward Bryce's trailer.

Bryce had never been big on upkeep. Maintenance just wasn't in his vocabulary. As long as I'd been coming up here, not much had changed except the worsening condition of everything in sight. From the exponentially growing trash piles to the flaking paint to the bent speaker poles to the cesspool that Bryce called a trailer, the entire place was racing down one giant spiral toward uninhabitable. It was no wonder he never married. If Health and Human Services had ever come up here, they'd have condemned the place.

To say that Bryce was a pack rat would be kind. Problem was, he packed most everything in huge piles that dotted the landscape—gigantic mounds of twisted metal, car parts, wood scraps, and pretty much anything he'd ever used. His property looked like a bad marriage between a garage sale and a city trash heap. I never could tell the difference between what was trash and what wasn't. Bryce never bothered with that distinction.

When I crested the hill and exited the woods that once served as the parking lot for silver screen number one, I looked around and couldn't believe my eyes.

To start with, the piles were gone. Not a single scrap of trash could be seen. Anywhere. Except for one smoldering burn pile down the hill a few hundred yards, the place was spotless. The grounds had been mowed and edged, and every square foot of concrete had been blown or swept meticulously. And I don't mean the grass had just been *cut*. It had been cut, raked, then picked up and discarded someplace else. And not a weed grew anywhere within sight.

Everything that could be painted, starting with the three movie screens, had been painted, and now sat sparkling white. And that's another thing: there were now three screens. Two had been mysteriously rebuilt. In all three parking lots that spread out like a star from the concession/projector house, all the speaker poles had been repaired and evidently rewired. On closer inspection, the projector house, too, had been cleaned. I climbed the stairs to the projector room and what Bryce had fondly called the "film library." The several hundred reels of movies that had at one time been filed in a mound on the floor were now rolled up, sealed in round metal cases, labeled, and filed alphabetically on specially built shelves.

Outside Bryce's trailer, a clothesline stretched between two poles standing seven feet tall and sunk some forty feet apart. Four pairs of military-issue camouflage BDUs hung equidistant across the line along with three pairs of bleached white boxers and two pairs of tube socks. Each item was stretched taut between two clothespins and hung without a wrinkle. Everything smelled of detergent. On his front steps sat two pairs of black GI boots, sparkling like granite countertops.

I stepped inside the trailer, and the smell of bleach and Pine Sol hit me like a wave. I could have eaten off the floor. Outside the back door, the mop bucket had been turned upside down and leaned against the house. Next to it leaned the mop, which had quit dripping but was still moist.

I studied the trailer, my jaw at my waist. Bryce's bed was made, which astonished me because I'd never seen sheets on the mattress before today. Towels were hung in his bathroom, his toothbrush sat in the holder, the toothpaste cap was screwed onto the tube—which had been rolled from the bottom up— and his closet would have made Martha Stewart proud.

If I thought the bedroom and bathroom were amazing, the kitchen was a totally new revelation. New appliances, new linoleum, new exhaust fan, new bar stools at the counter, new silverware, new plates, new everything. The whole kitchen gave the impression that someone was actually using it—or could. I shook my head and then opened the fridge.

First, there was food. Real food. Vegetables, eggs, milk that was not cottage cheese, orange juice, fish, bottled water, Gatorade, chicken. Second—and this was the most glaring sight—there was no beer. Further, as I looked around the trailer and in the trash cans that stood orderly alongside, there were no beer cans—empty or full—anywhere.

But if the absence of beer was glaring, then there was one other absence that was as difficult to miss as the detonation of an atomic bomb. I looked around the trailer again and made sure. I looked behind doors, under the bed, through all the closets, and on the rack where they usually sat, bright, polished, and on display. Regardless, I found no bagpipes and no kilt anywhere.

I stepped out the back door and onto the porch. Scratching my head, wondering what in the world was wrong with Bryce, I saw a used foot trail that I'd never noticed before. It led into the woods on the back side of the hill where the drive-in sat.

I turned around to walk back into the trailer and noticed a glass frame encasing what looked like an aerial map. I looked closer and saw that it was actually two aerial photos. One was a photo of the drive-in proper, covering what looked like a distance of maybe a thousand square yards. The second looked more like a satellite photo that included Bryce's entire piece of property. I don't know how many acres or square miles it comprised, but I'd say the bottom of the map probably covered twenty miles, while the sides stretched up for closer to thirty. At the bottom was a little dot that looked like the drive-in, and at the top was the unmistakable Salkehatchie River. In between sat tens of thousands of acres of forest and swamp that few men had ever ventured into, much less through. It was a no-man's-land. It you wanted to hide, it'd be a great place to do it. It'd also be a great place to get lost if you were trying to hide and didn't know what you were doing.

I descended the steps leading off the porch and followed the trail out into the woods where the pines grew up like bean stalks. Another hundred yards and the trail led me into a clearing covered by about twenty gargantuan oak trees towering some sixty feet above the ground.

It was like walking into the Astrodome. The forest floor had been cleared for several acres, mulch had been spread along what looked like a running path, and along the perimeter of the canopy ran what looked like a fitness course. From tires to ropes to barbed wire to cable crossings over water holes to wooden walls that must be scaled to towers that must be rappelled, the obstacle course looked difficult by design.

To me, it looked as if the participant started by climbing over a sand hill covered in barbed wire, then over a hundred yards covered in hurdles, pipes, and tires elevated off the ground, then up a free-hanging rope that ended at a tower, where the then-exhausted participant must rappel down, only to climb along a tightrope that had been stretched between two trees some sixty feet apart. Falling would get you wet. Then through a series of ladders, up, over, and under a series of walls, around some pilings, and between some poles with seriously sharp points.

I had no idea how long Bryce had been working on it, but I guessed it had taken him months, maybe even a year, to complete it. The trail headed off into the woods far beyond my view, but I'd seen enough. I backtracked to the trailer and kept my eyes peeled.

I walked back through the trailer and noticed something I hadn't seen before. On the desk sat a manila envelope with "Caglestock" written in Bryce's handwriting on the front. I opened the envelope and saw that Bryce had signed in all the places where Caglestock's secretary had stuck the "Sign here" stickies. I stuffed the envelope under my arm and started back down the hill.

Toward town, I stopped at a pay phone and dialed our number. After six rings, the machine picked up. "Hey, this is Maggie and Dylan. Leave us a message, and we'll call you back."

After the beep, I said, "Hey, it's me. If you're there, pick up." When she didn't, I said, "Well, guess you're outside or something. I've got to see Caglestock and thought maybe we'd go together, get a bite to eat in—"

Just then, the phone picked up. Maggie was breathing hard. "Hey," she said, laughing and trying to catch her breath. "I was . . . in the stall." She tried to catch her breath again. "That pig has gotten big . . . Phew! She stinks too."

"Tell me about it."

"Did you say something about lunch?"

I smiled. "Something like that."

"I'll be waiting on you when you get here."

I paused. "You know, it'll take me about ten minutes to get there, and maybe . . . I was just thinking . . . well, you might feel better if . . ."

"I'm going now." The phone clicked silent, and I leaned against the pay phone glass, thinking of my wife, muddy and content in her overalls.

chapter ten

WE ARRIVED IN WALTERBORO JUST AFTER THE lunch crowd had exited Ira's Café. Ira, decked out in turquoise blue, met us at the door looking like a color swatch. She hugged Maggie and gave me a huge wet kiss on the cheek, which I wiped with my sleeve.

She pointed her coffeepot at me. "You best not be wiping off my kisses. I don't give too many out."

"Take my word for it," a guy in the kitchen hollered. "She's telling the truth."

"Hey, Ira," I said. "Good to see you."

Ira winked at us, smiled, smacked her gum from side to side, and then adjusted her left bosom with the V in her elbow, kind of lifting it back into place. Evidently business had been good in the last year, because they were bigger, and she looked as though she was trying to get used to them getting in her way. She pointed us to a booth. "You just missed Amos, but sit down and I'll stir up some lunch."

We sat in our booth and watched the Walterboro lunch crowd scurry across the town square en route to their jobs or in search of the next pocket of gossip. Across the square sat the town hall and what looked like both Amos's truck and Pastor John's Cadillac.

Ten minutes later, Ira delivered a lunch that looked a whole lot like breakfast. A mound of steaming eggs, piping hot biscuits, fresh sweet cream butter, honey, and cheese grits. She even threw in a few slices of salty fried ham.

It took us nearly an hour to eat it all. We washed it down with syrupy sweet tea, and when I asked Ira for the check, her face became contorted.

"Look here, you little whippersnapper, you get cute with me and I'll take a broomstick to the side of your head." She looked down at my backside. "Among other places." She sloshed the coffeepot at me again. "Now, don't you come in here and start snapping your fingers at me. No, sir."

I left twenty dollars on the table and grabbed two toothpicks at the counter—one for now and one for later—and we walked out. While I picked my teeth, we stood in the center of the sidewalk, gauging our level of fullness.

Maggie turned to me and shaded her eyes from the sun. "You know, that sounds gross."

I pulled the toothpick from my mouth. "What?"

"That." She pointed.

I stuck the toothpick back in my mouth and kept picking while she watched my fingers work. Then she ran her tongue over her teeth, sucked through them, and looked up at me again. "Does it really work?"

I nodded and offered her my second toothpick. She eyed it, stuck it in her mouth, and started picking. Finally she mumbled something I couldn't understand and nodded.

We turned toward the truck and walked directly past the alley where I had vomited breakfast about a year and a half earlier. Vomited because I'd eaten a huge breakfast with Amos and then realized that I'd gone forty-five minutes without thinking of my wife lying in a coma at the hospital. I looked at the ground where I'd stood that day, remembered the feeling in my stomach and the splatter on my boots, and felt it return when I remembered that I'd cut that scene out of Maggie's version of my story.

She clenched my arm more tightly, and her eyes innocently searched mine. "You okay?"

I swallowed hard and lied again.

We backed out of our parking spot and eased around the corner, where Amos and Pastor John were just exiting the courthouse. I waved and pulled up along a No Parking zone, thinking they'd walk up to the window and act sociable, but once I got a closer look, their faces told me otherwise. When they reached the sidewalk, Pastor John patted Amos on the shoulder and said something I couldn't hear, then they walked directly to their cars.

Amos, dressed in SWAT black, looked as if he'd been up all night. The stubble on his face and head was at least a day over-grown, and his clothes were stained with salt rings where he'd been sweating. He looked tired and aggravated. He stepped up into his truck, pulled down his glasses, held an imaginary phone to his ear, and then pointed at me and drove off, quickly.

Pastor John opened his car door and stepped in, but I waved him out and tried to break the tension that was thick in the air.

"Pastor John!" I pointed toward Amos. "If that guy causes you any trouble, I know where he lives."

He halfsmiled and waved. If I thought Amos looked tired, then Pastor John looked like a man who'd spent three days walking through the desert without food or water. His face was drawn and his eyes bloodshot. He tried to smile again and cupped his hand around his ear as if he were having a hard time hearing me because of the other cars.

"You two okay?" I hollered.

Pastor John looked toward the courthouse, brushed some pollen off the top of his car with the flat of his palm, and said, "Son, I'm looking over my shoulder . . ." He took what looked like a deep, painful breath and shook his head. Then he slid into his seat, shut the door, and drove off.

Maggie raised an eyebrow. "What was all that about?"

I followed his license tag with my eyes and then saw him place a cell phone to his ear. "I don't know, but evidently whatever it was didn't go very well."

chapter eleven

I SAT IN THE OFFICE CHAIR, MAGGIE'S HAND ON MY knee, and fidgeted. We had come to make sure the pink lines weren't lying. I slid Papa's watch from my pocket for the fourth time since we'd sat down. I eyed the face, and it told me that Dr. Frank's office was overbooked and running behind schedule. It was a twenty-one-jewel, Hamilton railroad pocket watch, and if I kept it wound, it lost only two to three seconds a month. Nanny had given it to him as a tenth-anniversary gift, and I don't ever remember a day that he didn't carry it. When he died, I thought about burying it with him, but then I wound it, heard the ticking, and thought better of it.

Catty-corner to the hospital, the professional office building sat brimming with people. I looked out the waiting room window and across the parking lot toward the hospital. I spotted the window of Maggie's room down at the far end of the hospital and thought of all the times I had looked down from it. It didn't take me very long to realize that I liked the view from Dr. Frank's office better.

I looked around the office and took notice of all the pregnant women and their husbands. And not just pregnant, but busting-at-the-seams, could-go-anytime pregnant. I whispered to Maggie, "Why are there so many people in here?"

She looked up from her magazine and cocked one eye. "Why do you think?"

"I know that. But why now? I mean, last time we were here, the place was empty. Today it's packed."

She shook her head and put down her magazine. "You're killing me, Doc."

"What?"

She rolled her eyes. "Can you count backward?"

"Yes."

"Well, count nine months backward from June."

I used both hands, opening each finger. Messing up once, I had to start over. "October." I shrugged.

"Right." She closed her magazine. "What happens in October and November?"

"Monday Night Football?"

She shook her head and whispered, "It gets colder."

It took me a few seconds. "Oh."

A nurse walked into the room and called, "Maggie Styles?"

Maggie stood up, and all heads turned toward us. I stood and reached for her hand, but she smiled. "I'll be back," she whispered. "You can't really help with this."

She walked to the door, where the nurse handed her a small plastic cup with a screw-on lid. A few minutes later,

Maggie poked her head around the corner and motioned for me to follow.

The nurse led us to a small examining room and handed Maggie a gown. "It's less than flattering, but here . . . The doctor'll be here in a minute."

Maggie stood behind the curtain, stripped down to her birthday suit, and handed me everything but her socks. "If he wants my socks, he's going to have to ask." She came out, turned, and lifted her hair off her shoulders. "Tie me?"

I gathered the gown around her waist and watched goose bumps appear at the base of her back, along the outline of her hips, and on the backs of her thighs. When I messed up tying the third bow, Maggie shook her head slightly and whispered, "You did that on purpose."

Busted.

I said nothing, pulled fresh paper out of the roll on the table where her bottom would be, and then helped her step up onto the examining table. I stood alongside, holding her hand and looking at the stirrups folded out of sight. Maggie saw me staring and leaned over. "Hey, you in there?"

Busted again.

I had a few things on my mind. First, there was the physical side. Given what her body had endured both in delivery and in the atrophy of the coma, could Maggie handle the next eight months and what they led up to? Second, could she handle it emotionally? Eight months is a long time to wonder if those will be your last months on earth, and if you'll be leaving your widowed husband to raise an only child alone. Or, even worse, just alone. Maggie was strong, but was she that strong? I had my doubts. Both about her and about me.

Which brings me to my last issue. While I was uncertain about Maggs, I was relatively certain about myself. I knew beyond a shadow of a doubt that I was going to suffer hell until I knew the answers to the above.

While the knot in my stomach grew and ground against my nerves, the door opened and Dr. Frank walked in wearing an exasperated face. Given the state of the waiting room and all the hormones that came with it, I'd have looked that way too.

He sat down on the rolling stool and scooted up to us, taking in and then letting out an enormous breath. "Hey, guys. How're you two doing? You holding up?" He shook my hand and put his other appropriately on Maggie's knee.

We nodded.

"I guess I don't need to tell you what you already know."

Maggie tilted her shoulders. "So those little sticks really are telling the truth?"

He nodded. "They usually do."

She looked at me. I scratched her back and looked at him, not wanting Maggie to see into my eyes.

"Hey, it's a walk in the park from here," he said. "Just sit back and enjoy the ride. Your body will take care of the rest."

I never knew that one man's words could be so prophetic.

He inserted the earpieces of his stethoscope and spoke while he listened to Maggs's heart. "You picked out names yet?"

"Haven't gotten that far."

"You've got time." He paused and moved the stethoscope to her back. Maggie breathed deeply without being told. He examined her back and the muscles in her shoulders that had returned over the last year. "Maggie, you really are healthy. Whatever you're doing, keep it up, because you're looking great."

The nurse came back in and helped him slip his hands into two whitish rubber gloves that each made a distinctive *smack* as he pulled them tight. Maggie lay back on the table and placed her feet in the stirrups while the nurse covered Dr. Frank's fingertips in jelly.

I held her hand, noticed that Maggs had painted her toenails bright red sometime between last night and this morning, and then watched her wince as he examined her.

"I won't lie to you; you've got some pretty good scar tissue that will take some stretching." He pulled off his gloves, pitched them in the trash, and helped Maggs sit up. "So as the baby grows, understand that it will feel different from last time. Little aches and pains that will make you wonder. But that's normal. So take a deep breath"—which Maggie did— "and start painting the nursery."

He followed the nurse to the door and stood in the doorway, smiling at us. "I'm excited for you guys. I've been waiting for this day."

Maggie was beaming.

"But take it easy. No marathons. Just live your life. Get as much rest as you want, eat right, and make sure you take enough time for each other." He pointed at me. "Go on a date every couple of days, like it or not."

Maggs squeezed my hand. "We can handle that."

The nurse reappeared over his shoulder and looked at Maggie. "I forgot to weigh you. Come see me when you get dressed."

They shut the door, and Maggie wrapped a bear hug around me. We stood in the doctor's office several minutes just holding each other. Maybe everything was going to be okay. Maybe I was just being a little paranoid. Maybe . . .

A few minutes later we walked out the door, and Maggie headed toward the nurse and the scale.

Seeing his moment, Dr. Frank tapped me on the shoulder

and motioned me around the corner. "You want it sugarcoated or straight?"

I looked down the hall toward the sound of Maggie laughing with some nurses. "Straight up."

He lowered his voice. "Sometimes, when women who've suffered some type of trauma become pregnant, their bodies will reject it."

I leaned in closer, and he put a hand on my shoulder.

"If so, it's got nothing to do with you two. It's the body's natural reaction to protect itself. Honestly, I'm amazed it let you get this far this soon. But that is one strong woman. I know I'm not telling you anything you don't know, but the next few weeks are critical. No bumpy tractor rides, no car wrecks, no scary movies, no nothing that will shock her system and make it unconsciously want to shut down and protect itself."

He looked down the hall to where Maggie was stepping off the scale. "If you've ever protected her," he said, looking back at me, "now is the time to do it."

I shook his hand. "Thanks, Dr. Frank. We appreciate you. We'll keep you posted." When I turned and walked down the hall, the sweat cascaded down my back.

chapter twelve

EVERY MORNING WHEN MY GRANDFATHER WOKE, he'd sit on the edge of the bed and run yesterday's sock between his toes like a shoe shine. Once his toes were clean, he'd walk to the window and look out across the fields. Then he'd walk to his dresser, pick up his pocket watch, and wind it. He'd wind it slowly, adding tension to the spring with every turn, always stopping just one turn shy of too much. That was the trick. Too much and it would lock up, seizing internally, and that meant a trip to the watchmaker, but after years of practice, Papa had the feel for just right.

Maggie and I walked out of the doctor's office, underneath the magnifying glass and across the parking lot. Her face shining like a glow plug and her feet barely touching the ground, she bounced as she walked. Except for the long hair, she reminded me of Julie Andrews dancing atop the mountain at the start of *The Sound of Music*. And when she pulled her sunglasses down over her eyes and smiled at me, she looked like Audrey Hepburn in *Breakfast at Tiffany's*. I opened the van door and she climbed in, bouncing up and down on the springy seat like a puppy in the window of a pet store. Only then did she remind me of Papa's watch spring. Problem was, I didn't know where she stood in relation to too much.

Maggs put her feet on the dash, tucked her knees tight into her chest, smiled, and began pointing her finger. That meant we were going in search of something to eat. When we got there, her stop-sign hand would let me know.

Her finger led us to the drive-through window at Dairy Queen, where I ordered two large vanilla cones dipped in chocolate. Maggie wanted hers covered in sprinkles, so I passed it back through the window and shrugged, and the guy doused it with rainbow sprinkles.

Licking circles around our cones, we rolled down the windows and headed toward home. Maggie finished her ice cream before I'd eaten half of mine. She took a deep breath and slid her sunglasses up over her head, pulling her hair back behind her ears. "I think we can let the cat out of the bag now."

"You sure?"

She patted her stomach. "Well, pretty soon it's going to become obvious."

"Okay."

"Ooooh," she said, sitting up quickly and pointing at the grocery store, "pull in here."

I did as directed and parked in the fire lane while Maggie ran in, smirking. Minutes later, she ran out laughing, barely able to put one foot in front of the other. That's my Maggie, just cracking herself up.

"What's so funny?"

She pulled out a notepad, wrote "Guess what?" on the top piece of paper, and then pulled a baby bottle from her bag. She unscrewed the nipple, slid the note inside the clear plastic bottle, and screwed the nipple back on. She held it up, triumphant. "The message in the bottle."

I looked at the bag. "How many of those you get?"

She shook the bag and what must have been a dozen bottles. "Enough."

First, we pulled into Bryce's and parked at the gate. If he was around, we knew he'd want to know. Besides, Maggie really wanted to tell him. She grabbed a bottle and held my hand, and we tiptoed up the drive. The woods were quiet, and it was cooler beneath the tall canopy of oak arms that had overgrown the cracked drive up the hill to Bryce's compound. Where the limbs shadowed us from above, the roots had broken the asphalt and turned most of the hardtop into what looked like a road map of the United States.

When we cleared the trees, Maggie took in a deep breath and said, "Holy smokes! You weren't kidding. What happened?"

I shrugged. "No idea."

We searched the grounds, even the obstacle course, but found no fresh evidence of Bryce. Maggie looked around, shaded her eyes, and pointed atop the second screen. "You ever see that before?"

I looked up, and my eyes widened. The second screen had been rebuilt, larger than an IMAX screen—probably seventy feet tall. Erected across the top was, for lack of a better term, a crow's nest. Fed by a ladder and a metal walkway, it looked large enough for one man, and because of its position atop the hill on Bryce's property, it would give anyone up there a rather advantageous view of Digger.

I shook my head and shrugged. I didn't know much about military tactics or training, but judging from the level platform, and the length of it, the ladder leading up the side, and the idea that high ground is best, I started putting two and two together. Given Bryce's history, or what little I knew of it and the mystery that surrounded it, compounded with the stories I'd heard from Amos that rose out of his SWAT sniper training, I started to wonder. But I said nothing to Maggie.

Thinking he'd return to his trailer sooner or later, we left the bottle hanging from a string on the front door. We walked back down the hill, underneath the tentacled arms of the oaks and beneath the shade of the canopy. While our feet crunched dried acorns, I had a strange feeling that just because we hadn't seen Bryce didn't mean he hadn't seen us. This wasn't something I knew but rather something I felt—kind of like static electricity.

One question kept popping up across the backs of my eyelids: *Why?* I had now been here twice and was pretty sure Bryce knew about both trips, but he hadn't showed. Granted, Bryce had never been a very social person. He prized his own company, avoided most other human beings on the planet, and had no real friends to speak of. But for some reason, all that had changed when it came to Maggie and me. Especially Maggie. In fact, he'd made efforts to see us when he didn't have to. All that, coupled with the sight of Bryce's compound, put a wrinkle in the center of my forehead that Maggie would have seen had she not been working on her note to Amos and Amanda.

We headed toward home and pulled into their drive, and

my giddy wife hopped out and dropped a bottle in the Carters' mailbox. She climbed back in, propped her feet up, and kicked the dashboard.

"What'd the note say?"

She smiled and leaned her head back. "Dylan's got a secret."

chapter thirteen

At 11:00 p.m. I heard a faint tap on our bed-room window. When Amos is your neighbor, you learn to live with these things.

I looked out the window and saw him motioning me toward the front porch. Given Maggs's little gift we left in the mailbox, I'd been expecting a visit. I covered Maggie, who had been asleep since a little after nine, and stepped into my jeans. Blue hopped off the end of the bed and followed silently behind.

When I slid open the door, Amos was sitting on the porch railing, looking out over the corn. He didn't look at me, and when Blue brushed up alongside the railing, he didn't seem to notice. From the side, his face looked thin, and his eyes were sunk back in his head. He pointed at the cotton. "It's pretty in the moonlight."

I nodded and moved around the side where the moon lit the sweat on Amos's face and shone off the badge that hung on a chain around his neck. He looked tired. His waist was hung with all sorts of police paraphernalia: a SureFire flashlight, black, nonreflective; handcuffs; a retractable baton; his Kimber in .45 auto; several clips; and a few other odds and ends that I couldn't place.

I spoke softly. "You been up awhile?"

He nodded. "Couple of days."

"You want to talk about it?"

Amos shook his head. I walked inside, grabbed two cups and the pitcher of sweet tea out of the fridge, and returned to the porch. Pouring a glass, I handed it to him and sat on the railing next to him. Blue hopped up on the swing and pointed his nose at us.

"Thanks." Amos wiped his face with the fat of his palm and looked up at the ten trillion stars looking down on us. Then he looked at me. "You still got Papa's Model 12?"

I nodded.

"You remember how to . . . ?"

Amos trailed off, and I nodded again.

"You might think about . . . keeping it handy."

Papa's Model 12 was a pump-action Winchester twelve-gauge with a thirty-inch barrel and a full choke. The longer barrel and full choke gave it a tighter pattern at longer distances—good for shooting geese, turkey, or deer. According to Amos, it was reliable and gained in popularity with inner-city gangsters in the 1940s and 1950s. Starting in the '60s, law enforcement adopted it to clear houses and hallways, and in Vietnam, marines and Rangers alike used it in the tunnel networks.

What had started out as a hunting shotgun evolved rapidly into a rather potent self-defense weapon. The only difference between theirs and mine was that most of them had cut twelve inches off the barrel so the pattern spread more quickly. The sound of the pump action sliding a round into the chamber is definitely distinct. If you were breaking into a house and heard that sound somewhere in the darkness around you, it'd get you to thinking.

I looked at him. "Ebony, feels like there's a whole lot you're not telling me."

He nodded and glanced over his shoulder to where Maggie lay sleeping. "You two got enough to worry about right now." He stood, lifted his belt, and pulled his car keys from his pocket. "Just keep it close. You hear me?"

"I heard you the first time, but that doesn't mean I understand you."

He looked off across the pasture. "The sound alone might do you as much good as the business end of it." He grabbed his bag and started down the steps. Then he stopped, shook his head, and reached into the bag. He pulled out a small gift tied with a bow and set it on the railing. "Got this for you." He feigned a smile. "It'll come in handy."

He looked at his house across the street. "'Manda'll be over tomorrow with something for Maggie. She's over there now, dreaming up something."

Amos walked down the drive and across the street into his yard. I watched him dodge the toys and then disappear through the front door. His status among local and federal law enforcement had increased a lot in the last two years, and his broad shoulders carried a lot more than just the shirt on his back. And I loved him for it.

chapter fourteen

AMOS AND I WERE NINE, AND IT WAS SUMMER BREAK.
We were dressed up like cowboys, walking through Dodge City
while keeping our eyes on Boot Hill.

Marshal Amos had seen the bad guys run behind the general store, which looked a lot like our barn, so he told his
faithful companion, Texas Ranger Dylan, and we slipped
around back and ducked into Papa's soybeans. If we could
corner them in the barn, they'd have to jump from the hayloft
and we'd get them in the air on the way down. It was the
fourth time this week they'd chosen that escape route.

Sure enough, they had climbed the ladder inside the barn
and were already taking shots at us. That meant we had to face
them. Man-to-man. Amos and I straightened the bandannas
around our necks to keep the dust out, checked the caps on

our pistols, and loosed the holster fob. We licked the sights on our carbines, and then we walked out of the shoulder-high plants, challenging all comers. We sprinted around the barn, dove into the sawdust, rolled, shuffled behind the Evinrude motor clamped to the motor mount, and aimed at the sun just cracking through the slats in the hayloft.

I looked at Amos, he nodded, and we came out blazing. Like Wyatt Earp at the OK Corral, and John Wayne in *True Grit*, we bit down on our bandannas like halter reins and started slinging lead. We worked the levers on our faithful Model 94 Winchesters and popped as many caps as our fingers would let us. When they were empty, we threw down our carbines, pulled both six-shooters, and kept pouring the lead at them. When the remaining two finally leaped from the loft, Marshal Amos squeezed off a fantastic shot behind his back, leaving him out of ammo and me to deal with the worst of the outlaw gang alone.

I stepped quietly, crunching dried hay, and when that notorious outlaw came swinging down the rope with a knife in his mouth and a pistol in each hand, I shot his hat off to blind him, then shot him through both hands. Amos and I handcuffed the entire gang, locked them in the jail (where chances were good they'd attempt a jailbreak tomorrow), and walked to the saloon for some sweet tea.

We never suffered from lack of imagination. We could shoot the same outlaw ten times, and he'd always come back meaner and nastier—which was just fine with us. Bring them on; we could get more caps. The fight of good versus evil got us out of bed in the morning, and the promise of another shootout sped us through our chores and out into the fields, where we'd lasso rustlers, rescue fair maidens in distress, and warn the stagecoach that the bridge was out.

And if there was one thing in this life that we spent hours dreaming about, it was a Model 69 pump-action Winchester in .22 caliber. With that in my hands, not a squirrel, raccoon, or armadillo in Digger would be safe. I had cut the advertisement out of *Field and Stream* and pasted it on the wall next to my bed. Amos had too. But the gun had a price tag of $129, and I was at least two summers away from being able to afford it.

Amos and I walked up the steps of the saloon just as Papa came walking out the back door. Before he could blink, and before I had time to think, I beat him to the draw and blasted him with both six-shooters. And it was there, with smoke trailing out of both barrels, that it hit me. Caught up in the moment and the game we were playing, I had just violated cardinal rule number one: *Never, absolutely never, point any gun, play or not, at a real person. Imagine all you want, but never in real life.*

Papa stuffed his hand in the open side of his overalls, half-closed one eye, chewed on his lip, and nodded us both inside. I dropped both guns out of fear of what was about to happen to my backside. He pointed to the kitchen table, where we unbuckled—*No guns at the table*—and then sat obediently. At minimum, he'd take my guns away for a few weeks, increase my chores, and tan my backside. At most, well . . . I'd rather not go there.

He picked up the phone and dialed Mr. Carter, and the two talked in hushed tones for several minutes. Before he hung up, Papa said, "You'll make the call?" He waited a second. "Good. We'll meet you down there."

Nanny had been shelling peas on the front porch, but she poked her head in when Papa appeared. Papa shook his head and waved her off with his hand. She returned to the porch, and Papa walked to their room; slid his wallet, change, and truck keys off the dresser; and then pointed us to his old, beat-up Dodge Power Wagon.

His failure to speak was a bad omen. My palms grew cold and clammy, and my stomach jumped up into my throat. The look of accusation and blame on Amos's face was almost more than I could handle.

We drove downtown in total silence. We had been warned. The time for talking was over, and I knew it. To make matters worse, my indiscretion was about to earn Amos a butt blistering too. The fact that he had not drawn would mean little to Mr. Carter. He was a part of it. The look on his face told me that idea had not been lost on him.

Papa parked the truck just off the town square and ushered us up the sidewalk and down another side street. At the first nondescript building on the right, he held the door and nodded us in. He still hadn't spoken a word, and his silence told me that I was in more trouble than I'd ever known in my entire life. In our house, guns—play or not—were respected. And when I fired off both caps at Papa, I hadn't.

The building was painted battleship gray, and the inside was very cold. The receptionist wore a sweater, which was odd given the fact that it was the middle of summer, and the whole place smelled like bleach and something else. Mr. Carter was sitting in a chair reading a magazine with his glasses on the end of his nose. When we walked in, he nodded at Papa and didn't say a word to either one of us.

We were dead meat. When their heads were turned, Amos glared and mouthed, "Nice going, butt head!"

The receptionist led us down a long hallway to a room that was well lit and looked like a hospital operating room, but without all the doctors and nurses. A man in blue scrubs met us in the back. He had a flashlight strapped around his head, but his apron looked like a butcher's. I remember thinking that if he was a surgeon, he sure was messy. With his hands covered in bloody white rubber gloves, he led us to a metal table, where a spotted white sheet covered what looked like somebody sleeping. The person's head was covered; I could tell his mouth was open, and I remember thinking it must have been difficult for him to sleep without feeling smothered.

About then it hit me that he might not be sleeping. Amos and I walked around the end of the table, and our eyes grew as wide as Oreos. The man's feet were sticking out from under the sheet. They were grayish-blue, and while the left pointed straight up, the right had sort of flopped over to the right. On his left big toe, somebody had tied what looked like a luggage tag. We walked around the other end, and Mr. Carter nodded to Papa, who nodded to the "doctor."

He set me on one side and Amos on the other, not more than six inches from the man's shoulders. Then he pulled back the sheet. He looked at both of us and then at the man on the table. "This . . . is what happens when you play with guns."

And I've never looked at one the same way since.

In the span of a millisecond, I learned that a firearm—no matter what kind—has one purpose: to kill. Period. No two ways about it. No matter what the movies teach you, and no matter how romantic the notion might be, if you point a gun at someone and pull the trigger, at the end of the day that person is dead. You can't pause, rewind, and replay. The blue man on the table taught me that.

Papa and I drove back to the farm in quiet, listening to the rhythmic sound of a pebble lodged in the tire tread. Back at the house, Papa was pensive. He returned to his tractor, where he usually did his best thinking. I started on tomorrow's chores, and when I finished those, I did anything I could think of that was helpful and would look as though I was paying penance. The thought of the whipping I was still sure of getting was a great motivator, and when Papa finally parked the tractor at a little after four, I had that barn looking like a showroom. Problem was, if Papa noticed, he didn't let on.

He hopped off the tractor and disappeared inside the house, and I stood just outside the door, waiting for him to call my name. With my heart pounding like a war drum, I stood against the frame and waited. A few minutes later he walked out the back door, kissed Nanny—who was drying her hands on her clean white apron—and then loaded back into the truck.

I couldn't quite tell, but Nanny didn't seem to have an angry look on her face. She almost looked as if she were trying to hide a smile. I wanted to ask if I could stay with her, but Papa cranked the engine and waved me into the front seat. This was not making sense. If he wanted me to suffer, he'd done the trick.

I opened the door. "Papa?"

He looked at me, his sun-wrinkled eyes bending downward at the edges.

"If I'm gonna get a whippin', I'd just as soon get it over."

He looked out the windshield, and when he looked back, I saw that his eyes had watered up. He patted the seat, swallowed, and nodded. He wasn't smiling, but he wasn't frowning either. Papa had something on his mind, and whatever it was seemed more important to him at the moment than blistering me, so I climbed in.

We drove back to town, something we rarely did twice in the same day. We parked on the street in front of the hardware store, and Papa led me between the aisles filled with garden tools and bolt bins and finally to the far corner of the store.

Mr. Steve, one of the four brothers who owned the place, was working behind the counter where they kept all the hunting and fishing stuff.

Papa leaned against the counter and extended his hand. "Steve."

Mr. Steve switched his cigarette to the other hand, brushed a few ashes off his shirt, and extended his hand. "Mr. Styles." He nodded at me and smiled. "Dylan."

Papa pointed his nose at the wall. "I've come to pay you what remains."

I looked at Papa, the confusion in me growing.

Mr. Steve nodded, smiled at me again, then looked back at Papa. "Yes, sir, eight months is a long time on layaway." He turned, walked to the only rifle I'd ever cared anything about, and pulled the Model 69 Winchester off the wall. My eyes grew as wide as bowling balls.

Papa pulled out a twenty-dollar bill and handed it to Mr. Steve, who punched the buttons on his cash register, pulled the handle, and stood back as the bottom drawer sprang open. He pulled out a single dollar, pulled the rifle off the wall, and slid the action downward, proving to both himself and Papa that it was unloaded. He handed it to Papa, who also checked it, and asked, "You want the box?"

Papa shook his head. "No." He looked at me and almost smiled. "It wouldn't last very long. Besides, we don't have very far to go." He hefted the rifle in his left hand, ever careful to keep the barrel down, then gently grabbed my left hand with his right, and we walked out while my teeth carved drag marks in the linoleum tiles.

Papa loaded me into the passenger's side and laid the rifle, barrel tip on the floor mat, next to me. My heart was pounding so hard I thought it would explode. He walked around, climbed in, and cranked the engine. He pulled his white handkerchief from his back pocket and wiped the sweat beading across his forehead. He methodically refolded it and then turned toward me. His face had turned serious again.

I swallowed, looked at the rifle, and swallowed again—afraid to hope. I saw now that Papa intended to hang this thing on the wall, where it would sit for two years, reminding me daily of my indiscretion. I'd have preferred a spanking. "Papa?"

Papa shook his head and put his hand on my shoulder. He thought for a moment, then said, "Yup, you messed up today, but . . . I did, too, when I was your age."

I almost smiled, then thought better of it. I wasn't out of the woods yet.

He lowered his voice. "I don't want to break the spirit of the kid in you; that's a precious thing." He took a deep breath. "But it's time we start making a man out of the boy I see before me."

That night, after we'd shot an entire box—fifty rounds—at more than our fair share of cans down at the river, Papa took me into the kitchen and laid the new rifle across the table. He sat me down and then laid down the law. His tone of voice told me that if I ever violated it, he'd take that rifle away for as long as I lived in this house.

"*Never* bring a loaded gun into the house."

"Yes, sir."

"Never point one at anybody—floor or ceiling only, unless you're shooting at a target and intend to pull the trigger."

"Yes, sir."

"Make sure of your target and what's behind your target. If you miss, what will you hit?"

I'd heard all this a hundred times before, but I wasn't about to interrupt him. "Yes, sir."

He sat back and patted the rifle, then pointed his finger at my face and inched his nose closer to mine. "Always, always, *always* treat a gun as if it's loaded, even when you know it's not."

"Yes, sir."

The kitchen smelled of Hoppe's solvent, Winchester oil, and Vicks mentholatum—Papa's choice of lip balm. Papa dipped the brass brush in the solvent, then ran it down the barrel, removing the gunpowder. Then he ran several quarter-sized, oiled white cloths down through the barrel until they came out looking as white as when they'd gone in. He brushed and oiled the action, the barrel, the trigger assembly, and finally the stock itself. Then he toweled it off so it wouldn't be too slick. When finished, the rifle lay on the table—clean, oiled, and empty. The thing that had filled my nights and days with dreams of heroes and grand deeds now lay on the table before me much like that man had.

Papa leaned forward. "You see that?"

"Yes, sir."

He paused, measuring his words. "By itself, that is harmless. Can't hurt a flea. The most dangerous thing about that . . . is you." He gently grabbed my hand and placed it on the stock. "You understand?"

I nodded. "Yes, sir."

"Does it scare you?"

I nodded.

He set me on his lap and wrapped his arms around me. I needed that hug. "Don't fear it—respect it." He smiled. "That way, you'll live to be my age, and older."

Later that night, the world seemed a lot bigger than it had when I'd woken up that morning. We were all sitting on the front porch, listening to the whippoorwill. Nanny and Papa swayed on the front porch while I stretched out across the top step.

"Papa?" The smell of his pipe wafted around us and filtered into the woodwork.

"Yes."

"You think it's okay with God if we have guns?"

Papa clinched his teeth about his pipe, pulled his yellow-handled Case Trapper from his front pocket, opened it, and began scraping his fingernails. Over his shoulder, nailed to the wall of the house, was a wooden plaque with the Ten Commandments etched onto it. He thought several minutes, nodded, and said, "I have thought a lot about that, and I think the answer is yes."

Knowing that he could quote each one by heart, I said, "Why?"

He didn't flinch. "'Cause not all men are good."

AMOS'S AND MY CHILDHOOD FASCINATION WITH GUNS HAD been killed that day, and that man lying cold and still on the stainless steel table took more to his grave than he intended. When I think back on it, it was one of the best lessons I've ever learned.

Amos asked me if I still had Papa's Model 12, and then asked if I remembered how to use it. I did. And he knew that I did. His question spoke volumes that both of us understood yet neither of us needed to voice. It told me that Amos had thought about it ahead of time, weighed asking me against not asking me, and asked anyway. And that, more than anything else, told me he was scared.

I looked toward the house, imagined the Model 12 leaning against the back wall of my closet, and tried to digest our conversation. I sat on the top step, leaned back, and noticed the small package perched above me on the railing. I lifted it, untied the silver bow that lay shining in the moonlight, slid off the lid, and found a child's pacifier.

With the pacifier lying on my left, Maggie asleep behind, Papa's Model 12 not too far away, uncertainty all around, our conversation swirling about inside me like smoke fumes, I sat in the middle and tried to make sense of it all.

When morning came, I still had not.

I stepped off the porch steps and walked around the side to the faucet beneath our bedroom window. The faucet had been running all night through a slow-leaking soaker hose that stretched through Maggie's vegetable garden. She had wrapped it around the base of a dozen or more tomato plants.

The window above gave me a clear view of Maggie stretched across the bed, tacked down at each corner. I smiled and tapped on the window. She didn't even budge. I tapped louder. She pulled a pillow over her head and waved me off. Blue rolled over and stuck all four paws in the air. I tapped a third time, and she threw a pillow at the window.

Laughing to myself, I reached down, turned off the dripping faucet, and froze. I studied the dirt path that ran between the house and the azalea bushes, and the closer I looked, the more unsettled I became. Footprints, lots of them, made by a barefooted person, covered the footpath.

As I followed them, I walked back and forth several times, finally coming to a stop beneath our window. Based on the length and depth of imprint, they were too big to be Maggie's and—I placed my bare foot inside the outline—too wide to be mine. I knelt, crawled around, and looked more closely. They couldn't be Amos's, because these had a defined arch and Amos was flat-footed. Maggie had been back here yesterday afternoon to turn on the faucet, but these prints covered hers.

All this told me two things: I didn't know what Peeping Tom had made these prints, and they had been made sometime between yesterday afternoon and this morning. I looked over to the porch where Amos and I had talked, just ten feet away, and felt cold.

chapter fifteen

THE PHONE RANG AND BROUGHT ME OFF MY KNEES. I poked my head above the azalea tops and listened. It rang a second time. Chances were good that a phone call this early had to be Caglestock. He rarely slept—one of the self-inflicted disciplines of managing Bryce's millions. "Hello?"

"Dylan, it's John." He sounded as if he'd been up awhile, and based on the speed with which he spoke, as if he'd already consumed a pot of coffee.

"Morning to you. How're things?"

"Good. Thanks for getting us those documents." Caglestock paused. "Hey, Dylan, how much do you know of Bryce's past? I mean, how much do you really know?"

I considered his question. "Ummm, only what you and he

have told me. Really, just the highlights. Bryce plays his cards pretty close to his chest."

John stalled. "Help me with that one."

"He only tells you what he wants you to know, or doesn't bother you with what he thinks you might not be interested in."

"That's my experience too. Which got me to thinking. We've done some digging, asked a few questions, and I wondered if you could come have lunch with us. Can you do that?"

"Sure. When?"

"Today." His tone had changed.

"Everything all right, John?"

"Don't know, but it'd be good if you were here. Still no word from Bryce."

I hung up the phone to the sound of Blue licking my toes and Maggie walking down the hall, covered in sleep. Her weight made the boards creak, and her calloused heels scuffed the bare floors. She walked up and leaned against me—sign language for "Good morning. Love you. I need a hug." Her hair was sticking in fifty different directions and floating on static electricity. If I hadn't known her, she might have scared me.

I hugged her, thought how warm she was, how soft her breasts felt and yet how firm her back had become, and finally, how perfectly she fit in the space between my shoulders.

"Who was that?" she mumbled.

"Caglestock. Wants me to have lunch with him."

She nodded, pulled the OJ from the fridge, and drank straight out of the jug. Then she pulled the bread out of the hamper, made two PB&Js, began eating one, and simultaneously started scrambling some eggs. While spreading cheese over the eggs, she ate the other sandwich. Every few seconds she'd take another swig from the OJ jug.

I leaned against the counter, hovering over my coffee mug

and watching. Maggs wasn't entirely awake yet, but in the last week or so, her appetite had become voracious. If something was edible and wasn't nailed down, she'd eat it.

When the eggs were fluffy, hot, and steaming, she ate them—directly off the skillet. She stood over the sink, scooped up a forkful, and blew across it. Not waiting long enough for it to cool off, she bit down, then stood with her mouth open trying to blow out the hot air. When she bit into a bite that was still too hot, she'd dance around a little like someone who'd swallowed a jalapeño.

Her short cotton nightgown fell an inch or so below the fold where her thighs met her bottom. Her long legs had begun to tan in the sun, and every day I marveled at the transformation. Her dance continued for several minutes while she polished off the eggs. After she'd cleaned the skillet, she peeled a banana and ate it in three bites. She washed that down with another swig and then stood holding the fridge door open.

She shook her head. "I need to get to the grocery store. There's nothing to eat here."

I raised an eyebrow and blew steam off my cup. "Tell me about it."

Eyeing the newspaper on the table, she pulled out a jar of pickles, sat down, and began reading the front page and fingering pickles into her mouth. She ate like a chain-smoker.

I tried not to laugh. "Honey, you want me to get you something to dip those in?"

She was reading the headlines and didn't pay me much attention. She shook her head, shoved another pickle into her mouth, and didn't look up. "No thanks."

I shook my head, kissed her on the cheek, and walked to the shower.

When I got out, I heard two women giggling and talking. The hyena laugh mixed with the muted snicker told me all I needed to know. I poked my head around the corner and saw Maggs and Amanda arm in arm, tears streaming down their faces, sitting on the floor of the den with a pint of Häagen-Dazs between them. Each was armed with a spoon and a handful of Kleenex.

"You girls okay?"

Amanda worked her spoon into the hard frozen ice cream and spoke over her shoulder. "Hey, Professor."

Despite the many changes in our lives and the multiple times I'd told her otherwise, Amanda just couldn't get past calling me Professor. By now, it had become a term of endearment.

"Hey, Amanda. How're things?"

"Good," she said, stuffing a spoonful into her mouth.

Maggs swallowed and pointed a loaded spoon at me. "You and Mr. Clean better get ready, 'cause dirty diapers don't change themselves."

I dressed, lifted our bedroom window, and, looking over my shoulder, quickly and quietly slid the long-barreled shotgun out and leaned it against the house. Blue looked at me as if I'd lost my mind.

Then I kissed Maggs, who'd decided to stay and talk children with Amanda, and waved to them both as I slipped out the back door. They had finished off the ice cream and were now standing in the nursery talking about window treatments. I walked around the house, grabbed the shotgun, slid it along the floorboard behind the backseat of my van, and idled out of the drive.

The air had turned hot, reminding me of things I missed. I turned off the AC, rolled down the windows, sped up, and remembered things I loved. The scanner sat beside me on the seat, crackling with numbers and codes that I was slowly learning to translate.

With sweat soaking through the back of my shirt, I drove the long way to town. It was Monday, Pastor John's day off, but when I drove by the church, his Cadillac was parked by itself around back. I looked in my rearview, saw nothing, and kept driving. A few more back roads and I drove by Bryce's locked gate. The chain and lock were still shiny with that just-off-the-shelf look. In the last year, confederate jasmine had grown across the gate and was now thick with fresh green leaves. It blocked any sight beyond the gate.

I drove by, felt the tug, and realized how much I missed seeing Bryce. I missed his deep, resonating brogue, his unshaven face, his reddish hair, his fat, burly chest, and our one-sided conversations that I seldom made sense of. I missed the sound of his pipes, his emerald green eyes, the taste of a cold beer shared in a Styrofoam cup. And, I'll admit, I even missed the comical look of him in a kilt or next to nothing at all.

Bryce was his own person, and to his credit, he didn't care what the world thought. There were times when I admired him for that. I didn't have time to stop then, but I told myself I would on the way back.

Lorraine met me at the door and led me to the conference room, where Caglestock introduced me to a man decked out in military dress and covered in medals.

"Dylan, this is Colonel Max Bates. He works in the Pentagon."

Colonel Bates wore a beret and a face that told me he'd seen more than his share of barrels pointed in his direction. He was in his midfifties and erect with a lifetime of military discipline. It seemed hardwired into his DNA.

The colonel extended his hand and nodded. "Dr. Styles,

good to meet you. John's told me about your friendship with Sergeant McGregor."

I shook his hand. "Yes, sir, Bryce is . . . well, he's someone I consider a friend, as much as Bryce is friends with anybody."

While we ate, Caglestock retold Colonel Bates of my friendship and working relationship with Bryce—how I handled his funds, how Bryce had given me power of attorney over most of his affairs, and how I tried to check in on him regularly.

The colonel listened, ate, and seemed to make mental notes. When Lorraine delivered a plate of chocolate chip cookies, Caglestock turned the conservation over to Colonel Bates, saying, "Max, I think it'd be helpful if you'd tell Dylan, tell us both, what you know about Bryce."

Colonel Bates swallowed, sat back, and thought for a moment. Finally he spoke. "Much of Sergeant McGregor's record is confidential. Top secret. Not even I, as his commanding officer, have enough clearance to read it, but since I saw most of it personally . . ." He shrugged and then shook his head. "When it comes to the psychological exams and reports, I won't have much for you." He picked a strawberry off the side of the cookie plate and ate it.

"Bryce Kai McGregor joined the Marines in 1970 for reasons I never did understand. Back then, he looked a lot like you. Clean-cut, full of life, innocent to an extent." Bates swiveled in his seat. "Maybe he was trying to earn his inheritance—I've seen it before. Rich kids wrestling with how to handle Daddy's money. We put him through the ropes, trying to get rid of him before he got himself killed, and he proved us wrong. The harder we made it, the better he did. It was like the kid had never been tested and had been waiting his whole life to be discovered. We laid him out at the range on the thousand-yard targets, and he dropped a few jaws. The kid could shoot like nothing I'd seen before or since. Boy had a gift." He paused, scratched his nose, and said, "And sometimes I wished I'd never discovered it."

He swiveled again. "Fast-forward a few years. Bryce, or Scotty, as he became known, was leading an elite team of specialists. Kind of like the Green Berets or Rangers, but more like what we now call the Delta Force. We didn't really give them a name, but we sent them any- and everywhere. Before Vietnam got so ugly, they'd been on missions all over the globe. And just as he did in training, the worse the conditions and the more impossible the mission, the more Bryce excelled. Fast-forward again to Vietnam, 1975, right at the end."

He paused again and chose his words carefully. "We had inserted Bryce and his team of eight in a place from which they were not expected to return. We told them that, we explained to them the value of the target, and we gave them the choice. They voted—unanimous. They were just like that." Bates teared up and shook it off. "For several reasons we lost radio contact. At the rendezvous, Bryce and his team never showed."

"Do you know what happened?"

He nodded. "I do—but that information is found in that part of the file I can't talk about." He folded his hands. "This is what I can tell you. Five months later, some three months after the U.S. had pulled out of Vietnam, I got a phone call. Three minutes later, I went straight to the top, we sent in two planes, extracted him, and brought the boy home—alone."

Bates took a handkerchief from his pocket and wiped his eyes. "I wished to God I'd never sent that kid in there. Of all of them, I should've . . . I knew he'd never leave a man behind. No matter the orders." He sat back, refolded his handkerchief, and stared out the window. "If you read the

whitewashed version of his record, you'll find a highly deco-
rated veteran who was and is missed by his country. If you read
the version you can't read, you'll find a one-man killing
machine, who's killed God only knows how many people, and
who, in the end, saw and had to do things that few men in history have ever been asked to do."

Silence spread across the room as the picture of Bryce,
passed out on his lawn chair before a John Wayne movie,
flashed before me.

Bates continued, his voice falling slightly. "We tried to reha-
bilitate him. Tried therapy, drugs, electroshock, you name it.
Anything we thought would help, we offered. Finally he left to
face his demons alone. I guess he's been facing them ever since."

"You make him sound like Rambo."

"I wish it were that simple."

Caglestock spoke up. "Would you describe him as having
post-traumatic stress disorder?"

Bates tilted his head and shook it. "If that were the extent
of Bryce's problem, I'd be jumping up and down. The military
can handle that. Bryce could too."

"If there's been a change in Bryce, why now?"

"If I knew the answer to that, I'd get my own talk show. In
my experience, men like Bryce are ticking time bombs. Some
just take longer than others to go off."

I didn't know what to say.

Bates looked at me. "I can see it on your face, so let me spell
it out. Bryce can kill you or any other human a thousand different ways with his thumb. Give him this pencil, and he can
kill you from the other end of the room. Give him a weapon,
and, well . . . if Bryce cracks or has already cracked, as we've
seen in a few others just like him, I don't think you're safe
going up to his place." He waited while the gravity of his words

settled in. "Actually, nobody within hiking distance is safe."

"What's hiking distance?"

He sucked through his teeth and calculated. "Bryce has covered a hundred miles without sleeping."

"What do you intend to do?"

He shook his head. "I can't tell you that. But if he contacts you, you'd do well to keep your distance. And under no circumstances should you take your wife or any other female up there."

"Why? I mean, what's the—"

He held out his hand like a stop sign. "If he's in the state I suspect he's in, the sight of a female might trigger some things you don't want to trigger." He sat back and placed both hands on his thighs as though he were ready to leave. "I've said enough." He stood and extended his hand. "I thank you for all you've done."

I nodded and shook his hand, and Colonel Bates walked out to the click of hard heels on tile floor. Caglestock led him to the door, said a few words in hushed tones, and then returned to the conference table, shutting the door behind him.

John took a deep breath as if he were still trying to digest the story. He poured us each a cup of ice water and sat back down. "What do you think we ought to do?"

I didn't hesitate. "I have no doubt that Bryce can kill me a hundred different ways from Sunday, but I'm leaving here, making one stop, and then going by to check on him."

Caglestock nodded. "You want me to go with you?"

I shook my head. "No. No offense, but I think I'd better go alone."

He nodded. "Call me if you run into him."

I stood to leave. "And if I find him, and call you, are you going to call him?"

I nodded out the window at Bates's car backing out of the parking lot.

Caglestock followed the red taillights with his eyes. "I don't know." He shook his head. "I don't know."

I DROVE THROUGH AN OLDER SECTION OF WALTERBORO AND passed the hardware store where Papa had bought me the Model 69 so many years ago. I parked along the street, grabbed Papa's Model 12 shotgun, slid the chamber slide open so that it not only was unloaded but also looked unloaded, and walked into the store—barrel down.

This would have seemed abnormal except that I carried it in my left hand, and folks were always carrying weapons in here. Vince, a crusty Korean War veteran and one of the best gunsmiths in South Carolina, worked here three days a week. Guys came from all over the South just to pass him their valuables across the countertop and hire his magic touch.

Vince had been working on firearms since the military taught him how in Korea. He could and would work on most anything, but he was partial to fine custom shotguns and double rifles. He also did all the custom work for most of the police and SWAT teams in two or three of the surrounding states. He and Amos were on a first-name basis, and because of that, so were he and I.

In the far corner of the store, the gun counter was usually dotted with men leaning against it like a bar. Mostly they talked about guns they wanted, or if they got tired of that, they talked about guns they had—which only led them back to ones they wanted. Vince seldom responded or initiated the conversation. He just nodded, lit another cigarette, and stared out the window of the store.

I walked up to the counter. "Hey, Vince."

"Dylan." He eyed the Model 12, and I passed it across the counter.

Vince, hanging the cigarette from his lip, took the shotgun and started looking it over. He worked the action, eyed the receiver, clicked the safety back and forth, slowly cracked the trigger, and then slid the action open once again. He said nothing, but the smile on his face told me he liked the feel of a fifty-year-old shotgun, and his eyes asked, *Can I help you?*

I looked over both shoulders and leaned closer. "I, uh . . . I think I want to change the choke on that."

The choke of a shotgun does just what it sounds like. It chokes the flow of shot. Think of a brass hose nozzle with a twist stream. Squeezing it down makes for a tighter stream. Opening it wide makes for a spray. What I handed Vince was a squeezed-down stream. What I'd come to get was a wide-open stream.

There was only one way to get this. I knew this, Vince knew this, and he knew that I knew this.

He eyed the tip of the thirty-inch barrel. "It's full now." He moved the cigarette from one corner of his mouth to the other. "With this barrel, even screw-in chokes won't make much of a difference."

Screw-in chokes were a development in late-model shotguns that allowed a shooter with a fixed barrel, or one shotgun, to screw in varying chokes to suit his or her hunting needs. The determining factor was the distance to be shot. In short, quail and skeet, usually close-in game, required a "skeet" or "improved cylinder" choke. Doves, a bit farther out, required more of an improved cylinder, while geese and turkey, sometimes shot from as far as forty or fifty yards, required a "full" choke.

I looked over my shoulder again and wrestled with what I wanted to say.

Vince read my face and asked, "You thinking about opening day of dove season?"

I shook my head.

He eyed the shotgun again. He knew no one in their right
mind shot quail with a twelve-gauge, so he asked, "You taking
up skeet shooting?"

I shook my head again.

He laid the shotgun on a velvet cloth laid out across the
countertop. "You hunting something else close-up?"

I bit my lip and half-nodded. There was one choke wider
than skeet. It was called cylinder bore and was used primarily
by law enforcement. It gave the widest pattern in the shortest
distance and really had only one purpose.

Vince looked at the shotgun. "Police and SWAT carry theirs
down to fourteen inches." He ran his fingers along the blued
steel. "But us normal citizens can't go below eighteen." He
shrugged. "Unless you want to apply for a special permit, or
your buddy comes in here and puts it on his books."

I shook my head. "Let's just go eighteen, maybe even eighteen and a quarter." I laid my hand across the barrel. "Legal,
but . . ."

Vince picked up the shotgun again and interrupted me.
"You sure you want to do that to this? They don't make them
like this anymore."

I nodded. Given the right machinery, cutting off a shotgun
barrel took about thirty seconds. Vince had the machinery
that could cut, sand, and polish it.

He stubbed out his cigarette and said, "Give me about ten
minutes."

I shopped the aisles and then returned to the counter as
Vince was pulling off his black apron and oiling the shotgun.
He handed it across the counter.

"I saw a lot of those in the war."

"What do I owe you?" I asked.

He shook his head. "Nothing. But if your greens or water-melon come in this year, I'll take whatever you got."

"Will do."

chapter sixteen

I SHUT THE DOOR OF THE VAN, EYED THE NOW-shorter shotgun, and decided to leave it behind the backseat. I shuffled under the fence and up the drive. I smelled smoke and saw the white cloud wafting up just beyond the trees. When I cleared the canopy, a trash pile was smoldering not far from Bryce's trailer. It was mostly ashes and soot, meaning it might've been lit sometime yesterday.

I walked up to the trailer and knocked on the door. No answer. I walked around to what was now Bryce's film library and projection house. No answer. I walked around back toward the obstacle course and whistled, then I walked back to the trailer, pushed open the door, whistled inside, and waited. Nothing. I turned around. And almost peed in my pants.

Not three inches from my face stood Bryce, and it took me

a second or two to recognize him. He had lost weight. A lot of weight, maybe fifty pounds. He was chiseled, clean-shaven—both his face and head—and he wore military BDUs. They were camouflage, starched, and ironed to a crease. His black boots were polished to a mirror shine, and he carried what looked like an ivory-handled Colt 1911 in a shoulder holster.

He stood looking at me, studying my face and features as though we'd never met. While he studied, he reached into the pocket on his thigh and pulled out a pack of chewing gum—the kind with the little pockets protected by foil. He popped all twelve pieces out of the sheet of gum, tossed them into his mouth, and started chewing with great labor.

The smell of spearmint was overwhelming. Bryce chewed for several seconds, swallowing what was obviously extreme production by his saliva glands, and continued to study me while his eyes watered. When he had the gum in a manageable wad, he looked me over and said, "Dylan."

I stepped back. "Hey, Bryce."

His sleeves were rolled up and buttoned, exposing arms that were suntanned and rippling with muscle and veins. On the opposite strap of his shoulder harness he carried a large silver-handled, brass-butted survival knife. The thing was at least a foot long. The handle hung down toward his waist and could be slid from the sheath with a simple flick of the tab that locked it in place. Both the knife and the pistol were oiled and appeared to have had their fair share of use.

I eyed the weapons and Bryce, who was still chewing vigorously. Without a word, he turned with precision, hopped off the steps, grabbed a rucksack that I had not noticed, and hoisted it onto his shoulders. It was fully loaded, probably weighed a hundred pounds, and Bryce didn't even seem to notice it. He cinched down the straps and waist belt, nodded,

turned toward the woods, and began what can only be de-
scribed as a cross between a march and a jog.

"Bryce!" I managed.

He stopped, double-timed it back up the hill, and stopped
once again just inches from my face. He was sweating, the vein
along the right side of his brow was throbbing, and he looked
magnificent.

"I just . . . we just . . . , ummm, Maggie's pregnant."

Bryce stopped chewing, looked from me to the ground to
the treetops and maybe to an image in his head. "Maggie?"

I nodded. His brow wrinkled a bit, then control took over
once again. He stuck out his hand, and I took it. Or rather, he
took mine.

I'd never felt a hand that strong. It was a vise. If he had
wanted to crush mine, he could have. The muscles in the
palm were thick and covered in callus. But like the rest of
Bryce, his hand wasn't dirty. He was meticulously clean and
smelled of deodorant and aftershave. He grasped my hand,
shook gently, turned, and then disappeared into the trees.
Within seconds, I couldn't even hear him walking.

chapter seventeen

An hour later, I pulled into the drive and idled around back. I admit, I was growing accustomed to air-conditioning and cruise control—but the minivan couldn't hold a candle to my truck. Maybe my identity was too closely linked to some rusted metal and a few working parts, but the absence of my truck had left a sour taste in my mouth. I missed it: I missed the musty smell of sweat mixed with oil, the way it sounded when I cranked it, the way it needed a few minutes to warm up in the morning, the way I knew when to add to or change the oil, the play in the steering wheel, the way the door sounded when I shut it, and the sound the window made when I lowered it.

I put the Honda in park, shook my head to get out the bitter taste, and then imagined my wife strapping our son or daughter into the child-restraint seat behind me.

It was late, and the sun had already fallen behind the trees. I grabbed my scanner—now my constant companion, since Blue seldom left Maggie's side—and stepped out of the van.

First thing I saw was Maggie sitting on the back steps with a large carving knife in one hand and a chunk of watermelon in the other. Her feet straddled a huge melon that had been whacked down the middle and already had most of the heart cut out of it. She had red juice smeared onto both cheeks and dripping off her chin. Her cheeks were so stuffed with watermelon that she looked like a chipmunk. Blue was licking the right side of her face.

I rested my foot on the first step and eyed the watermelon. "Where'd that come from?"

Maggie took another bite and smiled earlobe to earlobe. She took another enormous bite, squeezed juice out the sides of her mouth, and forced her lips into a funnel. She leaned back, lifting her heels off the steps, then lurched forward, spitting the seed high over my head and into the grass.

Blue jumped off the steps and started sniffing the grass. I wiped my face where Maggie had just covered me in watermelon puree. She pointed the carving knife out across our pasture toward Old Man McCutcheon's farm, which bordered ours.

Old Man McCutcheon was rather particular about his watermelon crop. Not only was growing watermelons a science that he studied; it was also something he protected—vehemently. And it had been this way as long as Amos and I could remember.

Sure, we'd stolen a few back in our day, but that ended with us tangled in an electrical fence after being spotlighted like two deer in the headlights. After McCutcheon cut the power and relieved us of the melons we'd been trying to steal, he sat us down in his kitchen, handed us the phone, and made us call our folks. And since stealing was stealing, that ended poorly too.

It would be years before we ventured back into his fields, and then only when we were certain beyond any shadow of a doubt that he and Mrs. McCutcheon had driven their motor home north for their every-two-years ten-day vacation.

Evidently Maggie had no such inhibition. She pointed the carving knife behind her. Stacked up like firewood sat five more watermelons just as large as the one she was currently dissecting. Given their size and weight, and what I knew of her size and weight, that meant she'd made no fewer than six trips across Old Man McCutcheon's fence and into his fields. One trip and you might get lucky. Two and you're tempting fate. Six and you're courting the dark side.

I smirked. "You go shopping?"

Her mouth was packed. There was no way on earth she could form a complete sentence. Maggie bit again, squeezing out more juice. "Uh-huh."

"Wow," I said, sitting next to her. "Must have been a long walk home from the grocery store, since I had the van."

Maggie's only reply was to lean back, lift her heels, inhale deeply, funnel her lips, and lurch forward again, sending the seeds out farther than the first. I looked closer and noticed that the ground was covered in shiny black dots. I got up and grabbed a melon, set it between my legs, and pulled Papa's yellow-handled Case Trapper from my back pocket. I slit the melon down the middle, cut out the heart, and buried my face in sweet South Carolina. Few things are better, and knowing she'd robbed Old Man McCutcheon made it all the sweeter.

By dusk, about the time the first of the wood ducks screamed overhead en route to their roost somewhere south along the river, we'd covered the grass in seeds, spit, laughter, and watermelon rinds.

It grew dark, and the fireflies lit up the night. They danced in silence over and in between the cornstalks, filling our eyes with wonder and lazy amazement. A gentle breeze ushered in and blew off some of the dust and heat. I grabbed a black plastic trash bag and began picking the rinds off the grass. The breeze shifted and swirled about the house, bringing with it an earthy smell and . . . the smell of smoke.

I stood, sniffed the air, and followed it toward the direction it had come from. Smelling smoke in the country was nothing new, but doing so on a breezy night like this, when the forest service never would have issued a burn permit, gave me pause. Then I smelled the unmistakable tinge of kerosene, which meant one of two things: a gas station had just blown up, or somebody's old house, made of heart of pine, also known as "fat lighter," was burning to the ground. Given the conditions and the absence of a gas station within ten miles of my house, I guessed the latter. When the scanner crackled five seconds later, it confirmed my fears.

I ran inside, jumped into my firefighting pants and boots, slid the suspenders over my shoulders, and ran back out the door, carrying my helmet and jacket and tripping over my own feet. Maggie was sitting on the porch listening to the scanner, and her eyes told me that the seriousness of what she was hearing outweighed the sight of me in my suit. She ran with me to the van and said, "I'll check on Amanda."

I threw my stuff in the back and took a long look south. The black billow of pine burning hot clouded the night sky, but it was the sight of the flames almost four miles away that really got my attention. I kissed Maggie, jumped into the van, slammed it into drive, and spun the front tires out the driveway. I turned onto the blacktop and nearly collided with Amos's truck as he spun sideways out of his own drive. I corrected and let him straighten out, and then I, too, punched the accelerator to the floor. I only looked down once, but when I did, the speedometer was pressing against the plastic somewhere north of eighty-five miles an hour.

We pulled into the parking lot that was swirling in red flashing lights and firemen running around like ants. I threw on my helmet and started toward the source, but the heat was so intense that we couldn't get any closer than the front steps of the church. Pastor John's Cadillac, parked right up front, had already been consumed by the flames, and when I looked up, the steeple was just beginning to fall. The collapse of the narthex sent a huge flash of flame and sparks out onto the men holding the hoses, all of which were trained on the base of the flames.

The fire must have started in the narthex, because not much of it remained. Based on the flames shooting out of the roof, half the pews were gone and the altar wouldn't be far behind. The church offices backed up to the rear of the church, and even in the darkness I could see smoke billowing from every orifice, window, or soffit.

Amos hit the ground running and tapped the first guy he found holding the hose. "Where's John?" he demanded.

The guy shrugged, and Amos took off for the back of the church. He returned a few seconds later, coughing, and grabbed an ax from the side of the ladder truck. With the ax spread between both hands, he disappeared again. I grabbed an air tank and a second ax and followed.

When I turned the corner, the flames reflected off the river and lit the shape of a man climbing out of the water. I couldn't see his face, and he was draped in something, but his eyes told me all I needed to know. He stepped out of the water as though he lived in it and began climbing the bank toward us. He was just a few feet away, but I didn't have time to wait or ask questions, so I put my head down and followed Amos.

Amos reached the door, braced his feet, and took one huge Paul Bunyan swing at it. The door literally came off at the hinges and flew backward into the smoke. Amos ran through the door into the smoke and disappeared. I lost sight of him, but he didn't have air and wouldn't last long. I followed.

I ran down the hallway, shouting, but couldn't hear or see him. The heat was intense, as was the sound of crashing timbers in the church and flames overhead. I'd never been in something this hot, but I knew we had a minute or so at best and a few seconds at worst. If Pastor John was in here, chances were good he was long dead from smoke inhalation—and if Amos didn't turn around right now, he would be too.

I ran down the hall toward John's office, turned right, and tripped on a body. I gathered myself, shone my light, and saw Amos's bloody face. A cross timber had come through the roof and hit him across the shoulder and back of the head. Pastor John's door was next to him and shut. I tried the handle, but it was locked. I kicked it, but it didn't budge. Smashed at it with the ax, and one hinge busted loose. Hit it again in the middle and loosened it again. Finally I swung as hard as I could and broke it free enough to wedge the ax in and hack it off the hinges.

I shoved the door out of the way and dragged Amos into the room, where the air was less smoky and a window AC unit was blowing outside air in. I figured that gave us about thirty more seconds. I heard another huge crash and jumped on top of Amos, covering him with my body, as sparks and flames exploded through the roof. I was hot inside my suit, and Amos wasn't wearing one, so I knew his skin had to be boiling. I shone my light around the office and saw no trace of John.

Time was up. If I didn't get Amos up and over my shoulder right now, we were both dead, because the roof was about to come in on us and I could barely see my hand in front of my face. I tried to lift Amos, then heard a cough and a thump behind me. I crawled around the side of the desk, and there lay Pastor John. His eyes were closed, his face had been beaten badly, his clothes were torn, his hands and feet were tied, and he was covered in blood.

I looked from Pastor John to Amos and back to Pastor John. I had time to get one person out of this hellhole before it swallowed us. I crawled over to Amos and slapped him in the face. *"Amos! Amos! Get up! Wake up, Amos!"*

He was as limp as a sack of potatoes and just as responsive. I screamed again, but neither man moved. I grabbed Amos by the strap of his shoulder holster and Pastor John by the ropes tied around his feet. I dragged both to the door, but the two of them were more than I could drag out. The smoke had gotten inside my air mask and was killing my eyes; the heat was so intense. I took another deep breath, grabbed each man again, and tried to pull them through the door, but the roof came in above me and something very heavy hit my helmet and sent me to the floor. I blacked out and tried to get up on my hands and knees, but the room was spinning out of control and looked upside down and backward. Something big and fiery had fallen across Amos, and the flames were starting to climb up his legs. I crawled across him, tried to stamp out the flames, but it was no use. Flames were all around us, and sparks were burning my skin around my collar and between my sleeves and gloves.

I threw the flaming thing off Amos, pulled Pastor John over next to us, covered Amos's body with mine, and cradled his head next to mine. I didn't know where the door was or used to be. I didn't know how I got in or how to get out, and the blow to my head had made me nauseous. I tried to control the urge to vomit but could not. When the first heave came, I started crying. I didn't want to go this way, and I didn't want Amos to either. I stood, made one last attempt to throw him over my shoulder. Then I took another look at Pastor John, and the tears came. How was I going to explain this?

I stepped over Pastor John, took one last look, and ran smack into Bryce. He was dripping wet, covered in a blanket that was also soaking wet, and in his arms he carried what looked like another. I grabbed him by the blanket, shouted above the roar of the flames, and pointed. *"Bryce! Pastor John!"*

Without blinking, Bryce lifted Pastor John over his shoulder, turned, and shoved me in a direction I didn't want to go, and we lurched through the flames together. When we came out the other side, we were standing in what used to be the hallway. Bryce pushed me again, and eight steps later we were running into the spray of the ladder hose that was falling down across the church. We turned through one last burning frame, jumped, and landed on the dirt outside Pastor John's office. I guess we'd just run through what used to be his wall. Amos landed on top of me, we rolled, and when I came to my feet, I saw that his pant legs were on fire. I was standing just a few feet from the river, so I picked him up, hugged him to my chest, and ran down the bank.

The weight of Amos's body pushed me down into the black, cool water. The hole was deep, much deeper than my six-foot height, and I had no footing. I threw off my helmet, wrestled myself out of my tank and jacket, and pushed Amos's head up and out of the water. I kicked hard, but my boots made it nearly impossible. I reached, grabbing for anything, knowing I needed air.

I pushed Amos as far as I could and then felt him yanked out of my hands with a force I didn't know existed in another human. Amos left the water as though he'd been propelled by an engine. My pants had filled with water, as had my boots, and they were pulling me down. It'd been a long time since I'd had any air, and I needed it now. I saw the flames beyond the water, reached toward them, and felt a powerful, muscled hand grab mine. Bryce lifted me from the water as if I were a feather and flopped me on the beach next to Amos, where I lay sputtering and coughing as the flames that had engulfed the church lit the beach.

I looked around and knew the paramedics were working on Amos. Looking up the hill, I saw them loading somebody onto a stretcher and wheeling him toward the back of an open ambulance. The guys fighting the fire had backed away and were now attempting to contain rather than extinguish. The church was gone.

A paramedic jumped across me and pointed a light in my eyes. I grabbed it and shone it toward Amos. I tried to reach for him to check his vitals, but the paramedic pressed my shoulders into the ground and said, "Hey, Superman, we'll take it from here."

I took one last look around, but Bryce was nowhere to be seen. Somewhere in there, everything went black.

chapter eighteen

WHEN I CAME TO, AMOS WAS GONE. THE PARAMEDICS
had my clothes off and were gingerly checking me for burns.
Evidently I had escaped real damage. I'd been singed pretty
badly, but I'd heal. They let me breathe some oxygen a few
minutes to clear my lungs, but my tank had taken pretty good
care of me. My throat was scratchy, my skin felt as if all the
moisture had been sucked out of it, and in general I felt like
a piece of smoked barbecue.

I walked up the bank in my boxer shorts and accepted a
blanket from a paramedic who was handing them out. The
ambulance carrying Amos disappeared down the road, and I
knew I needed to collect Maggie and Amanda and then get to
the hospital. I knew Amos had been breathing when we started

out of the church, but after that, I wasn't so sure. And as for Pastor John, I wasn't so sure either.

I took one last look at the church, but there wasn't much to see. Nothing standing but some charred remains and a black residue that in the nighttime spotlight of the fire trucks looked like tombstones in a cemetery. I jumped into the van, pegged the accelerator, and wished for some Gatorade.

Amos's house was quiet and dark. I pulled into our drive and around the back of the house and parked the van. I ran up the back steps calling for Maggie, then came to a sudden halt. The screen door had been ripped off the hinges.

I stepped into the kitchen, which looked as though it had been hit by a tornado. The table sat upside down, two chairs were missing, and the other two lay on their sides in the hall-way leading to our room. Pots and pans littered the floor, drawers had been pulled from the cabinets and dumped, and every utensil we had lay scattered like leaves around the room. What glasses we used to own now lay in ten million shards across the floor.

"Maggie!"

I tiptoed my way through the kitchen and stood in the den. My drum that had been sitting atop the mantel now lay on the floor with a kitchen knife sticking through the middle. The coffee table lay upside down, and the couch was turned on its side.

"Maggs!"

I ran down the hallway, dodging furniture, shoes, and lamps. Whatever had happened here, Maggie had put up one hell of a fight. I reached the door to our room and heard Blue growl-ing. I turned the corner, and there in the corner sat Blue, crouched over the figure of Maggie, who lay crumpled on the floor in a bloody mess.

"Maggs!"

She was breathing, but her face was puffy and purple. Her lips were cut, her eyes almost swollen shut, and her shirt had been ripped off. Blue whined and nuzzled me, and he, too, was bloody.

I gently picked her up, bringing gurgled coughs and moans of pain from her bleeding mouth. She put one arm around me while the other hung limp. I carried her gently to the van and laid her down in the back. Blue hopped in and lay down next to her, careful not to nudge her. I climbed into the driver's seat, cranked the engine, and pulled out of the drive.

And then I saw the smoke trailing out of the soffit above Amos's kitchen. Shining through the window, a single flame rose up toward the ceiling. I looked down at Maggie's swollen and bloody face and shoved the stick into drive. I didn't let off the accelerator until we reached town.

I drove into the emergency room entrance and found one of Amos's newest deputies directing traffic. He tried to route me into the parking lot, and I almost ran him over. I pulled up in front of the double glass doors and opened the side door to lift Maggie out. The deputy ran up alongside me and shone a light in my face. When he saw it, and Maggie, he got out of the way and told others to do the same.

I put my hand on his shoulder and said, "Fire at Amos's house."

I lifted Maggs from the car and walked through the doors, Blue close on my heels. The receptionist took one look at me and immediately got on the phone. Two seconds later she punched a button and pointed, and the door marked Medical Personnel Only opened. I walked through and followed her to a brightly lit room that was filling up with nurses and techs. One nurse pointed at the bed, and I laid Maggie down gently.

I brushed the sticky hair out of her face, and she tried to smile. She said something, but I couldn't understand. I leaned over, and she tried to speak again, but she coughed, spitting blood. Finally she pulled me closer and whispered, "What took you so long?"

That's when the tears came.

God, please take care of my wife.

A nurse was cutting off Maggie's jeans, and another put her hand on my shoulder and led me away from the table. Amanda walked in then, dressed in flowery scrubs.

The nurse sat me down in a chair nearby and then returned to Maggie's bedside. When they finished cutting off her clothes, Amanda brought them to me and laid them next to my chair. She touched me gently on the shoulder and returned to Maggie.

I wondered about Amos and her dad, but her being here told me enough of what I needed. I picked up the clothes and studied them. The seat of Maggie's jeans was sticky, stained dark red, and under the light, I noticed that the tops of my arms were too.

THE STAFF GOT MAGGS COMFORTABLE, WASHED HER CUTS and nicks, gave her something to take the edge off, and put several pads beneath her. Then they rolled her down the hall for X-rays and a CT scan. Everywhere she went, Amanda went too. I sat in the room staring at the terrazzo.

A few minutes later they wheeled her back in, and I stepped up to the side of her table. Maggs had been crying, but she was doped up pretty well. Amanda, holding a fresh pad, nodded at me. I gently lifted Maggie's bottom off the bed and held her there while Amanda pulled off the old and put down the new. Amanda's face was pain-stricken.

I tried to speak. "When I left, your house was . . ."

She nodded but didn't take her eyes off Maggie. "I know."

Dr. Frank walked in soon after, spoke with the attending physician, and walked to the other side of the bed. A nurse followed, rolling what looked like an ultrasound machine.

They squirted a bunch of jelly across Maggie's tummy and then began waving the wand around her belly button. Maggs was having a hard time keeping her eyes open.

Amanda walked around the bed, tears rolling off her cheeks, and locked her arm inside mine. She stood next to me while Dr. Frank watched the screen.

The other nurses talked in hushed tones, and not even Dr. Frank said much. I heard a shuffling at the door and turned to see Amos standing in the doorway, wearing a hospital gown and leaning on a crutch. An oxygen mask loosely covered his mouth, while a nurse held an ice pack to his head. He looked as bad as I'd ever seen him. Some red-colored goo covered both his ankles and calves, and his head looked as though it had been hit with a bowling ball.

He shuffled over, sat next to me, held the oxygen mask close to his face, and breathed deeply. He coughed, breathed deeply again, and said nothing.

Amanda took the ice pack from the other nurse and held it gently on the back of his bald and blood-smeared head. He grabbed her hand, she squeezed his, and still neither one said a thing. Amos sniffled, bit his lip, and pulled the mask away from his face. His eyes were beyond red, and I noticed that his eyebrows and eyelashes were singed and had been mostly burned off. He breathed again. "I came as soon as I heard."

I thought for a minute. The room was mostly quiet. Whenever someone spoke, they did so in a reverent whisper.

People seemed to tiptoe around. I looked from Amos to Maggs and back to Amos. "Heard what?"

A tear fell off Amos's face. He pointed with the oxygen mask. "That . . . that Maggs was . . . was . . . is . . . losing the baby."

chapter nineteen

I KNELT NEXT TO THE BED AND BRUSHED HER HAIR behind her ear. Maggie's eyes were closed because they had given her something to relax her and help her sleep. They'd found at least three broken ribs and thought she'd do better if she could sleep eight hours or so. Her face was pale and bruised and still needed cleaning. I turned to Amanda and opened my mouth, but I didn't even need to ask.

Amanda brought some gauze pads and solution, and I gently cleaned Maggs's face and shoulders while Amanda washed her arms and legs. Amanda looked tired and worried.

I spoke softly. "How's your dad?"

She nodded and reached for my hand. "He'll make it. They'll keep him tonight, but it's just routine. Momma's with him now."

When we finished, I patted Maggie dry, covered her with a new gown and several blankets, and then lifted her again while Amanda changed the pad beneath her. It was spotted dark red and dotted with blackish clots.

Amanda rolled the pad inside itself, placed it in a bag, and looked at me with tears pouring off her face. Her bottom lip was quivering. Amos stood looking out the window, blinking a lot and crying.

Dr. Frank came in and pulled me aside. He was wearing jeans, running shoes, a team shirt for what looked like his kid's T-ball team, a white coat, and his stethoscope. He said, "Her injuries are many, but physically she'll recover. Whoever did this was pretty strong, but Maggie's tough." He tried to smile. "She's proven that." His forehead wrinkled with concern. "As for the pregnancy . . ."

He pointed at Amanda, straightening the pads beneath Maggie. "This will continue for another hour, maybe longer. Women's bodies do this at different paces." He looked as if what he was saying pressed down on his shoulders and made it difficult to breathe deeply. "We just have to wait it out." He sat me down, placed the clipboard on his lap, and said, "There's one other thing."

I tried to listen, but it sounded to me as if he were talking out of a barrel. The echo in my ears slurred the words, and all I wanted to do was cradle Maggie's head in my hands and tell her everything would be okay. We'd be okay. As long as she woke up, we'd make it.

Dr. Frank turned a pen over in his hand. "Has she been running a fever?"

I shook my head. "No." I looked at Maggie. Her temples were sweating, and yet her face looked pale. "Well, I don't think so."

"She has one now. Low grade. 'Bout a hundred. But based on her blood work, I think she might have had it awhile."

"What do you mean?"

He shook his head. "I don't think whoever did this"—he waved his hand across Maggie's bed—"did that." He pointed to the pad. "I don't think they're connected. The one might have brought on the other a bit faster, but I think the clock has been ticking and this would have happened, or was in the process of happening, anyway. I need to run some more tests."

He put his hand on my shoulder. "Let's get through tonight. We've got her on some antibiotics now, so let's worry about tomorrow, tomorrow."

Amanda dipped herself under Amos's shoulder and helped him limp out of the room.

When they got halfway to the door, I whispered, "Hey, Ebony?"

Amos turned.

"Your house was . . . ."

Amos nodded, and they walked out, leaving me alone with Maggie.

The machines that I had come to hate were now monitoring her every movement, breath, and heartbeat. I sat next to her wanting to unplug every single one, scoop her into my arms, and disappear out the front door. I'd put in my time here, in these halls, these rooms. I had no desire to do it again. I whispered in her ear and laid my hand beneath hers.

After an hour or so, I checked her feet, then searched the room for some socks. I changed her pad and cleaned the backs of her legs and bottom. Then I straightened her gown, pulled up the covers, laid a second blanket across her feet and shins, and pushed the nurse's call button.

In a moment a woman's voice said, "Yes?"

"Hi, um, do you know if there are any socks around here for the patients?"

The voice hesitated, then crackled back over the speaker, "Honey, give me a few minutes. I'll find you some."

Ten minutes later I heard heavy footsteps and then a slight knock on the door. A familiar face looked in. "May I?"

It had been almost eighteen months since I'd seen her, working the nurses' station on Maggie's hall. She had cut her hair, lost a few pounds, and was wearing makeup. She grabbed the tip of her name tag and held it under the light so I could read it: ALICE MAY NEWSOME, SERVING 40 YEARS.

I stood, realized that it hurt to do so, and braced myself against the wall. "Hi, Allie. You look good. It's good to see you."

She hugged me and handed me a pair of socks. "Hey, honey, how's your girl?"

I shrugged. "She's tough, but . . ." I accepted the socks and gently tugged them onto Maggie's feet.

Allie had disappeared. In a few minutes she was back with a really hot cup of coffee, another blanket, and a pair of scrub pants.

"For you." She pointed at my clothes. "Thought you might be cold."

I looked down for the first time since being in the hospital and noticed that I was still dressed only in my boxer shorts and the socks I'd been wearing beneath my rubber boots.

JUST BEFORE DAYLIGHT, AMOS RETURNED. HE WAS LIMPING; his right calf and shin were wrapped in gauze and looked goopy with some sort of greasy brown medicine. All of it was held in place via some fishnet-looking thing.

His flip-flops, shorts, and aftershave told me he'd showered, and the small black duffel bag tucked under his arm told me he'd been by my house. He handed me the duffel, and it smelled like smoke.

Amos put his hands together and rolled his head around as if he were trying to pull the words out. "Last night, after we got here. Whoever they were, they came back to your house." He shook his head. "Your buddies got there within a few minutes, but . . . Some of the guys went back this morning and covered the hole in the roof with a tarp. You got insurance, right?"

I nodded.

He put his arm around me and pointed to the bag. "Thought you might want some clothes."

"Thanks."

"Your shower stuff is in there." He tried to smile, but he looked more anguished than happy.

I walked into Maggie's bathroom, pulled the curtain behind me, and tried to wash off the last twelve hours. I washed off the smoke and the sweat, and I scrubbed off Maggie's blood that had caked on my forearms, but the rest wouldn't come out.

I dressed in jeans and a T-shirt and walked back out into the room to find Amos standing guard over Maggie. The picture of our smoldering house was just starting to sink in. I wanted to know more. "How bad is it?"

Amos didn't look at me.

I tugged on his arm. "Hey."

Both sweat and tears were running down his face. "Let's get through this right here first."

I looked at Maggie and prayed to God the fire hadn't touched the nursery. "Where'd it start?"

Amos looked at me. He could tell I wasn't letting up. "Back of the house."

There were two rooms in the back of the house, ours and the nursery. "Which side?"

Amos raised his chin, his eyes glistening in the blue light of Maggie's machines. "Both."

I thought a minute, the anger bubbling. "Why? Why, Amos?"

A tear fell off Amos's face and landed on the sheet near Maggie's foot. "Why does somebody like that do anything? It's just meanness. That's all."

Moments passed in silence. I held Maggie's limp, hot hand and wrestled with disbelief. "How's your place?"

Amos shook his head. "Even the toys in the front yard are melted." He studied Maggie's face. "Did she say who did this?"

I shook my head.

Amos paused, letting the automatic blood pressure cuff expand, measure, and then deflate itself once again. "John said he didn't see who hog-tied him and set the church on fire. Said he was sitting at his desk, turned to grab a book out of his credenza, and then somebody whacked him on the head and turned out the lights. Next thing he knew, we were rolling on top of him and the room was full of smoke. Said his eyes were burning so bad and the roar of the fire was making so much noise that he didn't know who we were till we landed outside in the mud."

I looked at him. "You got any ideas?"

He nodded, stared through me, and said nothing. Then he looked at Maggie. "We should know more once Maggie wakes up." He walked to the door, turned, and looked as if he were replaying last night. "How'd you get us out of there, anyway?"

I shook my head. "I didn't."

Amos's eyes grew wider, revealing his confusion.

"Bryce did. Covered in a wet blanket. He threw Pastor John over his shoulder, and I grabbed the back of the blanket and followed him out."

Amos nodded. "I've got a meeting down at the station. I also got a call from Vince at the hardware store, said he wanted to talk to me. He said that you'd been in . . ."

I nodded and looked at the floor.

Amos stood in the doorway and waited while a few nurses passed in the hall. He lowered his voice. "You okay?" Even with all he had going on, all he was worried about, all the pain the burns on his legs were no doubt causing him, Amos was still checking my pulse.

"Yeah." I pointed at his leg and head. "You?"

He shrugged it off. "First degree. Nothing more. Give me a Band-Aid and I'm good. Besides," he said, smiling, "'Manda said the women from church are already dropping off casseroles and pies at her folks' house. You'd think I'd had a baby or something."

Amos pulled the door behind him and left me alone with Maggie. I pulled the chair up next to the bed, rested my head on the mattress, sank my hand beneath hers, and closed my eyes. In the dim light of the machinery glowing about her, the sick feeling of familiarity fell on me, and I did not like it.

chapter twenty

A COUPLE OF HOURS LATER, I FELT SOMEONE'S FINGERS running through my hair, gentle and soft. I sat up to find Maggs looking at me. Her eyes were heavy, her face flushed, and the monitor on the wall said her fever had risen to 101 degrees. Her breaths were short, and her face told me they were painful if she inhaled too deeply.

"Hey, you," she said, fighting off a shiver.

"Hey."

"I held them off as long as I could." Her voice was little more than a whisper. "I threw everything I could get my hands on, but . . ." She blinked, and a tear trickled off her cheek. "I just ran out of stuff to throw." She looked in the corner of the room where Blue lay, his tail tucked up under his back legs, his nose pointed at Maggs. "If he hadn't been there . . ."

"I got held up at church."

She nodded. "Amos told me. He was here when I woke up an hour ago."

Her face was still puffy, and her eyes had turned black and swollen. I wanted to touch her, but I was afraid I'd hurt her.

"Did you tell Amos what they looked like?"

Maggs shook her head. "He said he'd come back. But they won't be hard to spot."

"How's that?"

"Tattoos. They're covered." She tried to smile, but the cuts around her mouth and the swollenness of her lips made it difficult. I stood and kissed her. Her lips felt taut and swollen.

I tried to reassure her. "Amos has got everybody in South Carolina looking for them." I slipped my hand beneath hers and tried to change the subject. "Has Dr. Frank been in?"

She shook her head. "Not yet."

I stroked her hand and knew I needed to quit stalling. "Honey, you . . . we lost the . . ."

She placed her finger on my lips. "Shhh . . ." She nodded, and her bottom lip quivered. She tried to hold it together, but soon the sobs came. It was the most painful wail I'd ever heard pour out of another human.

Her cries brought Amanda running down the hall. She peeked in the room, saw me cradling Maggie in my arms, and quietly shut the door.

Maggie looked up at me. "I'm so sorry."

"Hey, hey, it's got nothing to do with you." I looked around the room, grasping for comfort. "We'll try again." I pushed the hair out of her face and brushed a tear off her lip. "We're good at that."

She reached up and clung to me. Her thin arms were shaking.

Maybe thirty minutes passed while she lay with her head next to mine. She closed her eyes, holding my left hand with both of hers. Eventually the tears dried, only to surface again like a rising tide.

I picked an eyelash off her cheek. "Honey, there's something else."

She looked up.

"Have you been running a fever?"

She tilted her head to one side.

"How long?" I asked.

"Four or five days. Just low, around a hundred."

"Why didn't you tell me?"

"I thought it was just a virus, thought it would pass. I didn't want you to worry."

I laid my chin on the bed and looked up at her. "You've got to tell me these things." I tucked her hair behind her ear. "No more secrets."

She smiled and nodded slightly. "No more secrets."

As the words slid off her tongue, my hypocrisy slapped me in the face.

She looked up at the ceiling and pressed her knees tight together, and her eyes welled.

I slid my hand behind her head. "Maggs."

She faked another smile. "Someday you're gonna make a great dad." The words slipped off her tongue, and the sobs came again. Her ribs made it impossible to mask her pain, so she cried harder and louder. The crying started in her toes, and her entire body shook beneath the sheets.

The sound brought Amanda running again. She checked the machine behind the bed, stepped under the single light, and slid her hand into Maggie's. She cradled the pale white hand in her brown, tender palm and checked the IV.

"Daddy wants to know if he can come see you."

Maggie nodded, and the tears continued to fall. Soon Amanda, too, was crying. Her tears fell onto the rounding top of her belly, and she brushed at them in embarrassment.

Maggie reached out, placed her palm flat against Amanda's tummy, and said, "How's everybody doing?"

Amanda smiled and nodded. "We're good. I just can't eat enough." She blew her nose. "I've never been so hungry."

A few minutes later, Dr. Frank walked in. He sat opposite us and laid his clipboard on the bed near Maggie's feet. "I heard you guys were having a good cry, so I thought I'd come join you."

Maggie held out the box of tissues and then nodded toward the call button. She sniffled. "If you run out, push that button."

"Yeah, I've been wanting to get one of those buttons at home, but I think my wife would kick me out of the house."

We tried to laugh, but we all knew we were just trying to delay the inevitable.

He looked at me, then at Maggie. "You should have passed everything by now." He pointed to the pad. "We'll keep this here today, but when you feel up to it, I think it'd be best if you got up and walked around some."

Amanda nodded and slipped out the door.

"When can I go home?" Maggie asked.

Dr. Frank checked the monitors on the wall behind her. "Tell me about this fever first."

"Four or five days, low grade. I just thought it was a virus."

"I want to run some more tests, try to get the fever down and get control of the infection. That means I might keep you a few days. You can't go home yet anyway—not until your husband cleans up the mess."

We were quiet for several seconds.

"Your lab results tell me there's something going on with

your blood that I can't get a handle on. I don't know what kind of infection or where it is, but it's a bugger, to say the least." He eyed the IV bag above her. "We're attacking it now with a broad-spectrum antibiotic, but I want to keep you where I can monitor you."

"What's a girl got to do to get something to eat around here?"

Dr. Frank scribbled on a notepad. "I'll have them send something up, but you only eat what I send up here. You got it?"

Maggie nodded and crossed her fingers across her chest.

He shook his head. "No kidding." He eyed the digital readout that listed her body temperature. It had risen to 102 degrees. "I need to monitor everything going into you until I get my hands around this infection. Deal?"

Maggie nodded and uncrossed her fingers.

He stood, patted her gently on the hand, and said, "I'll let you eat, then start the tests."

He stepped out, and Maggie put her head on my hand.

"Why don't you sleep some?" I said.

She closed her eyes and fidgeted around the tenderness of her ribs. Within a few minutes, she was asleep.

AFTER DINNER PASTOR JOHN CRACKED THE DOOR. HE pulled up a chair on the opposite side of the bed and patted Maggie's leg. We sat there in the darkness, waiting on Maggie to wake up. Thirty minutes later, she did.

Her eyes were glassed over, telling me the same thing as the machines on the wall. Despite Motrin, her body temperature hadn't changed. The fever was taking its toll.

She rolled her head toward Pastor John and smiled. He stood up, kissed her forehead, and sat back down.

Pastor John was in pain, but it wasn't physical. He patted

her leg again and said, "Maggie, I need to tell you a story." He pulled out his handkerchief, wiped his nose and the corner of one eye, and began.

"I wasn't always a pastor. When I was younger, more than twenty years ago, I fell in with three guys looking for trouble. Problem was, we were good at both getting into it and getting out of it. And because we liked what the money bought us, which was mostly an identity as something other than what we were, we stole anything we could get our hands on. Especially me." He let that sink in.

"I was smart, and gifted at being a thief." He shook his head, fighting the memories. "A couple of years later, our luck ran out." He smiled. "Maybe the Lord had had enough of our foolishness."

Tears rolled off Pastor John's face, and Maggie slid her hand out from underneath the sheets and grabbed his, pulling it close to her chest.

"We were put in jail, and somewhere in that cold cell, I got tired of lying. So I started telling the truth. Because of the way that works in the legal system, I got out early and they stayed in longer." He tried to smile. "The other guys weren't very happy with this. Evidently, they're still not."

He reached into his coat pocket and pulled out a stack of postcards held together with a rubber band. "Over the last several years, they've written me about once a month to tell me how ungrateful they are." He placed the cards back in his pocket, and his huge shoulders rolled forward. He unfolded his handkerchief, wiped his face, and then looked Maggie in the eyes. "I . . . Maggie, honey . . . I'm sorry."

Maggie reached out and hugged Pastor John. He cradled her and rocked her as she wept in his arms. He bit his lip and managed, "Some sins I'm still paying for."

We sat there a long time. Finally Maggie tried to sit up and said, "I'm sorry about your church."

Pastor John shook his head and looked out through the window into the moonlight. "We can build another building, but we might need some help with the steeple."

I nodded. "Yes, sir."

Pastor John leaned over and kissed Maggie's forehead. Then he stood and placed his hand on her head. He whispered, but not really to us. Finally he took my hand, spread it across Maggie's tummy, and covered mine with his. He looked at us both and spoke quietly, the weight of what he was saying pressing in on his voice. "In Isaiah God says, 'Fear not, for I will pour water on him who is thirsty, and floods on the dry and barren ground. I will pour My Spirit on your descendants, and My blessing on your offspring. They will spring up among the grass like willows by the watercourses.'" He walked over to the door, stood for a moment, and then slipped out.

ON TOWARD MIDNIGHT I HEARD A SOFT RAP ON THE DOOR, as though someone either was afraid to come in or was a southern gentleman of the sort who never barged in on a lady. It turned out to be the latter.

I opened the door, and a man dressed in a bright orange bow tie, white oxford shirt, starched khakis, and gold wire-rimmed glasses extended his hand. Jason Thentwhistle, hospital financial officer.

He pointed down the hall toward the nurses' station and doctors' cubicle. "If they want to run a test, or do anything at all, you let them. We'll work out the other side of it on the other side." He turned and walked about four steps.

I reached out and caught him by the arm. He looked at me guardedly, as one stranger would look at another.

"Jason, thanks for coming. We appreciate it."

He smiled, half nodded, and continued walking down the hall.

chapter twenty-one

BY MIDAFTERNOON OF THE NEXT DAY, MAGGIE'S
body finished doing what it was doing and no longer needed
the bed pad beneath her, so I helped her into the shower. It
took awhile to get her cleaned up because she was bruised
from head to toe.

She put on some hospital scrubs, and we took a slow and
gentle stroll around the halls. Maggie leaned on me and
hooked her arm inside mine. When we came to the large view-
ing window of the nursery, she leaned against the glass and
stared at the six babies sleeping inside. When she pulled away,
her tears slid down the glass and came to rest on the windowsill.

At dinnertime Amos walked in dressed in his SWAT gear,
and despite the singed hair and skin, he looked as though he
hadn't skipped a beat. In his hands were two chocolate shakes.

He walked over to the bed, set them down, and pulled two straws from his shirt pocket. "I checked with Dr. Frank. He said it was okay."

He knelt next to the bed and slid one huge palm under Maggie's shoulders. "How's our girl?" he asked. The assurance in his voice was worth a million dollars.

Maggie smiled lazily, physically tired and emotionally drained. She took a sip of the shake.

Amos put on his law enforcement face. "Maggs, I need to know who did this."

Maggie leaned forward while I adjusted the pillows behind her back.

"I've never seen them before. Two men. Black. Maybe late thirties, early forties. Both covered in tattoos. One guy had his shirt off, and his whole chest and back were nothing but tattoos."

"Could you recognize them?"

She nodded.

Amos pulled two pictures from his shirt pocket and held them in front of her.

Maggie looked at the pictures, sipped again, then nodded.

"Anton, as he likes to be called, and Felix became tattoo artists in prison. Now most of both their bodies are covered in ink—making them pretty easy to spot. They both look like that dude in *Moby Dick*." He snapped his fingers. "The one that was in the coffin."

"Queequeg," I said quietly.

Amos nodded. "Throughout their time in prison, they traded their services for information, which meant they were never too far from the pipeline. They kept pretty good tabs on John."

"Pastor John said he had three partners."

Amos nodded. "Third one's name is Whittaker. Nobody's

seen him. His name in prison was Ghost. Due to a sick twist in
fate, overcrowding brought him two cells down, and the three
got reacquainted. Oddly enough, that same twist brought a
former Hollywood pyrotechnics expert next door to the twins,
which would explain their newfound love of bonfires. From
what investigators have gathered, the former partners became
rather vocal about their post-prison plans."

"But why me? Why our house?"

Amos shook his head. "I'm working on that. Right now, I
have no idea, other than you live across the street from me."

Maggie nodded and looked at me, then back to Amos.
"Where are Amanda and Li'l Dylan?"

"Amanda's down the hall. Momma's got L.D. We're staying
with them in town for a while."

"You scared?" I asked.

He looked at me, at Maggie, then back at me, and shook his
head. "No. Not scared. Worried? A bit. Angry?" He spoke
softly, as if he were talking to someone who wasn't in the
room. His voice dropped and his eyes narrowed, telling me
that one way or another, there would be a reckoning. "Yes."

chapter twenty-two

AFTER DINNER I DIMMED THE LIGHTS AND LEFT
Maggie napping in her room. Amanda had gone home for the
evening, but the on-call nurse had stuck her head in the door
and let me know she'd be checking on Maggie.

I knelt down in the corner of the room and scratched
Blue's tummy while he moaned and flopped his ears back. I
rubbed his muzzle and picked off the specks of dried blood
on the top of his head. I pointed outside. "You gotta go?" The
magnolia outside the window caught my eye. "Mark some old
territory?"

Blue tucked his nose up under a fold in the blanket, let out
a long sigh, and looked away.

I turned into our drive, aimed the headlights at the house,
and parked.

Shining my flashlight, I stepped through the door and noticed, above the smell of my burnt house, the unusual and lingering scent of cheap aftershave and lots of it. I checked the rooms, found the house empty, and then opened all the doors and windows, hoping the house would breathe itself free of the stench.

In the race to save the house, the screen door had been torn off, the back door broken off its hinges, and most of the inside sprayed with water under very high pressure. The water put out the fire, which had bubbled much of the paint, while the pressure behind the water peeled many of the blisters, making our walls look leprous.

From what I could see, most of the inside was wet and stained black. I walked down the back hall and looked overhead. The ceiling had caved in, exposing the rafters and pieces of hanging insulation. I made it to the doors that led into the bedroom and nursery, but there was no need to go in. Whoever had started the fire had evidently done so in both rooms.

The other half of the house—which included the kitchen and den—escaped everything but hose drag marks, overspray, and muddy footprints.

In our room the walls had burned to the studs, the furniture was nothing but soggy, charred cinders, the mattress on our bed was little more than a crumbling mess, and the ceiling and roof were gone. The motor for the Hunter fan that once hung above our bed now sat at an angle in the middle of the mattress, its wires sticking up like an insect's antennae. The moonlight shone through the blue tarp and gave the room an eerie blue haze.

I was afraid to look into the nursery, but I knew I had to. All the stuffed animals were little more than charred remains, and the rocker had all but disappeared. The crib sat at an angle, as if one leg were shorter than another. The books of nursery rhymes were crumbling and wet, and all the baby clothes in the closet lay in pieces on the floor, blackened scraps of cotton.

Between the two rooms, my writing closet, its door marred and bubbling from the heat, remained locked. I didn't know what it looked like on the inside. As for Maggie's orchids scattered around the house, they had not fared well. They were nothing but naked stems without bloom or petal.

I was standing in the kitchen surveying the damage when the phone rang—which surprised me, given that the guys had disconnected the electricity at the street to avoid an electrical fire.

"Dylan, it's John."

I knew Caglestock had become comfortable with me when he started calling me by my first name. I also knew that if he was calling me at close to ten thirty, he had something on his mind.

I sat down. "Hey, John."

"Listen, we've got to move one of Bryce's accounts from one trading house to another. We can get a better rate, so it makes good sense. But, as with any transaction of this type, it will produce a commission—of about $45,000." He let that sink in.

I understood. It was the cost of doing business, and Bryce understood this.

"No matter how or where I move them, I'll end up paying a commission to move these funds." He let that sink in too. Then he said what he'd called for. "I want to know if you will let me hire you for a day to make one transaction."

I looked out through the kitchen window overlooking the pasture.

"Dylan," he continued, "Bryce's estate, his LLC, or any of

the partnerships we've formed would pay this commission to anyone regardless of their affiliation with him."

He was right. And in terms of Bryce's account total, which now ran in the hundreds of millions, it wasn't even a drop in the bucket.

"I want to hire you for a day."

I took a deep breath. "John, I made a promise to Bryce that I would never seek to profit from him or the management of his funds."

"Yes, but given the good decisions you've made now over an almost-five-year period"—John paused—"do you know how much money you've made him?"

"John, I gave him my word."

"I don't think this qualifies as—"

"And second, I don't ever want Bryce to think I want any part of his money. I don't. Not one penny."

"That makes you different from most of the people who've befriended Bryce."

"That makes me *me.*"

"It might also make you poor."

"John?" I knew he meant well, and his intentions were good, but I also knew that wasn't good enough. "Just because it's legal doesn't necessarily make it right."

He started to say something, but I cut him off. "I was maybe ten, standing with my grandfather in the grocery store checkout line, when the lady at the cash register handed him his change. He counted, paused, recounted, and then handed a twenty back to her and said, 'This one was stuck to the other one. You gave me one too many.' To say the least, she was pretty relieved when she realized he was right. We got in the truck, and I asked him why he didn't just keep it. She'd never know. You know what he said?"

"I'm listening."

"He said, 'I'll know.' He must have seen the confused look on my face, because he said, 'Son, I won't sell my word, my integrity, for twenty dollars. Not today. Not ever.' He stuck his face real close to mine and said, 'Words are what men live by, and once you sell them, not all the tea in China can ever buy 'em back.'"

John chuckled, and I could hear his chair squeak as if he'd just sat back and propped his feet up.

"I would have liked to have met your grandpa."

John was an honest man, and I knew this. Every audit of his firm and, specifically, his firm's work with Bryce's money, had produced nothing but praise from every auditor we'd ever met. Bryce had been good to him, but maybe more important, he'd been good for Bryce.

The problem was not the legality of the action he proposed; of course it was legal. The problem it posed for me was the gray area it presented with respect to my relationship with Bryce and my promise to him.

"I think you two would have gotten along well," I said.

I hung up the phone and leaned against the kitchen sink. I took a deep breath, let it out slowly between my teeth, feeling the pressure in my cheeks, and wondered if my grandfather and I were just plain crazy.

Knowing I needed to quit carrying a loaded shotgun around in the van, I brought it inside, unlocked my writing closet, and slid the gun onto the floor just above our "safe." I locked the doors and walked outside onto the porch. It was close to midnight, but a flicker in the distance caught my eye and told me something about the world was distinctly different.

I stepped off the porch, walked out into the cotton, and ran my fingers along the tops of the white flowers. Beneath the moon, spotlight-bright above me, the cotton field shone with thousands of moon-white flowers, waving ever so slightly in the cooling breeze. They had opened in the last few hours and would remain that way for twenty-four more, in which time a single, microscopic grain of pollen, carried on the breeze, would come to rest inside, pollinate the flower, and start once again the mystery that grows inside.

Maybe it was then that it really hit me. The loss reached up out of the earth, and I felt cold and lonely, like low, dark clouds before rain. I squatted in the cotton, eye-level with the blooms, and the tears came in a flood.

All the world had bloomed, and Maggie had not.

chapter twenty-three

I CRACKED MAGGIE'S DOOR AND STUCK MY HEAD IN, and froze. A large, broad-shouldered man stood in the darkness next to her bed. He stood ironing-board straight, towering over her.

But Blue hadn't moved.

The man stood with his hands behind his back, at ease. As I stepped into the room, he turned to face me. He had showered, shaved, cropped his hair higher and tighter, splashed with aftershave—a smell I recognized—and put on clean, starched, and creased BDUs. His boots were polished to a mirror shine. In his right hand he held a black, cylindrical-looking thing about fourteen inches long. The end closest to me reflected light and looked like small circles of glass.

I stepped into the dim glow of the fluorescent light coming

from the bathroom, and the reflection told me that Bryce had been crying. Tears clung to his drawn cheeks and puddled in the bottoms of the wrinkles around the base of his eyes. He blinked and sent the puddles falling off his face. I stepped up alongside him, and we stood overlooking Maggie, who slept peacefully beneath the covers and whatever medication Dr. Frank had prescribed. I glanced at the machine above her bed and saw that her temperature had climbed to 102 degrees.

Standing next to Bryce, I noticed that the baton in his hand was actually a rifle scope. The bluing had worn in spots, and because of the rings and brackets, it looked as though it was rigged with a quick-release mechanism that would allow it to be quickly attached or detached from the top of a rifle.

In months past, as Amos became proficient with more types of weaponry, he had shown me the SWAT team sniper gear. One thing that struck me was the rifle scope. Most were large, came in adjustable powers, and could deliver a projectile with great accuracy up to eight hundred yards, even farther. Many had two protruding adjustment knobs that allowed the shooter to make last-minute adjustments depending on distance, wind, and various other conditions. They were state-of-the-art.

If Amos's gear was fifth- or even tenth-generation, then Bryce's scope looked like a first generation. It was longer, thinner, probably a fixed power, and didn't have the protruding adjustment knobs. He carried it the way a sailor might carry his spyglass.

Bryce didn't say a word. After a few minutes he knelt next to the bed, stretched his neck, and leaned over Maggie. He lowered his head ever so slightly over her tummy, finally pressing his ear against the blanket as if he were listening to a railroad track. He rested there several seconds, close but not pressing into her. After a minute he rose, kissed her forehead, and tiptoed out of the room.

I sat up the rest of the night, eyeing the temperature reading on the machine above her bed. Twice it bounced up to 103.5 degrees, but it spent most of the night at 102. Somewhere in the middle of the night, Blue hopped off the bed and licked my face. I cradled him in my arms, and I guessed we dozed off there.

At daylight, Dr. Frank walked in and nudged my arm. Blue hopped down, and I stood up, balancing myself with a hand on Maggie's bed.

"When was the last time you slept in a bed?"

I scratched my head, smiled, and shook my head. "Can't recall."

"You need to." He stepped closer to the bed and slid his hand under Maggie's wrist, feeling for her distal pulse. He could read it plainly on the machine on the wall, but he seemed to be in thought, and his measurement of her pulse was more subconscious than conscious.

I whispered, "Most of the night it hung around 102. A couple of times it hit 103."

"I expected that. It'll always rise at night. Her body's doing what it should. Fighting."

I nodded, and a few seconds passed. I tucked one long strand of hair behind Maggie's ear. "She is a fighter."

Maggs stirred, and her eyes blinked open. "Hey, guys." She shivered and pulled the covers up over her shoulders. "You two planning on hanging meat in here?"

I grabbed another blanket while Dr. Frank instinctively felt her forehead with his hand. He pulled his rolling seat up to the side of her bed and said, "Well, you want the good news or the bad news?"

"Good news, and let's just skip the bad. We've had enough of that for a while." Maggie's hand appeared from under the covers and grabbed mine.

When I think about my wife, one word comes to mind. *Indomitable.*

"The good news is that my son's team won his game last night and put us in the play-offs. The bad news is that I have no idea what's causing your fever. Your blood work will only tell me so much." He eyed the IV hanging above her. "We're throwing some pretty strong stuff at you, and it should have kicked in by now."

Maggs moved slowly and looked tired, as though the fever was really working her over.

"I have an idea," the doctor said, "but I wanted to check with you first, since it's your body."

Her eyes opened slightly, the sleep almost falling off the edges of her face. "I'm game for most anything that allows me to stay in this bed. I'm afraid I'd fall flat on my face if I had to get out of it."

Frank nodded. "It's just the fever. It'll pass as soon as we get on top of the infection." He patted her foot. "Since your first delivery, have you had any pictures taken of your insides? Uterus, ovaries, etc."

"Other than that really kind lady doctor you sent us to, no." Maggie smiled. "I could've spit nails."

"Yeah, sorry about that. I called her this morning, and she doesn't have what I need." He repositioned himself on his chair. "I want to take some pictures, look around a bit. We'll sedate you."

Maggs nodded. "When do you want to do this?"

Amanda rolled in a cart loaded with medicines and needles. She walked up next to the bed, hooked one arm inside mine, and patted Maggie's leg.

Dr. Frank said, "How about now?"

We heard the seriousness in his voice. Maggie turned toward me, took my hand with both of hers, and looked at me. "You'll be here when I wake up?"

I knelt, my eyes level with hers. "Always."

Dr. Frank nodded, Amanda inserted the needle into Maggie's IV, and in five minutes, Maggs was in that sedated place that fell somewhere between partly awake and mostly asleep. Amanda pushed the cart back out into the hall and clickety-clacked down the terrazzo while Dr. Frank escorted another nurse into the room, pushing an entirely different machine complete with an LCD screen.

I helped him turn Maggie onto her side, and then I stepped back while the nurse prepped her. Frank pulled out a long, cylindrical tube that could flex and bend like a joystick, and while I was thinking, *You're not sticking that thing in my wife,* Amanda walked back in with a hot plate covered with aluminum foil.

"When was the last time you ate?"

I shrugged.

She set it on the countertop behind me, patted me on the shoulder, and checked Maggs's IV. She changed the fluid bags, inserted a catheter, and emptied Maggs's bladder, and then Frank inserted his camera. He turned the screen so that I could watch along with a second doctor I'd never met, who'd appeared just for consultation.

While Frank moved the camera via the joystick, he pointed at the screen with his other finger. "This is Maggie's uterus." He moved the camera. "This is the cervix." He moved it again. "The fallopian tube."

He said something to the other doctor, and while I'm sure he was speaking English, I didn't understand a word. Amanda watched and listened, and the consternation on her face told me that she understood more of that screen than I did.

Maggie's face was pale. When Frank moved the camera, extending it farther into Maggie, she moaned and gripped my hand more tightly. I turned to Amanda and raised an eyebrow. Amanda shook her head and brushed Maggie's forehead with her fingers.

"She's okay. These are pretty good drugs."

Dr. Frank was speaking quietly to the nurse technician who stood alongside him. He nodded at the screen. "That one." He moved the camera slightly. "And that one too."

Twenty minutes later, he pulled the camera out and printed out several pictures from the machine. As the nurse rolled the cart back out into the hall, he called behind her, "Ask the lab to run that to the front of the line."

Then he turned to me and held up the pictures. "Nothing I didn't expect, except maybe this one." He held one up closer to the light. "This is Maggie's fallopian tube, and these are cysts along with some scar tissue from the first delivery." He shrugged. "Many women have them; sometimes they're nothing, sometimes they prevent people from ever getting pregnant, but in this case . . ." He turned the picture sideways to get a different look. "We biopsied these two because most cysts don't look like that."

"What should they look like?"

He rolled his shoulders and shrugged. "Not like that. The lab will send results as quick as they can. We'll know more then."

I pressed him again. "What might they tell us?"

He chose his words carefully. "They'll either tell us it's nothing or tell us it's something."

"Frank, define 'something.'"

He took a deep breath, blinked, and folded his arms. "Best case, just an abnormal cyst that I can remove with little problem."

I grabbed his arm. "And worst case?"

He took another breath. "I don't know, Dylan. I just don't know. Let's wait on the lab."

"Frank, you're hiding something."

"Dylan, Maggie's body is hiding something from me, from all of us. And I think that cyst might be a starting point. Let's wait on the lab."

"So if you remove the cyst, will it lower the fever?" I was grasping at straws.

Frank shook his head. "That's the bad news. Normally, a cyst wouldn't cause a fever like that." He looked at my dinner growing cold. "Why don't you try to eat something? I'll check back in a while."

He walked out and left me alone with Amanda, Maggie, and Blue.

After several minutes, Amanda spoke. "When I get to heaven, I'm going to ask God why it's so easy for some and yet so difficult for others."

"What's that?"

She patted her tummy. "Just doing what He made us to do." She placed her palm flat across Maggie's forehead and whispered, "Why, when some want it so bad, and deserve it so much, is it so difficult to get?"

She leaned over, kissed Maggie's temple, and then eyed the call button. "Holler if you need me."

I sat down, rested my chin on Maggie's bedside, my face just inches from hers, and watched her breathe. I could smell the last remaining whispers of her perfume beneath the waves of antiseptic. An hour later, I looked at the wall of lights. Maggie's temperature had risen to 104 degrees.

TRUE TO HIS WORD, DR. FRANK WALKED IN WITH THE LAB results in his hand, but he wasn't alone. He'd brought most of the hospital with him. Five nurses, dressed in various versions of surgical scrubs, immediately walked to the bed and began prepping Maggie. They worked quietly and efficiently.

Frank pulled me aside. "I'm taking Maggie to the OR."

"Right this second? Why?"

"Because Maggie's body needs help getting rid of the baby."

I was confused. "I thought . . . I thought she'd already done that."

Frank nodded. "She had, in part. Problem is, Maggie was having twins. She had a heterotopic pregnancy. In layman's terms, there's one still in there, and she's being poisoned from the inside out. I'll explain after surgery."

He turned and followed the nurses, who pushed a sleeping Maggie out the door on a rolling bed. I stepped forward to kiss her, but she was gone. I watched them roll her down the hall, then turned to look at Amanda, who was shutting down the monitoring machines. The last one she clicked off was the temperature, reading 105.5 degrees.

I sat down in the hospital room and sank my head in my hands. *Twins?*

Amanda sat down next to me, looped her arm beneath mine, and rested her head on my shoulder. About that time, Amos came running into the room. He was sweating, breathing heavily, and almost slid onto the floor beneath me. "I came as soon as I heard."

I looked up, unable to focus. The world was spinning. "We were having twins."

Amos swore silently. He stood up, wrung his hands together, then finally pulled me up with him and bear-hugged me.

chapter twenty-four

I SAT NEXT TO THE BED, REACHED BENEATH THE covers, and touched Maggs's hand. She was hot to the touch, and her face was flushed. When she opened her eyes, they were glassed over and heavy. The machine on the wall told me her fever was now only 102.5. I rubbed her hand gently and tried to open my mouth, but the words wouldn't come.

She fidgeted, but her ribs were tender, making movement difficult, and her face was still puffy, slow to heal. She saw me struggling and touched my lips with her fingers. "I was having a dream about you."

"Yeah?" I tried to smile.

"You were sitting on the tractor with our daughter, driving to the river. She was blonde, had your eyes, my toes."

I bit my lip, gritted my teeth, and tried to hold back but

could not. I choked and wiped my face with her sheet. Maggie
eyed the wall, her temperature, and then me. Her movements
were slow. She looked as if she'd just delivered a child and run
a marathon.

I tried again. "Dr. Frank had to . . . you see . . . we were . . .
you . . ."

She breathed deeply and turned toward me, pressing her
forehead to mine. She placed her palm on my cheek and whispered, "Shhh." She tried to swallow, but her mouth was dry.

I held the glass of water while she sipped through the straw,
then she pulled me close. I held her several moments, her
eyes studying mine, mine studying hers.

"I want to grow old with you."

"Maggie," I stuttered, "we were having twins."

Her eyes narrowed, and her head tilted like Blue's when he
didn't understand. I could see the pieces falling into place.

"The second baby got caught in your tube, and it was just
growing and . . ."

Maggie shook her head vehemently, placed a flat palm over
her stomach as if it could tell her the truth, and started whispering, "No. No. No!"

I placed my hand on her shoulder. "Honey, Dr. Frank had
to remove your . . ."

The words I'd spoken registered somewhere in her foggy
mind, and she laid her head on the pillow, unable to hold
back the sobs. They came loud and in waves. I tried to hold
her, to wrap my arms around her, protect her from the world
and take away the pain, but I had no defense strong enough.
She rolled into a ball and pounded the bed with her fists.

Amanda came running, pulled a syringe from her pocket,
and quickly inserted it into Maggie's IV. The medicine hit her
veins, and within thirty seconds her eyelids were heavy and

her movements slow and incomplete. They'd given her medicine for the pain in her ribs and the stitches in her uterus. But Maggie was teetering on the edge, and only the oblivion of sleep could give Maggie respite from the pain in her heart.

The last words she screamed before the lights went out were unintelligible. Lost in transmission. But while I couldn't understand the words, I understood the emotion.

chapter twenty-five

MAGGIE LEANED AGAINST ME, THE AIR-CONDITIONING cooling our faces as Amos drove us home slowly in his truck. He pulled into our drive and around back, where we climbed out and stood looking at the house. The smell of smoke, burned pine, melted rubber, and soured water met us under the searing heat of the sun.

Maggie couldn't hide her shock. She was too tired to be angry, but that was there, too, just beneath the surface. A blue tarp covered half the roof, the screen door had been torn off, about half the windows were broken, and black smoke scars stained the upper portions of the windows, eaves, and soffits.

She turned and studied the rolling pastures. On one side grew the corn—tall, green, and tasseled out. On the other sat the cotton. She looped her arm inside mine, and we walked toward the rows and finally between them. She chose the cotton, waist-high and gently swathing our legs. Maggie ran her fingers across the tops and then scanned the horizon where the pasture bled into the trees almost a mile away.

In a manner of speaking, cotton is the only flower that blooms twice from the same bud, or "square," as it is technically called. A cotton flower blooms, or opens, only for twenty-four hours, during which time it must be fertilized by a pollen grain to produce the cotton. When the flower opens, it is white; a day later it turns a fleshy pinkish red; and after four or five days, it turns a crispy mauve or purple. At the end of the first week, the petals litter the row in which it grows. Depending on growth conditions, it takes another month or more before the seed capsule, called a boll, develops and opens like popcorn.

Maggie turned, teary and tired. "Did you know that cotton is in the same family as hibiscus?" She pointed without looking toward some shoulder-height bushes planted against the house.

I shook my head.

"When the flower opens, it has exactly twenty-four hours to be fertilized by a single grain of pollen, or there will be no cotton."

I said nothing.

She nodded and picked a fallen flower off the soil. "It's pretty."

I looked at my wife. "Yes."

Maggie walked into the house behind me, followed closely by Amos. She went into the nursery, stood a moment, placed a hand on the crib, and shook her head. Then she walked into our bedroom and stood beneath the tarp where our bed lay. Water dripped off the tarp and splattered about her feet. She took a deep breath, walked back to the doorway, and eased her shoulder under my arm.

"Amos?" She looked around the house, then turned and poked him in the chest. Her voice grew strong and direct. "You catch the people who did this to my house. You hear me?"

Amos nodded. "Yes, ma'am."

He walked out onto the porch, and I laid a watermelon in the back of his truck. "You mind taking this to Vince? I owe him." Amos nodded and pulled out of the drive.

Maggie stood on the porch and looked at me through squinted eyes. "Why do you owe him?"

I retrieved the shotgun and showed her the barrel. She eyed the change, and I didn't need to explain. I held it out. "You remember how?" She palmed the shotgun and slid a shell in the chamber while I placed the smallest of the melons on the grass in the yard.

I eyed the target and then behind it, which was eight hundred yards of corn pasture down to the river.

Maggie shouldered the shotgun, clicked off the safety, and squeezed. The watermelon exploded into a million red and green pieces and sent Blue scurrying under the porch. She ejected the shell, smoke rising from the chamber, handed me the shotgun, and walked toward the barn.

chapter twenty-six

ALTHOUGH I'D OFFERED TO MOVE HER TO A HOTEL, Maggie didn't want anything to do with that. The electricity had been restored, and we still had a phone line and plumbing. I agreed to stay with one stipulation. "You point," I said. "I'll clean."

Knowing she was far too weak to dive into a house renovation, she didn't argue. We walked into the smoke-stained kitchen, and she said, "I'll put on some coffee."

While she filtered through the kitchen, I unlocked the closet, knelt beneath my desk, and pried the board loose with the tip of my knife. I lifted the silver box, opened the lid, and breathed more easily knowing my manuscript, wrapped in a dry plastic bag, lay safely inside. Somehow, being below the house, it had survived.

It took me almost two days to haul out all the wet, burned, or otherwise ruined stuff from our house. I carried everything into a pile out back, and on the second night we lit it and roasted marshmallows.

THE SUMMER BETWEEN MY JUNIOR AND SENIOR YEARS IN high school, Papa let me turn the hayloft into my bedroom— my first real foray into independence. We cut in a window, added a wall, stuffed insulation between the studs, put up drywall, carpeted the floor, and inserted an air-conditioning unit that blew both hot and cold air. We found some used furniture at garage sales and a four-poster queen-sized bed that looked as though it had come out of some Russian palace. It didn't fit Digger, but at twenty bucks, it fit my budget. When finished, the room looked a lot like an upscale garage apartment and would probably fetch a goodly sum in some place like New York.

Since Maggie and I had married, I'd used the loft to store stuff, but with the house uninhabitable, I got to work. We moved out the stored stuff—old furniture and boxes—and hung a ceiling fan. We bought a new-used mattress and even bought Blue a new bed and laid it alongside ours. I caulked some of the cracks in the floor and walls, rolled on a fresh coat of paint, laid new carpet, and replaced the ladder with steps.

The bathroom was little more than a thin-walled closet in the corner with just enough room for a toilet, a sink, and one person. I repiped the fittings to the water supply, installed a new wax ring at the base, changed out the flushing mechanism so it'd quit running, and put a 40-watt bulb in the fixture above the sink. Within a couple of days, our one-room flat was livable again.

Granted, it was not our house, but because of the height above the ground, the angle at which it faced the rising sun, and the unobstructed view to the river almost a mile away, it had one feature possessed by few homes anywhere. Each morning, when the sun came up over the river, it would light the pasture in that blueberry haze that occurred as the fog was lifting. It then crawled like a wave across the landscape to the barn, where it climbed up the sides, pierced through the window, and took your breath away.

I had swept the floor and adjusted the bed so Maggie wouldn't miss the sunrise. Below the loft, on ground level, I laid a pallet that allowed for better drainage and dragged Maggie's green garden hose through the window and fitted it with a soaking watering head. I hung a piece of cracked glass on the wall, to show half my face when I shaved. While our morning showers were cool to cold, by late afternoon the sun had heated the hose and provided about five minutes of luke-warm water—which I seldom had a chance to experience, thanks to Maggie.

I didn't really care. If Maggie needed hot water, I'd shower in ice cubes.

During all this, Blue chased something he shouldn't have, stuck his nose too close to its back end, and got sprayed. He then went and rolled in the dirt for about an hour trying to rub out the smell. When he finally made it to the house later that night, he was in a bad way. He came walking slowly up to the barn, dirty as he'd ever been and smelling worse. Even Pinky turned away.

Maggie got one whiff of him and gagged. "Oh my," she said. "Your dog needs you."

I grabbed some dish soap from under the sink and every can of tomato soup I could find out of what used to be the pantry. We cleaned him, then scrubbed the soup into his pores, turning our hands and his skin red. When we finished, he smelled like spaghetti sauce—which was better than the alternative. Midway through the scrubbing, I clipped a clothespin on my nose. Blue spent the next day licking himself and lying across the porch. He was red from head to toe and looked as though someone had played a bad trick on him.

OUR THIRD MORNING HOME, I STOOD IN THE SHOWER, leaning against the post while the water soaked my back. I reached up, cut off the water, and looked at myself in the triangular shape of glass I'd tacked to the wall for a shaving mirror. Pinky was looking at me through the slats in her stall like I'd lost my mind. She was probably right. I eyed a few nicks from a dull razor and settled on the wrinkle that had developed between my eyes.

A car engine startled me. I dried, dressed, walked out into the sun, and was met by a man wearing a suit and tie. He explained that he was with my insurance company. After showing him around the house, he expressed his condolences and wrote me a check for $5,000.

"This will get you started. We can get the other half to you just as soon as I file my report."

"What do you mean, the other half?"

"Well, your particular policy allows for $10,000 in replacement due to theft or fire."

"It does?"

He nodded and continued his explanation. "The police say their investigation is over, that arson is to blame, and that clears us up to get started here."

I thanked him, although I didn't feel very thankful, and

told him I'd be in touch, and he drove off. I was headed back into the loft when a second car turned into the drive. This time a lady, maybe midforties, stepped out, wearing a pantsuit and carrying a clipboard.

She reluctantly shook my hand. "Are you Dr. Dylan Styles?"

"Yes, ma'am."

She pointed at the house. "Is this your home?"

"What's left of it."

She made a note on her clipboard.

Maggie appeared in the barn door, barefooted and wrapped in a blanket and squinting. Pinky was squealing in her stall.

The lady's eyes grew a bit wider. "I'm with the adoption agency."

I cussed under my breath.

"I've come to assess the, for lack of a better word, *living conditions* of your home."

I spat and wished I had a toothpick.

I tried to reassure her. "That fellow driving off there is our insurance adjuster, and he's just cleared us to start work now that the police have finished their investigation."

"Police?"

"Yes, ma'am. See, we had a series of fires the other night, started apparently by some guys who like to play with matches."

She was not amused. Understanding that we were living in the barn, she pointed her pencil. "How long do you think this arrangement will last?"

"Just a couple of weeks while I rebuild."

She perked up a little. "So you've hired a contractor?"

I looked at Maggie, then back at the lady, who had yet to tell me her name. "Well, yes."

She waited, then said, "Who?"

"Me."

She looked at me over the top of her glasses, then through them, and made another note. "I see."

About then Blue walked out of the barn. She looked, then looked again. "What's that?"

"That's our dog."

"Good Lord, he looks like a demon."

"He got too friendly with a skunk. That red is the tomato juice; it neutralizes the smell."

She scribbled some more, and when Blue started trotting toward her, she stepped quickly back into her car without shaking my hand. She lowered her window about two inches. "Dr. Styles, you must know that I have to submit an accurate account to the committee, and that this"—she pointed from the house to the barn to Blue—"is likely not going to help you."

I nodded. "Yes, ma'am. But certainly the committee understands we had a fire that was not our fault, and given some time, we can rebuild." I waved my hands in a large arc. "Maybe run the porch around the whole house."

"Yes, but the committee will also want to look at the company you keep and whether or not those associations provide a suitable environment for children."

I nodded and decided it might be best if I just shut up. She flipped down her visor against the sun and drove off. I rubbed Blue between the ears and decided that this whole adoption thing was just about to hack me off.

Maggie walked out, nuzzled against me, and said, "Who was that?"

I watched the taillights at the end of our driveway. "That was the assessor from the adoption agency who came out unannounced to determine if our home is a suitable environment for children."

"You've got to be kidding."

"I wish I was."

"What'd she say?"

"It wasn't so much what she said as how she said it."

chapter twenty-seven

TWO DAYS LATER I WALKED INTO THE BARN AND found Maggie staring into my shaving mirror. She turned, curled her hair around her index finger, and said, "I think I need a haircut." I wasn't about to argue, so I drove her to town and sat in the waiting area while they cut her hair. The smell of shampoo and the sound of eight blow-dryers was too much sensory overload, so I walked out onto the street and let the heat off the asphalt cook the skin on my face.

An hour later Maggie reappeared, again looking like Audrey Hepburn. I wanted to ask, *What happened to your hair?* but I knew better than to open my mouth. A woman and her hair are a peculiar thing.

We stopped at Home Depot and bought, among other things, some two-by-eight trusses and aluminum sheeting for the roof. An hour later I sat on the porch, missing my own truck and waiting for the lumber delivery. When it arrived, the driver had the audacity to look around and say, "Can't believe you own a farm but don't own a truck."

You ever poured lemon juice on an open wound?

My plan for the house was to repair the roof and ceilings first, pay a painter to spray the entire inside of the house with KILZ and then a color of Maggie's choosing, and then move us out of the barn and back into the house while I concentrated on the finish work.

I walked outside, stepped off the back porch, and meandered through my cotton field, where the midmorning sun was growing high and the bolls were swollen taut with white gold inside. Behind me, Maggie threw open the screen door, tossed Blue out on the porch, and slammed the door, rattling the windowpane. Blue looked at the door, licked the sides of his muzzle, and followed me out into the pasture.

I rubbed his ears and said, "Hey, pal, don't blame her. She's just having a rough time right now. We've just got to give her some space."

Blue looked back at the house and then at me. He wasn't buying it.

I looked across the pasture and road into the blackened piles that remained of Amos and Amanda's house. Amos had hired a bulldozer to push everything into a pile and a dump truck to haul it off. He and Amanda had been staying at Pastor John's house since the fire, and I wasn't the only one who sensed their absence. Blue stuck his nose in the air and, smelling nothing, whined and walked a figure eight between my legs.

A few minutes later Maggie walked out of the house. The sight of her hair was still strange to me. It wasn't that I didn't like it; it was just a surprise, that's all. She stood on the porch, holding her pruning shears and studying the landscape. Then she walked off the porch and began weaving through the flowers.

Everything had bloomed weeks ago. That meant a lot of dead and shriveled flowers now hung limp on drying twigs. Maggie began pruning the garden that surrounded our house. The process looked painful. I grabbed an old plastic trash can and followed her, quietly picking up the pieces. When she got to the roses, she paused, second-guessed herself, and then quietly returned to work. Between her energy level and the number of flowers, the process took her the better part of the day.

Dr. Frank said Maggie had had a heterotopic pregnancy. A 1 in 50,000 oddity. He explained that while we were going to have twins, only one fertilized egg had made its way out of the fallopian tube and into the uterus, where it attached. The second fertilized egg, for reasons we'll never know, became lodged in the tube. As it grew, it burst the tube, destroying itself and beginning a process of rotting inside Maggie, poisoning her blood, killing the other embryo attached to her uterus, and sending her fever to 105.5 degrees. Frank removed the tube, the ovary—which had been destroyed—and our baby. He said another couple of hours and the septic shock would have killed her.

BLUE FETCHED THE MORNING PAPER. I SPREAD IT ACROSS the table, and only then did I realize that we'd missed the Fourth of July. It never even crossed my mind. Which was probably good, because we didn't feel much like fireworks.

While Maggie napped away the morning, Blue and I walked to the river and then north along the edge. Blue kept looking over his shoulder and following close at my heels. Stepping lightly, we walked beneath the oaks and around small bunches of wild iris that had grown up from bulbs Maggie planted three years ago and that had now spread a few hundred yards downriver. The temperature was in the midnineties, and the humidity was just shy of raining.

We came to a small bend in the river that made somewhat of a natural port, if you want to call it that, where Amos and I kept our raft. I hadn't been down here in months, and it looked pretty bad. The raft was covered in leaves and fallen limbs, and had I not known where it was, I'd have missed it. I uncovered it, brushed it off as best I could, and then lay down in the middle. Blue curled up alongside me, and we watched the sun rise above the cypress trees.

I watched the river moving slowly and silently alongside us. Despite the turmoil topside, its rhythm was never-changing. I dipped my feet in, letting the movement and coolness sift through my toes. Blue took a drink and then jumped in, swimming around long enough to cool off. He paddled back over to the raft, and I lifted him up. He showered me in dog-shake, which felt good, and we lay back down. Around noon, I heard footsteps.

Amos stepped onto the raft and sat down. He was dressed in cutoff jeans and a T-shirt, telling me that he'd taken a much-deserved day off. He pulled a soft-sided cooler off his shoulder and unzipped the top. "I've got PB&J, root beer, and Oreos."

I nodded, and he slapped a sandwich in my hand. I pulled back the plastic wrap, took a bite, and chewed without tasting it.

Amos looked at me curiously. "You look like you ain't eaten much lately."

He was right; it was the first thing I'd eaten in two days. I nodded again and stared at the water as if it were a nighttime campfire.

Amos popped the top on a root beer and handed it to me. "Thanks."

We sat on the raft, chewing, soaking in the sunlight and silence while I fed my crusts to Blue.

Amos pulled off his T-shirt and finally spoke. "Need to work on my tan. Been pushing too many pencils lately." He pulled his Kimber and holster out from behind his belt and laid them on the raft. After he finished his sandwich, he lay back and pulled his baseball cap down over his eyes.

We spent an hour in quiet.

AS THE CICADAS AND TREE FROGS TUNED UP THE PSYCHE-delic afternoon, Amos spoke. "We're taking 'Manda to and from work. She doesn't leave the house without one of us going with her. We've rented the house across the street, and some of my guys stare out the windows toward us at night."

I stared at him.

"No, she doesn't know that, but short of leaving town, it's the best we can do." He shook his head. "I've never staked out myself before."

Amos was pretty good at giving me only what I needed when I needed it. He was both friend and brother, but I needed more. I looked across the raft. "Amos, tell me about these guys. I want the *whole* story."

"As Pastor John told you, he got mixed up in some pretty bad stuff. Started out as petty theft in and around Charleston, but given time, and their appetites, it went up and out from there. They had warehouses all over the state stuffed with everything from diamond rings to classic cars. They were smart." He shrugged. "At least they started out that way. Like most criminals who can't keep a secret and love showing off how cool they are, they got greedy and sloppy. Really sloppy.

"They were hitting a jewelry store. Pastor John was the inside man. The other three were parked outside in a car, doping it up and waiting on the signal from John, when an off-duty police officer stumbled onto them. He smelled the dope, knocked on the window, and the driver, a fellow named James Whittaker III, self-proclaimed leader, rolled down the window, stuck a 9mm in the cop's chest, and pulled the trigger. John ran to the window, saw the car leaving pretty fast and a man lying in the street surrounded in streetlight-red. Our guys, having just pulled over a DUI about two blocks up, got there within a few seconds. When they arrived, they found a dead friend, the wiped-down Glock that the bullet had come from, and John Lovett crawling out the jewelry store window carrying a bag worth about a quarter of a million dollars."

I gulped.

"It gets better from there. While John Lovett was trying to explain to investigators how the dead police officer ended up in the street, the other three were feeling their oats. They crossed the state line into Georgia and went out boozing. James, along with two brothers named Antonio and Felix, started buying drinks all around and soon caught the ear of an FBI agent who happened to be in the bar trying to cheat on his wife. An hour or so later, another shooting occurred. This one is a little fuzzy, but according to witnesses, James wrestled the Bureau guy's .40 out of his hand, shot him, then shot the bartender 'cause he wasn't bringing the drinks fast enough. One of the brothers grabbed a bat from behind the bar and started swinging it at people. When the shouting stopped, three more people were dead, and the Three Musketeers drove off into the night.

"They ran out of gas an hour or so later on some forgotten two-lane. Too drunk to walk, they evidently got into a wrestling match, and all three passed out in or near the car. When daylight came, a soccer mom reported the car, along with the three guys sprawled around it, and an hour later they were booked in Georgia.

"It didn't take too long for investigators to put it all together. And while John was very much guilty of grand theft, he was not guilty of murder, nor was he an accessory. During the trial, the prosecution cut a deal, giving him a lesser sentence if he would simply state what happened that night. He did." Amos paused. "He also told them about the warehouses."

Therein lay the problem. Amos had told me several times that criminals don't forget, and they certainly don't forgive.

"When John identified his buddies as the three in the car, along with the locations of their warehouses, he received seven years, serving only four for, oddly enough, good behavior."

Amos dipped his hands in the river, washed his face, and then stood, letting the droplets cascade down his neck and shoulders. "Antonio and Felix got eighteen years, serving eighteen. James got life and served up until last month when his case was brought up for review by an ethics board. They were investigating the activities of the officers, who they thought were too bent on revenge and not justice for the death of their fellow officer, which they say colored the trial proceedings.

"The day you and Maggie saw us leaving the courthouse, we'd been watching video footage of the proceedings. It showed James marking on the table with his fingers, writing 'promises' to John Lovett and family. Seems James isn't too happy about having spent two decades in prison."

Amos pulled out the Oreos and offered them to me. I shook my head. He popped the lid on one, licked off the white center, and then ate the two chocolate sides. He did that for about eight cookies and then fed one to Blue, who was inching across the raft.

"And another thing," Amos said, "prison 'law' dictates that when someone rats on you, what they have becomes yours. That includes people."

After Blue and Amos polished off the Oreos, Amos tore open the wrapper and laid it in front of Blue, who chased it around the raft, wagging his tail and licking the plastic clean.

I looked at my watch and knew I needed to check on Maggie.

Amos put his arm on mine. "'Manda's at the house. Brought some dinner. She'll be okay."

I lay back down and watched the clouds roll overhead.

Amos stared down the river, then at me. "You gonna be okay?"

I shrugged.

"What's the doc say?"

"Says it might take some time."

"How much?"

"Who knows? Technically, we're waiting to see if her other ovary can do the work of two. When he closed her up, he wasn't too sure, so in a sense we're just waiting for her next cycle." I tossed a twig into the river. "If it happens, we'll know it's working. If not, Frank says she'll have to substitute with oral hormones. We'll know in two, maybe three weeks, give or take."

Amos nodded and popped another root beer. "Can you make it that long?"

I thought quietly. A month ago, we were crying at the sight of blood. Now we were hoping for it.

"Don't know."

Amos shook his head and then turned toward me as if he were afraid to ask. "What happened to her hair?"

I shrugged. I held out my hand, palm up. "Right now, life feels like it's just sand sifting through my fingers."

We walked back to the house in the twilight. When we got there, Pinky was grunting at me from inside the barn, so I dropped a bucket of corn in her trough and tried to rub her behind the ears. She rolled in the mud, shook her ears, and rubbed her four hundred–plus pounds against me. It was more of a shove than a love-rub. She wedged me against the stall, ground her muddy haunches against me, and snotted me. She was raising her leg when I hopped out of the stall.

Amos raised an eyebrow. "I thought you two had reached an agreement."

I brushed myself off. "That ended when we sold the piglets. Now she's back to being the devil."

"Can't say that I blame her."

"Feeding pigs ain't cheap."

I crept up the stairs, cracked the door, and peered into our bedroom. Maggie lay in bed, cocooned inside the sheets and sleeping. A pillow covered her head. I leaned my forehead against the doorjamb.

"Maggs, I'm taking Amos home. I'll be right back."

I heard a shuffle beneath the sheets, a creak of the bed, but no verbal response.

Amos loaded into the van for a ride home while I walked across to the house and grabbed the keys off the kitchen counter. The kitchen had been cleaned—Amanda, no doubt—but the nursery door was shut, as it had been since we got home.

Blue met me on the porch, and I pointed to the barn. "Stay." He whined and looked at the van. I knelt down and rubbed his muzzle and neck. "I know, buddy. Me too. But she needs you right now. You hang out here and keep an eye on things." Blue circled, curled into a ball, and kept an eye on the barn.

The ride to Pastor John's house was quiet. Amos said little, and I said nothing at all. I pulled up; he hopped out and leaned against the door.

"Next week, at the station house, we're having a boil. Pastor John wants to thank all the guys. You two are invited."

I nodded. Amos patted the top of the van, shut the door, and walked inside, where Amanda met him at the door with L.D. perched on her hip. Amos lifted him up. L.D.'s face lit up like a floodlight, and I drove off into the night. Alone.

I drove home the long way. Twenty minutes later, I pulled into Digger's outdoor amphitheater and cracked the gate. I walked down the aisle toward a seat in the middle. Clouds covered the moon, and the darkness blanketed me, so I bumped my knee on a few seat backs and tripped over a cup brimming with old rainwater. I tried to see the stage, but only the outline appeared. I sat a long time, listening, but I heard no pipes.

Toward midnight, I climbed back up the hill and cranked the van—a sound I had yet to grow accustomed to. I needed to go home, but I didn't. I drove past the church, but the bulldozer had already been there. Only the foundation remained.

Ten minutes later, I pulled into Bryce's drive and walked up the hill. I smelled the remains of a burnt-out trash fire, but when I prodded the coals, they were cold. I walked to the film house and checked the door. It was unlocked. I read the titles, grabbed a film canister, and loaded it into the machine. I hit the power switch, turned on the reel, and walked to the center of the field in front of the screen, where I leaned against an iron pole, the microphone just above my head.

I have a hard time watching John Wayne movies in which John Wayne dies. As a result, I don't usually watch *The Cowboys*, *The Green Berets*, *The Alamo*, or the one now rolling on the screen, *The Shootist*.

It's a simple story really. It was also the Duke's last. He plays a famed gunfighter named J. B. Books who rides into Carson City in 1901 to visit his old friend Doc E. W. Hostetler (Jimmy Stewart) in the last days of his life. Books is trying to hang up his pistols after he discovers he's dying of cancer, but like Poncho and Lefty, gunfighters aren't allowed to grow old. Only their legends do. Occupational hazard, I suppose.

I lay in the grass, my head resting against the pole, and watched as J. B. checked into the boardinghouse where the proprietor, an attractive widow named Bon Rogers (Lauren Bacall), and her son Gillom (Ron Howard) keep their distance and listen to the rumors surfacing about town. As the cancer eats at his body and the thought of a long, slow death eats at his soul, a few of the next generation of killers seek him out for a final fight. Then and now, what made watching more difficult was knowing that the Duke himself actually had cancer while filming, and it would be that same cancer that killed him soon after.

The movie continued through scenes of doctors' visits in which the Duke refills his prescription for laudanum to the scene at the barbershop in which the barber saves hair clippings to sell and then to conversations in which we learn that the undertaker plans to exhibit his corpse.

I lay on the grass and watched as the Duke walked into the bar. Even then, I wanted to scream like Gillom, "No!" The Duke bellied up to the bar, saw the flash of metal in the window's reflection, turned, and stood heroic one last time.

When my grandfather and I first watched this movie on television in the late seventies, I could not understand why the

Duke turned his back on the bartender. I knew that he knew the shotgun was under the bar. There's always a shotgun under the bar. As a kid, I jumped up off the floor and screamed at the television, "The shotgun under the bar!" But the Duke did not hear me, and he did not hear Gillom.

As I grew older, I understood. It was for that very reason he'd chosen the bar. The gunfighters couldn't get him; he was too good, and he knew it. But he also knew that if he turned his back, there'd be no way the bartender could miss. And he didn't.

Maybe death by shotgun was better than death by cancer. Maybe it still is. When the Duke fell against the bar, I jumped up off the ground and turned my back on the screen, walking down the drive while Gillom finished off the bartender and the end of the reel slapped the machine.

chapter twenty-eight

WHEN I GOT HOME IT WAS NEARLY THREE THIRTY IN the morning. All but the barn spotlights were out, and Maggie had left the sprinkler on. I walked around back, turned the spigot off, and in the dim light saw them a second time. Footprints.

I pulled a flashlight from the van, pinched it between my teeth, and crawled on my hands and knees alongside the house. There weren't as many this time, but they were there. And since Maggie had turned on the sprinkler after I'd left, the prints had been made sometime between when I left to take Amos home and just a few minutes ago.

I heard a stick crack in the pasture not forty yards from me and froze. Then I heard it again, followed by a shuffling and another crack.

I slid up onto the porch, unlocked the front door, and crept down the hallway to my writing closet. I unlocked it, slid my shotgun off the floor, and quietly worked the action, sliding a shell into the chamber. I grabbed my larger Maglite, like the kind Amos keeps in his undercover truck, and crept back outside. I belly-crawled off the porch, along the azaleas next to the spigot, and out over the grass next to our house.

When I neared the edge of the pasture, my heart was pounding so hard inside my chest that I thought it would explode out the front. Slowly I stood, holding the flashlight snug against the barrel and pointed in the same direction. I had yet to click it on, but I could with a flick of my thumb. The sound of cracking twigs had moved, maybe another forty yards closer to the river. It was slighter now, not so loud, and when I stepped into the rows of corn, it stopped altogether. With the wind at my back and rustling the leaves of the cornstalks that were two feet above my head, I stood and waited. I heard another shuffling, as if someone were crawling more quickly now, and still the sound was moving away from me toward the river. If he got to the river, he'd be gone. If I could head him off, or get to him first, I had a chance.

I stepped out of the cornfield and circled, the shotgun on my hip and the flashlight and barrel in my hand. The more quickly I moved, the more rapidly the sound out in front of me began moving through the corn. We were mirroring each other. The edge of the corn narrowed like a triangle toward the river, so given our current path, if I took off running right this second, we'd meet at the river. The moon had popped out from behind the clouds and threw my shadow on the dark grass before me. Trying to quiet my heart, I took a deep breath, gripped the shotgun more tightly, and took off running down the side of the corn rows.

Whoever I was chasing did the same, crashing through the corn like a bulldozer, trying desperately to get out the other side. The river was now just a hundred yards off, and based on the sound moving toward me from my left, he'd get there before me. I tried to run faster, but the grass was knee-high, and I'm not a very good sprinter in cowboy boots. He increased his speed, smashing through the corn, and every few seconds I could hear him breathing. Within forty yards of the river, I pulled up, the oaks on my right, corn on my left, and a small field of grass spread out before me and rolling down into the river.

North of me was Old Man McCutcheon's property, south of me a few hundred yards lay my son's grave, beyond that a couple of miles sat the church property, and sitting at a dead stop not ten yards from me in the corn, breathing heavily and sounding winded, sat someone who'd been peeping in my windows. I clicked off the safety, shouldered the shotgun, and placed my finger on the flashlight button. Unable to control either my breathing or my pounding heart, I stood and waited.

The barrel of the shotgun was moving wildly around the sight picture. I stared off into the darkness, trying to see the movement of outlines or images. Then a dark flash caught my eye. Followed by another. I looked straight at it and lost it entirely, so I looked at it out of the corner of my eye and saw the huge form crawling on his hands and knees out of the corn. He crawled out into the grass, trying to hide in the darkness, and when I was certain he had cleared the corn, I fired a shot into the air. The shot rang out and echoed across the river, turning me momentarily deaf, and the smell of burned gunpowder stung my nose and eyes. I quickly and loudly chambered another round, aimed at the shape, shouted, *"Stop!"* and clicked on the light.

Standing broadside, in all her corn-fed porcine glory, stood Pinky, a half-eaten corncob wedged between her teeth. She eyed me, sniffed the air, grunted, and ambled back into the corn, her big ears flopping happily alongside her. I watched her curlicue tail disappear into the corn, sat down on the ground, and breathed for the first time in five minutes.

I clicked on the safety, flipped off the flashlight, and lay down in the grass before I fell over. A couple of minutes later, I sat up, dusted myself off, and laid the shotgun across my shoulder. Then I stood, turned toward home, and ran square into the chest of a rock-solid man.

I dropped the shotgun, the light, and half my bladder before Bryce reached out and grabbed my shoulder. His face was painted in black and green stripes, and into his clothes he had tucked parts of cornstalks. He looked into my eyes, stared over my shoulder, sniffed me, and placed his .45 back into its shoulder holster beneath his left arm.

I picked up the flashlight and clicked it on, waving it wildly around the night and finally centering it on Bryce. The most striking feature was not the clothing, the cornstalks, the face paint, the sidearm, or the old scope dangling from twine around his neck, but rather his feet. His bare feet. I shone down, up, and down again. When I finished involuntarily emptying my bladder, I clicked off the light and said, "Bryce?"

He blinked. His voice was quiet and calm. "Dylan."

I stepped closer. Not smelling the fumes of alcohol I'd come to expect, I said, "You okay?"

Bryce nodded, checked the position of the safety without even looking, and handed it to me. The pungent smell of warm urine reached my nose and, evidently, Bryce's, because he grabbed the light, shone it on the front of my pants, and then clicked it off. He handed it back. "You?"

I took a deep breath, sat down again in the grass, and collapsed onto my back. Just then I heard the barn door slam and saw Maggie walk beneath the fluorescent glow of the light from the telephone pole that lit the yard between the barn and the house. Wrapped in a blanket, she strained her eyes, looking toward us.

I turned on the flashlight, shone it down onto myself, and said, "It's just me and Bryce." I decided it'd be better not to shine the light on Bryce, so I kept it pointing down on me, watching her. She craned her neck, muttered something, and disappeared again into the barn.

I flicked off the light again as Pinky crossed the trail in front of me, waddling her way back to the barn after what was apparently her nighttime feeding.

Bryce stepped closer to the corn and peered at the tops, shining black in the moonlight. He whispered, "They were a little taller than this. It was summer. I was chasing a man, and we came to a field." He raised his hands and touched the tips of the cornstalks.

"He had been assigned to me a month earlier, and I'd been chasing him ever since. That was the thirty-second day. When he cleared the corn and stepped into my row, he was forty-two paces." He pointed at the shotgun on my shoulder. "I'd been working some tunnels earlier in the evening, so I was carrying one of those. I placed the bead on his legs and squeezed." Bryce blinked but didn't flinch.

"He dropped, began spraying the corn around me with AK-47 fire, and one 7.62 round cut through my helmet but missed my head. I fired a second time, and the man stopped firing and clutched his feet. He was screaming. I walked within twenty paces and fired a third time."

Bryce dropped the imaginary gun and pulled the real Colt .45 from his holster. He clicked off the safety and, clasping it with two hands, walked farther down the corn row.

I followed, the shotgun over my shoulder, pointing away, the flashlight aimed on Bryce.

He walked to a spot twenty steps away and stood, feet apart, pointing into the dirt below him. He extended the pistol barrel into the air and stopped some two feet from the ground. He then began speaking in a language I'd never heard. It sounded like a loose cousin to what Maggie and I would hear when we went to eat sushi.

Bryce knelt, the pistol still clutched in both hands, and whispered, "I said, 'Where is she?'" He paused, waited, looked further into the memory, and spoke again. "Where is she?"

Silence followed as Bryce cocked the hammer on his Colt. I backed up one step, and Bryce whispered, pressing his ear hard against the memory of the man's face. He stayed there, listening, shaking his head, and nodding. Then, without another word, he stood up and pulled the trigger eight times. He fired all eight shots into the dirt beneath him, directly through the memory of the man's head. He ejected the clip, inserted a second, and flicked the slide forward, chambering another round. He clicked on the hammer safety, holstered the still-smoking weapon, and breathed in long, measured breaths. Finally he blinked, reached into the cargo pocket on his pants, pulled out a sheet of gum, and popped all twelve pieces into his mouth.

While I tried to make sense of this nonsense, Bryce worked the gum around in his mouth. The mixture of dirt, corn, gunpowder, urine, and spearmint added to the confusion.

"Bryce?"

He blinked and looked at me.

I shone the light on his feet. "Have, umm, . . . have you been, uh . . . do you always walk around barefooted?"

Bryce looked at his feet, the gum filling most of his mouth. "Only when I don't want to be heard."

"You know," I said, trying to sound casual, "if you're ever out this way and want to come in for a cup of coffee or a bite to eat, you can always knock. Or just come on in and have a seat at the table."

Bryce considered that for a moment, then said, "Okay."

I nodded. "Sure. You don't even have to knock."

Without another word, Bryce stepped off into the night. Within ten paces, I could no longer make out his outline. A few more, and both the sight and sound of him had disappeared altogether. Ten seconds later, I heard a covey of quail flush and rise down near the river beyond my son's grave, some two hundred yards away.

I walked back to the barn, stripped, and showered. Cleaner, I walked across the yard to the house and locked the shotgun back in the closet, and only when I'd sat down at the kitchen table, hovering over a glass of orange juice, did I realize how badly my hands were shaking.

When I cracked open our bedroom door, I found Maggie snow-angeled diagonally across the middle of the bed. Her breathing told me she was asleep, so I pulled the door quietly shut and spread out across the front porch with Blue. A few hours later, I woke inside a dew-covered sleeping bag. Pinky was grunting at me from inside the barn, and Blue lay on his bed across the porch looking at me as if I were from Mars.

I sat up and looked at him. "What? What'd I do?"

He flopped his ears forward, laid his muzzle down across his leg, and let out a deep breath. Maybe now he would let himself go to sleep.

THE CALENDAR ON THE REFRIGERATOR SHOWED THAT IT was Tuesday, July 16. Another week had passed. Each day seemed like one long day that rolled seamlessly into another, where daylight and darkness had little meaning other than to suggest something I'd forgotten. According to my count, Maggie had been home eighteen days. Before all this stuff started, her cycles had been pretty regular at twenty-eight days. I wasn't sure, but I guessed we were another two weeks, give or take a few days, from knowing one way or the other. I tried to imagine each scenario. Neither was very good. Whatever the outcome, I wasn't sure how Maggie would react.

I pulled on my jeans, slid on my boots, and combed my hair. I walked around the front of the house and found her sitting in a rocker, wrapped in a blanket, and watching the bulldozer dump burned memories and brick into a Dumpster across the street.

She hadn't eaten much in a couple of days, and I was sure she had lost some weight. Her face was thinner, accentuated by her short hair, and her color was not too good. Her hollow face looked like a reflection of her insides.

I scrambled some eggs, made some cheese grits and toast, and walked out onto the front porch. She smiled, nibbled, but ate little. I kissed her forehead, she brushed my face with her palm, and we sat in the rockers, swaying.

chapter twenty-nine

THE PHONE RANG TWICE BEFORE THE HOSPITAL
receptionist picked up. "Hello?"

It was late; I cleared my throat. "Hello. I need to speak with
Dr. Frank Palmer, please."

"Hold just one minute."

Five minutes passed while the elevator music reminded me
that I hadn't been to the dentist in a while.

"This is Dr. Frank."

"Dr. Frank, this is Dylan Styles."

"Hey, Dylan. How's our girl?"

"Well, sir, she's not sleeping much. I was wondering if—"

"No problem. I'll have the nurse call in something. How's
everything else?"

I wasn't sure how to answer. Finally I stammered, "I—I just think it'd do her some good to get a good night's sleep."

"I'll tell you what," he said, "why don't you stop by the office. I'll have the nurse pull a few things out of the sample bin. Save you some money."

"You don't mind?"

"I'll have it ready when you get there."

"Thanks, Dr. Frank."

THE BUILDING THAT HOUSED THE DIGGER VOLUNTEER Fire Department No. 1 was little more than a tall concrete-block warehouse with four large front-and-back aluminum garage doors that allowed the trucks to drive through the building rather than just into it and one very tall flagpole that stood adjacent to Mr. Carter's dog kennels. He had donated the land.

Picnic tables and folding chairs spread across the lawn behind the building, and the enormous flag flapped gently in the 98-degree air. Three-foot standing floor fans sat in the middle of the firehouse, circulating the air through the doors and blowing across the red-and-white-checkered tablecloths covering the picnic tables. Newspaper had been spread across the tablecloths, and upright rolls of paper towels sat on top of all that, ensuring that nothing would float away. Mr. Carter's rolling barbecue pit, an old propane tank cut lengthways and set on trailer wheels—and big enough for a man to lie down in—sat smoking, lid open, currently heating three huge twenty-gallon vats.

Draped in a red apron that read "Fire Chief," Mr. Carter tended both the fire and the pots with the same stick. He'd poke the fire, stoke the flames, then dip that same stick into the water and poke the boiling food. He said the mesquite in the charcoal added to the flavor. Badger and Gus, two of Mr. Carter's older and most obedient dogs, had been let out of the kennel and lay at their master's feet.

I parked out of sight because I didn't want to explain the van, and then Maggie and I crossed the street and walked through the firehouse. There's no use denying it; it's pretty much a huge toy room for grown men. All of us signed up in part because of all the cool toys. From chain saws to axes to the infamous Jaws of Life, we are enamored with things that cut, bang, or smash. And what boy doesn't grow up wanting to drive a fire truck?

Mr. Willard, the owner of the corner gas station and grocery, greeted us at the door with a pitcher of iced tea and two glasses. Jim Biggins, evidently taking a break from his land-clearing and firewood business, walked around the side of the building with a hundred-pound sack of charcoal slung over each shoulder. Butch Walker and his boys, free between the morning and evening milking at their dairy, sat at a table laughing with a few guys I didn't know. John Billingsly, Digger's only computer guru, sat hovering over a portable bug zapper that stood like a six-foot chiminea with a purple head. Every three or four seconds it zapped.

The wives of these men all sat at one table, whispering, laughing, and trying to hide whatever they were talking about from their husbands. Which was also exactly what the men were doing, but both groups knew this, so the game continued as it had since Adam met Eve in the garden.

No matter how slowly I walked, Maggie walked a half step behind me, almost hiding behind my shoulder. She hadn't said she didn't want to come, but she hadn't seemed too excited either. I looped my arm inside hers, and we walked to the nearest table, where Amanda saw us and came to our rescue. She grabbed Maggie and led her off to the women's table.

Maggie's eyes told me she didn't want to go, they told me she wanted to run very far away from here, but I silently urged her on, so she put on a smile and acted happy.

I sat with the boys, giving the obligatory laugh when needed, but my eyes, ears, and mind were with Maggie. The women's conversation had turned to children, whose child was in what grade, what sports they were playing, how far each mom drove the car pool each day, how many loads of laundry they washed in a week, and how much their grocery bill had increased because of the rising price of milk. Maggie listened, trying to look interested, but her crossed arms, crossed legs, and stiff neck told me she needed help.

Mr. Carter came to the rescue. Stirring the middle pot, he leaned back out of the smoke and said, "Amos and D.S."

We jumped up from the table and met him at the cooker. He gave us each a hot pad, and we lifted the first vat off the cooker. It was heavy, and I almost stumbled. Amos smiled, eyed my shaking arms, and shook his head. "You need to get busy."

I looked at my deflated biceps and compared them to Amos's. Not much comparison. We drained off the water, then dumped the contents directly onto the newspaper on the center table. Red potatoes, corn on the cob, carrots, shrimp, andouille sausage, Alaskan crab legs, and about four cans of Old Bay Seasoning spilled across the table and sat steaming in the shade of the magnolia tree that towered above us.

Amos and I returned for the other two vats while everyone else grabbed plates and started helping themselves to the mound on the table. We loaded up three tables with dinner and then sat around the tables eating with our hands. A true low-country boil does not involve flatware of any kind. We just bellied up to the tables, rested our elbows on the edges, and dug in.

Everyone, that is, except Maggie and me. We did what we were getting good at. We pretended.

An hour passed. The shrimp tails and crab shells piled up, and people began sitting back and passing around the toothpick cup. Inside the fire station, John Billingsly was tending his ice cream maker, which finished churning about the time someone started telling the story of Amos's and my heroic rescue at the church.

The guys laughed. One of them imitated me with my oxygen tank and rubber boots that were two sizes too big, while another mimicked Amos's attempt to kick in a stubborn door. While they prodded, Maggie, Amanda, and a few other ladies passed out plastic spoons and peach ice cream served in Styrofoam bowls.

While I listened and the fake smile on my face told the guys around me that I was enjoying their fun, my eyes watched Maggie, who had busied herself with cleaning the tables and the ice-cream machine. She tried to look helpful, look interested, look okay, but I knew her, and I knew that she was about ready to jump out of her skin and that when she did, tears wouldn't be far behind. She had held it together about as long as she could.

I threw my bowl away, looped my arm inside hers, and walked her slowly beneath the magnolia and along the grassy lawn that led down to Mr. Carter's duck pond. The shade felt good, the breeze felt better, and the farther we got from the tables, the more her shoulders relaxed and her breathing deepened. By the time we reached the pond, the wrinkle on her forehead had almost disappeared. We stood watching the ducks swim around the turtles and a few well-fed carp feed slowly through the weeds at the bank.

About ten minutes later, Amos and Amanda appeared behind us. Amos held an uncut watermelon on one shoulder. The four of us stood at the water, saying nothing and not feeling as though we had to. Maybe that's the sign of true friendship, when silence is not uncomfortable.

About twenty years ago, Mr. Carter had planted twelve weeping willows along the banks of his pond. Now they were tall, mature, and their branches swooped over and down into the water like Rapunzel's hair. We sat in the shade of one. I leaned against the tree trunk, and Maggie sat between my legs, leaning against me.

Amos drove his Benchmade down the middle of the melon, then cut out large chunks and passed them around. He sank his face into the heart and let the juice drip off his chin. Maggie did likewise, chewed, leaned back, and spit a seed out into the water.

Amos looked out across the pond. "The federal guys have put me in charge of the investigation here. We've got most every agent in the state trying to find them, which shouldn't be too hard to do given what they look like, but we haven't yet, and even when we do, we can't do anything, because technically, they haven't done anything wrong—at least that we can prove. It'd be Maggie's word against theirs, and we can question them but technically can't hold them.

"One more thing." Amos wiped his face, closed his eyes, and spoke as if it hurt. "Antonio and Felix were released from prison about three days before Amanda was kidnapped and tied to a tree in the woods two years ago."

We sat in the quiet a moment while the weight settled down into my stomach. He put his arm around Amanda, who seemed relatively unmoved by the admission. Evidently she'd heard this story before.

"A week later James received a postcard from Charleston. The front showed a picture of a rural country church that looked a lot like one that used to stand not too far from here. And on the back someone had drawn a stick figure wrapped around a tree."

"You think I should move Maggie someplace in town?"

Amos shrugged. "Hard to say. Criminals don't think like we do."

I stood and walked to the edge of the pond, dipping my fingers and then shaking them. I wiped them on my pants, plucked a tall weed from the bank, and began breaking it into smaller pieces.

I nodded. "You think they'll come back? I mean, to the house?"

"The cop in me doubts it." He tried to sound reassuring. "They're probably running now. I've known too many criminals who never make good on their word—even when it comes to revenge." He paused again and looked at Amanda. "But the husband in me does not."

Maggie looked at Amos. "Which one do you believe?"

"I believe . . ." He looked at Amanda, then put his hand on her shoulder, "the one who loves her."

We were quiet a minute.

"I'd keep Papa's 12 handy for a while."

MAGGIE DIDN'T SAY MUCH ON THE WAY HOME. NEITHER did I.

I parked in front of the barn and told her I wanted to check on the house. When I walked up the back steps and into the kitchen, the light on the answering machine was blinking. I pushed *play*, turned down the volume, and lowered my ear next to the machine. Mr. Sawyer from the adoption agency said the committee had reached its decision and would be sending out a letter in the next couple of weeks. When he had finished speaking, I pressed *delete* and walked slowly down the drive to the mailbox. It was empty.

Like me.

chapter thirty

BY MIDWEEK, I ADMITTED THAT SEVERAL THINGS
were bothering me and I could not shake them. I didn't like
having to live like two tramps in the barn; I was worried about
Maggie; I couldn't make sense of anything right now; and I
knew things were getting worse and not better. But at the top
of the heap of things that bothered me most, that woke me up
in a cold sweat at night, screaming out of the silence and calling me a liar, sat the story I'd written and given to Maggie.
And with Maggie growing more detached by the minute, what
troubled me was not what I'd left in but what I'd left out.

I leaned against the shower post and shut my eyes. The
water dripped off my shoulders and cooled my skin amid the
humid night. I didn't want to live this way. The wrinkle
between my eyes told me what was bothering me, but it also

said something else: it said I had grown angry and bitter that she had shut me out.

Pinky slammed her stall door, reminding me it was well past her dinnertime. I finally voiced to myself what I had been thinking for days but had not been willing to admit. When I looked at my life, at the torn and frayed quilted patchwork that had enveloped us, I wondered if any part of it could be sewn together again. Because as I studied it in my mind's eye, only tattered remnants remained.

I stood in the doorway, drying myself and studying the house. From the chipped paint to the squeaky screen door to the stick-and-twig ruins of Maggie's landscape design to the smell of Pinky's unkempt stall wafting across the back porch, the place looked and smelled the way I felt.

I leaned over the stall and looked down on Pinky, who was currently digging a hole to China in the corner. She looked at me, grunted through her snout, and flopped her ears forward.

I looked across the overgrown yard to the house and heard Maggie throwing things in the kitchen. I heard a glass break, a pause, then several more crashes for what I assumed was good measure. A door slammed. Blue looked at me, I shrugged, and his face told me what I already knew. We were nearing the end.

Something had been severed. It wasn't Maggie's voice that told me this. It was her eyes. When she looked at me, she was looking at the world beyond me where her dreams once lived. The brilliant light that had once been there was dim and flickering.

"What can heal the human soul?" I whispered.

Blue leaned against me and raised his cold nose to my hand. I stepped into my clothes and admitted that I had grown angry at something I could not see or touch. The irony of my life smacked me in the face: while I could protect Pastor

John from a raging fire, I could not protect my wife from that which threatened to kill her.

I walked out the back of the barn along the edge of the corn and tried counting the stars. I felt little and insignificant—one amid the many.

My sense of helplessness pressed down on my shoulders, grew tighter across my chest, and squeezed out the air. I could not escape the sense of blame. Like a wave of vomit I could not control, the ache cut my knees out from under me, sent me to the dirt, and then exited my heart like a cannon shot. I knelt, clutching the earth, gasping for air, and trying not to let the split in my heart split me.

MIDNIGHT CAME, AND I CRAWLED OUT OF THE FIELD. THE large green leaves of the corn slapped at my arms, and the tasseled tops towered now some two feet above me. I crept toward the barn, slipped through the garden behind the azaleas, and stood next to the barn door staring at the staircase.

Blue looked up at me and even shook his head, but I scratched him between the ears and told him, "I'm just checking on her." I climbed up the stairs into the loft. The room was cold and dark, and I could hear Maggie sleeping in the silence. She lay in the bed, mounded beneath the covers, breathing heavily under the oral sedation she'd grown accustomed to.

I tiptoed to the bedside table, picked up her bottle of sleeping pills, and clicked off the lid. One left. There were five this time last night.

I knelt next to the bed and slid my hand beneath hers. It was limp, frail, and did not respond to mine. I slid my hands beneath the sheets and found her cold feet. I pulled some socks from my drawer, slipped them over her heels, and covered her up. The fan was spinning like a tornado, and the AC was set on "snow." I knew our power bill would shoot through the roof, but I didn't adjust a thing. If that's what she needed, then that's what she needed.

I climbed down, walked across the yard, and found the answering machine light blinking quietly in the dark. The red light reminded me of the hospital and the machines that had monitored Maggie. Maybe we'd escaped the confining walls, but the monitoring continued. I pushed the button and heard Dr. Frank's voice.

"Dylan, it's Frank Palmer. Just checking on Maggie. I'm working the graveyard shift, so call me anytime tonight."

I dialed the number of the delivery ward and asked for Dr. Frank, and the receptionist paged him. A few minutes later he picked up the phone.

"Hey, Dylan, how're things?"

"I'm not too sure."

"Any sign of her cycle starting?"

"I don't think so."

Dr. Frank took a deep breath. "I don't want to give you any false hope. If you don't see something tomorrow, or the next day at the latest, I think, well . . ."

"I understand."

"How are her emotions? Is she on an even keel?"

I scratched my head. "No, not really."

"On a scale of one to ten, ten being really out of whack, where is she?"

"Reaching ten."

He paused as though he was checking his watch. "Today's Wednesday. Why don't you call the office Monday, and I'll tell the nurses to work her in. We probably ought to start her on a hormone replacement therapy. Like we discussed, it's routine for menopausal or sterile women."

The word *sterile* echoed through my head. "I'll call Monday."

He hung up, and I returned the phone to the receiver. When I turned around, Maggie was standing in the doorway, wrapped in a sheet. Her face was as white as a ghost, and she was barefooted. We stood looking at each other.

Finally she spoke. "What'd he say?"

"Who?"

Her eyes were dark and hollow. "Dr. Frank."

"He said he hoped we'd have a good weekend."

Maggie blinked and waited.

I shrugged. "He wants me to bring you in Monday."

"Why?"

"'Cause by the end of the weekend, we ought to know one way or the other."

Maggie's finger slid along the lines of the wall calendar. She reached what would be the end of the weekend, pulled the calendar off the wall, and pitched it into the trash. Then she turned and walked back to the barn.

I walked to the front porch and leaned against the screen door. The streetlight lit the mailbox and reminded me that I had not checked the mail in two days. I walked down the drive and filled my arms with junk mail, then walked back to the house. Sitting at the kitchen table, eyeing the barn door, I filtered through the pile.

The letter from the adoption agency was stuffed somewhere in the middle. I froze, eyed the hallway again, and then slit the top of the envelope.

"*Dr. and Mrs. Styles, We regret to inform you . . .*"

It was signed "*Sincerely,*" which I doubted, and then included a postscript, "*You may appeal this decision in writing,*" and gave detailed instructions on how to do that. The following page was a check in the amount of my deposit.

Over the last few weeks, the facts of my life had festered like a splinter and were now tender to the slightest touch. The letter was like somebody rubbing the tip of the splinter with sandpaper.

I'd had just about enough of this committee. I folded the letter, stuck it in my pocket, and closed my eyes. I needed to work on my appeal, pay off my debt at the bank, and figure out what I was going to tell Maggie.

chapter thirty-one

LAST JULY, AS THE HEAT OF SUMMER AND SWARMS of mosquitoes arrived in force, Maggie and I packed enough food for two or three days, whistled for Blue, and hopped on the raft. We shoved off, and I stood at the rear manning the rudder while Maggie lay across the deck tanning, talking with me, and dipping her feet in the river as Blue paced back and forth across the front spotting fish.

The first night we pulled into a small cove, anchored, lit the butane stove, fried fish, scrambled some eggs, and then sipped coffee while Maggie laid her head on my chest and the stars shot by overhead. Two magical days passed before we even blinked. And by the time we thought about returning, we'd been on the raft almost four days. It's a good thing the fish were biting.

Reluctantly we turned around, cranked the Evinrude, and began puttering home. On our trip north, Maggie began spotting flowers that had bloomed, blown off the stem, and landed in the water and now floated carelessly along. They were white and blue, and Maggie said they looked like some sort of iris. She began scooping them off the water, and in an hour or so she had twenty or thirty blooms.

She noticed that the blooms were spilling from the fingers of the Salkehatchie, and her curiosity grew. At the mouth of one narrow stream leading into the river, we saw half a dozen blooms floating single file behind one larger bloom, like ducklings following a drake. We pulled the raft up alongside a tree, marked the tree with a piece of rope, and puttered home.

The next day we borrowed Amos's fishing canoe, an Old Town, and returned to our rope-marked tree. Maggie wanted to find the source of those blooms, but the raft was too big and bulky, and walking was not an option. No one walked in the swamp. Well, not unless you were Jesus. You could be ankle-deep one minute, and in the next you'd be looking up from the bottom of a twenty-foot hole. The Salkehatchie has a way and a mind all its own, and you don't go in there unless you've got a strategy for getting out. Amos and I grew up listening to stories of lost Confederate gold, escaping slaves chained at the ankles, lost Germans manning a submarine, and Indians who lived in the trees.

Rain had overflowed the swamp and, like tidal waters along the shore, spilled over the edges into the larger body, the Salkehatchie River, that ran alongside it. The flooding happened to coincide with the blooming of what Maggie later learned was a rare iris that grew almost exclusively in a unique combination of two types of water that collided in the swamp. The compost created by the tannic acid in the water, the decomposition in the swamp, the water temperature, and the gentle flow of the water from an underground spring combined to make the perfect petri dish for what we soon dubbed Maggie's Iris. I'm pretty sure some botanist had already labeled it, but he wasn't around to correct us, so the name stuck.

The myths surrounding the swamp were many, but what we knew for certain was that the timber had never been cut, ever. Meaning that some trees in the middle were three or four hundred years old, and the canopy in some spots could be a hundred feet high and make the day seem like night. It was the quietest and most peaceful, untouched, virgin, ancient, and prehistoric land I'd ever seen. Few people had ventured far enough in to really get a look, because the first mile or so could be rather creepy. But when you're married to someone like Maggie, who's passionate about plants and where they come from, creepy just adds to the ambience.

We paddled in past our rope, up and into the swamp where the finger lost its boundary and bled into the landscape. Within a few hundred yards we were surrounded by nothing but trees and water. The trees, wide at the bottom and skinny at the top, grew up out of the black water like natural skyscrapers. Once in, everything looked the same, so I took a compass reading and poled slowly past the trees, the smallest of which were bigger at the base than the hood of Pastor John's Cadillac. While the silence engulfed us, Maggie pointed and I poled.

Behind us in the water, the pollen, which had fallen en masse and coated the water in a yellowish haze, was now marked by the wake of the canoe. If we wanted out, the only markers we had were my compass and that oozing trail back through the pollen, which, given a few hours, would bubble, roll, and flow its way along, covering up any track we'd made.

Meaning our trail in the pollen was about as effective as bread crumbs. Couldn't trust it for very long.

Occasionally we'd look into the water and see where an alligator or snake had rolled along the top of the water and made a similar cut in the pollen. The more I looked, the more I noticed that the surface of the swamp was marred with thousands of such scratches and cuts. Dotted amid all of this traffic atop the yellow brick road were the blooms that Maggie was chasing.

And me? I was chasing Maggie, and Oz lay somewhere in the distance.

I poled for hours, dipping under limbs, into the hearts of great canopies, around the bases of trees wrapped with vines and snakes, and over alligator holes and turtle perches. The coolness of the swamp did little to deter the mosquitoes, which had descended straight out of the Jurassic period. The farther in we went and the closer we seemed to get to the source of the blooms, the more Maggie beamed. After four or five miles, she was standing in the front of the canoe, leaning over the bow, pointing me onward like Lewis or Clark.

At dusk, I grew a bit antsy. I did not want to spend the night in the bottom of this canoe floating in this swamp, but I knew absent a miracle that was about to happen. We were almost out of insect spray, and when darkness came I had a feeling that the really big bugs would come out to play. And despite Maggie's Lewis and Clark mentality at the moment, the first really big bug that dropped on her during the night would end her tour of fun and send her across the top of the water like Peter on the Sea of Galilee.

Luckily, we never got that far. Thirty minutes before it grew too dark to see my hand in front of my face, Maggie pointed and started jumping up and down like a puppy in the window at a pet store. I poled another hundred yards and turned into a clearing where the moon, out early, was shining down like a God-sized spotlight. Maggie sat down, dropped her shoulders, and gasped.

A natural spring, flowing up out of nowhere, rose up like a small bubbling fountain and filtered through hundreds of wild irises that were hooked together via their roots and floating free above the spring. They were connected to nothing other than one another and evidently feeding off whatever was shooting up out of the earth. And given their defined perimeter, it was pretty obvious that they would grow only where the black swamp water met the clear springwater. As soon as the water diluted into the swamp, the flowers quit growing.

Maggie sat back on the bow of the canoe, sweeping her fingers through the tips of the irises in the emerald-green water and inhaling the pungency of the swamp through her lungs and into her limbs. She was surrounded by a sea of white and blue that looked almost fluorescent in the growing moonlight. It lit on her hair, which she had pulled back and up, and then cascaded down her shoulders and spilled into the water below. "Promise me that one day we can come back here."

The gates of the Emerald City opened, and I nodded.

I SIGNED MY APPEAL LETTER, DATED IT, AND STUCK ON THE stamp. It was noon, the sun was high, and Maggie had yet to emerge from our room in the hayloft, so I cranked the tractor, ambled across the road to the ruins of Amos's house, and pulled around back, where his shed stood lonely and isolated. I wedged open the door, picked my way through the banana spiders and cobwebs, and unearthed the canoe. I strapped it across the sides of the wheel wells and drove down to the river.

An hour later, draped in sweat and muscle ache, I reached the marked tree and noticed the first of the blooms floating atop the water. I turned into the swamp, took a compass reading, and began making my Osceola-like journey through the limbs and cypress stumps.

Two hours and five miles later, I had paddled my way into what some might have called the heart of darkness. Truth was, I was a long way from nowhere, but if this place had a heart, it was anything but dark. The farther in you paddled, the closer to the light you came—that's the secret of the swamp.

The blooms dotted the surface of the swamp like bread crumbs, just as they had the year before. I followed the trail and finally pulled up beneath the tree limbs, breaking into the cathedral canopy.

The sunlight lit the tops of the irises in a checkerboard of white and blue dotted with golden-yellow tips. The roots waved in the emerald-green water like mermaid fins. Somewhere high above me an owl hooted, and all around me the pungent ripeness of the decomposing yet perpetually reborn swamp filled my nose like menthol.

I worked quickly. The stalks were stiff, some three feet long, and I laid them in the bow of the canoe, blooms up. Within ten minutes I had about two armfuls. I turned the canoe, pulled hard on the paddle, and, thanks to the opposition of the current, landed the canoe on the riverbank below the house about two and a half hours later.

The sun was down, crickets had come up, and a light breeze lifted along the river. It would be a nice night. I grabbed the flowers, hopped on the tractor, and let third gear roll me home. I stopped at the barn, hopped off, and bounded up the steps, hoping I'd find Maggie awake.

She was sitting at the table, dressed in baggy sweats and

hovering over a cup of tea, her fingers nervously tapping the sides of the mug. Her face was thin and pale—like her eyes. She opened her mouth when I walked in, but closed it when she saw the flowers.

I was dripping with both sweat and river water. I didn't know what to say, so I walked to the sink, laid down the entire bundle of stalks, and start filling the basin with water. Her eyes watered, and she shook her head, then walked to the sink, gently feeling the blooms. She shook her head again and loosed a tear that fell like a BASE jumper down toward her once-painted toenails that were now chipped and peeling.

Her voice was hoarse as if she hadn't used it much. "Same place?" she whispered.

I nodded and watched her filter her fingers through the blooms as she would through the hair of a child.

"You follow the trail on the water?"

I nodded again.

She sat down, folded her arms, and looked at the floor as I leaned against the opposite countertop. There were six feet and a thousand miles between us.

When she crossed her legs, her bent knee raised her sweatpants just above the ankle, revealing a leg that hadn't been shaved in more than a week. Maybe two. I wanted to say something, anything to keep the conversation going. I pointed at the irises. "I wanted you to . . . well." Then I pointed at her stomach. "How's your tummy?" The words slipped out before I had time to take them back.

She reached up, grabbed a single bloom between her index finger and thumb, shook her head slightly, and then snapped off the bloom like a dead twig. She dropped the bloom in the sink, folded her arms again as if a subzero wind had just blown in through the cracks of the floor, and walked out on the porch, where the curtain seemed to be closing on the stage of our lives.

I looked through the kitchen window at the corn standing tall, still, and silent. The cotton was no different. I had only been to one Broadway show, *Riverdance,* with Maggie in New York, and when they finished that magnificent, glorious show, we jumped from our seats—our faces beaming and hearts racing—and clapped for fifteen minutes while the dancers bowed and smiled. Looking through the window, I heard no encore.

chapter thirty-two

I SHOWERED, SHAVED HALF MY FACE IN FRONT OF the cracked glass, turned and shaved the other half, and was sitting on the porch when Maggie walked out the door. She hadn't changed, still wore no shoes, and her hair hadn't been brushed out of her face. The only change showed in her eyes—they were red and puffier.

I stood up. I'd have taken her anywhere.

Blue circled behind her and licked her toes, and she pointed toward the river—her eyes lost beyond the horizon. "I'm going for a walk."

I set down my glass. "I'll go with?"

She held up a hand and shook her head. Without looking at me, she said, "I'll go."

I sat back down and watched her disappear into the corn.

Blue looked at me, and I whispered, "You'd better go with her." He slipped off the porch and into the corn just a few rows south of hers.

When dark came, I was about to go find her when Amos drove around the side of the house. His truck was muddy, he was driving fast, and he was half hanging out the window.

He tilted back his black baseball cap. "You coming?"

I had no idea what he was talking about.

"Come on, Ivory. Check the calendar."

I looked toward the house and back at him, but still nothing clicked into place.

He shook his head. "D.S., you need a keeper." He opened the passenger door and sat with the truck running. "Come on, get in."

I looked off into the corn, then back at Amos. "Where we going?"

"Pastor John's house."

"Why?"

He frowned and looked at his watch. "Dummy, it's your birthday." He let the words sink in. "I never met anyone who forgot his own birthday."

I looked toward the river. "My birthday?"

I pointed out into the corn to tell him why I couldn't come, when Maggie walked out. Her knees were dirty, and the hair on the sides of her face was stuck to her temples. She walked to Amos's side window and asked, "Is Amanda at home?"

Surprised, Amos nodded. "Hey, Maggs." He opened the truck door and slid off the seat. "How you doing, honey?"

Maggie walked up the porch steps, opened the front door, and turned around. A pained smile hung on her face. She crossed her arms. "I've got some things I want to bring her."

Amos looked at me, and I shrugged slightly. He nodded. "Well, I'm sure she'll like that."

Maggie walked inside and shut the door quietly behind her.

He spoke to me, but his mouth faced the door. "We thought if we gave you two some time, things might improve." Maggie's footsteps faded off into the back of the house. "Guess not."

I put a finger in the air just as Blue appeared out at the edge of the corn. "Give me just a minute."

I walked inside and down the hall through our construction site. The house was still a wreck. The walls and attic had been gutted, and if you looked up, you could see the underside of the new aluminum sheet roofing. I found Maggie sitting on the dusty floor of what was once our bedroom, looking out the back window toward the river.

"Maggs, Amos invited us to Pastor John's house tonight for dinner. You want to come?"

She turned, shook her head, and said, "No, you go." She paused and looked back out the window toward the oak that towered above our son's grave. "Tell Amanda I'll bring some things by tomorrow."

The thought of Maggie getting out sounded good, so I said, "I'll drive you. Maybe we could go to Ira's or DQ."

She nodded, but there was no conviction in it.

I stepped back out in the hall. "I'll check on you when I get in." I reached to pull the door shut, but she raised a hand.

"You can leave it open."

I stepped off the porch as Amos stepped out of the barn. "You ought to feed that pig every now and then. She might like you a bit more."

I nodded. "I think I'd better hang around here."

Blue hopped up on the porch and up onto the swing. He laid his nose on his front paw and let out a deep breath.

Amos shook his head. "I think that's about the smartest dog I've ever seen."

I nodded.

"And that pig is quite possibly the nastiest animal I've ever seen." He said something else, but I didn't hear him. Then he punched me in the shoulder and said, "Hey, you in there?"

"Huh?"

"I said, 'When did you move back into the house?'"

"Oh, that. Well, we haven't."

He looked toward our bedroom window where Maggie's shadow was moving around. "And?"

I shrugged. "She talks less, cries more."

Amos climbed into his truck. On the seat next to him sat a manila folder, thick with photographs. I leaned into the open passenger-side window and eyed the folder. Amos gathered the folder and set it on the dashboard. "Those will not help you sleep at night."

I looked at him. "Then how do you?"

"I don't."

"Me either."

chapter thirty-three

MAGGIE AND I SAT AT THE LAUNDROMAT IN
Walterboro trying to sift through several loads of clothing.
Mostly mine. I'm the dirty one. Our washer and dryer had
been out of commission since the fire burst the pipes that ran
through the crawl space in the attic. We thought the appliances themselves were relatively untouched, but we wouldn't
know until the plumber showed up, and that might not be
until next week. So we sat in the incredibly hot dryer room
while the television above played some soap opera. When one
of the short episodes flashed back to a woman who was trying
to get pregnant, I stood up and turned it off.

Trying to lighten the heaviness, I slipped a pair of my boxer
shorts over my head and poked my ears out the leg holes.
Maggie was not impressed, but she smiled, even laughed a bit,

and then threw a pair of jeans at me. I took the underwear off my head before someone walked in and I embarrassed us both. With my luck, Mr. Sawyer from the adoption agency would appear, and our chances of appeal would vanish.

Earlier yesterday I had stamped my appeal letter and asked for a hearing before the committee to plead our case. According to the letter I had received, an appeal was granted at request and they'd inform me via a phone call—which also had me scared—within two days of receiving my letter.

I pulled a white load from the washer and immediately realized my mistake: I had put a red T-shirt in with the whites. The entire load looked like a chemistry experiment gone bad. All of my underwear and T-shirts were red, which was sort of funny, but then Maggie's white cotton gown came out looking pink and splotchy. There was little we could do, so I threw the whole load in the dryer and started it spinning.

Maggie needed a few things, so I sent her on ahead to the drugstore next door and told her I'd finish folding as soon as things were dry. I fluffed, folded, and dropped the three baskets in the van before catching up with her.

The air in the store was filled with what sounded like three kids arguing over a toy. An overloaded mom with one child on her hip, one tugging on her shorts, and two more rolling in the aisle at her feet, fighting over a wooden airplane, was the center of attention and distraction.

I found Maggie two aisles over. Listening. Leaning against the greeting cards. She was trembling, trying not to lose it, and she fell on me when I walked up alongside her. She buried her face in my chest and clutched my shirt. I turned her, and we walked slowly from the store, having forgotten what we came for.

When we got home, Maggie had collected herself enough to walk inside and put on a pot of coffee. The answering machine was blinking at me, and I punched it without thinking.

"Hello, Dr. and Mrs. Styles, this is Kayla Sommers at the Charleston Adoption Agency."

Maggie froze, holding the percolator under the faucet.

"We received your letter of appeal and have set your date with the committee for Monday, August 13."

Two more weeks. I wasn't sure we'd last another day. Maggie's eyes were lost out the kitchen window, across the cotton toward the river.

Kayla continued, ". . . is scheduled for 10:00 a.m. Please try to be on time." Her voice fell to a whisper. "They prefer you are early."

Maggie set the percolator in the sink and walked quietly outside and onto the porch while the water overflowed the container.

I followed her. "Honey, I was going to tell you. I just . . ."

She touched my arm gently and shook her head. "That's—" She folded her arms and, despite the 94-degree heat, stepped into the cotton and didn't look back.

A LIGHT RAIN WOKE ME BEFORE THE SUN ON SATURDAY morning. I lifted my head and listened to the heavy drops as they pounded the corn and made their way to the house. Seconds later, they hammered the tin roof above. The warmth beneath the sheets told me Maggie lay beside me. I reached across the mattress and found her back turned to me and her body rolled into a ball. I doubted she was asleep.

I stood, scratched my head, and climbed downstairs, leaning against the barn door. The itch and high-pitched sound in my ear broke my gaze on the river. I swatted the mosquito, but he'd already bitten me. My fingers crawled around my neck and found that he hadn't been alone.

I hurried across the yard, sat on the railing, and rested my head on my knee, listening to the deluge. Rainwater gathered in the rows and trickled in tiny creeks down toward the river. With this much rain in such a short amount of time, the ground could not absorb it all. Most of it would run to the river and raise the water level a foot or so.

I grabbed one of Maggie's two remaining watermelons off the porch and slit it down the middle. Cracking it open, I gave half to Blue, who sank his muzzle directly into the meat. I sat my half on my lap and slowly began cutting out the heart. It was sweet, perfect, and only served to impress upon me the gulf that had spread between Maggie and me.

I grabbed a paper plate from the kitchen, cut a large piece of melon, and walked to the barn, where I climbed back up to the loft. I knocked quietly and waited. When she said nothing, I turned the knob and pushed. With the sun just coming over the pasture, I could see her lying in bed, turned on her side, facing away from me. I sat on the edge of the bed and held the plate in my lap, "I brought you some watermelon."

Maggie said nothing.

I placed my hand on her bare shoulder and shook her ever so gently.

She lifted the covers over her shoulder and covered her head with a pillow.

The ceiling fan above us had been set on "tornado," so I clicked it twice to "gentle breeze." I whispered, "Maggs?"

She made no response. Dr. Frank had said that while her emotions and hormones got squared away, I'd do well to give her some space. Well, I'd done that, and the more I gave her, the more she took. I shook her gently again. "Maggs?"

Without warning, she sat up in bed, turned toward me, and looked me square in the eyes. Hers were puffy and covered in red streaks, and they told me she'd been crying. I opened my mouth to say something, but she pointed her crooked, double-jointed finger in my face. Her voice was low and on the verge of cracking. "Don't."

"Maggs, I know you're hurting, but—"

"No!" she screamed. She grabbed the plate of watermelon and hurled it across the room, covering me in red puree. "You *don't know.* You can't possibly!"

"But why won't you talk to me?"

She turned, picked up the lamp from the bedside table, and hurled it across the loft. I ducked, and it, too, exploded on the wall behind me. Maggs lay back down in bed, pulled the covers up and the pillow over her head, and began a muffled sob.

I picked what was left of the watermelon off the floor, placed it back on the plate, and laid it on the bed. I stood there for a minute, watching her shoulders shake. One heel was sticking out from underneath the blankets, so I covered it.

I tried to make sense of it but couldn't. Maybe it was the hurt talking. I pulled a pair of socks from the dresser, set them on the bedside table, and walked out, pulling the door shut behind me.

chapter thirty-four

I HUNG AROUND THE HOUSE UNTIL LUNCH, BUT Maggs never showed, so I went for a drive. I pulled around the house and almost ran into the front end of Amos's truck.

Amanda was at the wheel. She rolled down the window. "She in?"

I thumbed over my shoulder at the loft. "Yeah, but I don't think she wants to see anyone right now."

Amanda nodded. "Maybe I'll try anyway." She tilted her head and chewed on her lip, sizing me up. "How're you doing?"

I shrugged.

"You sure?" She was getting more like Amos every day.

I turned toward the barn and said, "Make sure she knows it's you. Otherwise, get ready to duck."

I meandered along back roads until I found myself weaving

in a rather straight line to Jake's car lot. The closer I got, the faster I drove. I turned into the lot going a little too fast, hit the brakes, and slid to a dusty stop in front of his office. When I looked at my hands, my knuckles were white.

Jake walked out, holding the last bite of a hot dog. Both mustard and ketchup streaked across his white shirt and blue plaid tie. He shoved in the last bite and wiped his mouth with his tie.

"Well, hey, Dylan. Looks like you've grown to like the family minivan."

I hopped out and looked across the lot. My heart sank. I stuck my hands in my pockets and looked again. "Hey, Jake."

He pointed at the van. "How's she running?" He seemed to ask for both my sake and for his.

"Oh, fine, fine. No problems."

He rubbed his hands together and looked relieved. "Good, good. Well, what can I do for you?"

Jake was one of the unlucky follicle-challenged guys who had started losing his hair in high school. He was now combing one of his sideburns clear over to the other ear.

"I was just in the neighborhood and thought maybe I'd stop by and see if I left some old sunglasses in my truck. They're not worth much, but . . ."

He laughed. "Yeah, I know what you mean. I'll check the drawer in the office, but we searched that thing pretty good before we sold it. I don't think—"

"What?"

Jake stepped backward. "Yeah, we searched under the seats, in the glove box, everywhere. We do that with all the cars before we sell them."

That was the second time he'd said that.

"You sold it?"

Jake looked at me and tilted his head. "Well, yeah. Ummm, see, a fellow I never seen come in here, offered me cash, and drove out five minutes later. It was like he was looking for that exact truck, 'cause when he got in it, he just knew."

I leaned against the van and whispered, "You sold my truck?"

Jake pulled the three-by-five-inch card from his shirt pocket and said, "Well, if you're in the market."

"No." I waved my hand. "No thanks. I just thought . . . since I was driving by . . ."

His wife opened the door and shaded her eyes against the sun, and two kids pressed their noses against the glass.

"Hey, Dylan, you want some lunch? I just made some spaghetti."

The kids' fingers were covered in spaghetti sauce, as was the window.

I stepped forward. "No, ma'am. Thank you. I won't be a minute; thanks anyway."

Jake stepped forward and spoke softly. "Dylan, I'm real sorry. It's just that—" He pointed behind him. "This guy offered me—"

I shook my head and patted him on the shoulder. "No, Jake, it's not . . . I'm sorry. You did right."

"I know how you loved that truck. I was surprised when you wanted to trade it."

"Well, we're trying to adopt, and—"

"I can keep an eye out."

I stepped into the van. "Thanks. That'd be just fine." I cranked the engine and shifted the lever down into drive. "Thanks again."

Jake held an imaginary phone to his ear and called above the sound of crunching gravel. "If I see anything, I'll give you a holler."

I waved out the window and drove slowly toward Digger.

chapter thirty-five

A MILE OUT OF JAKE'S DRIVEWAY, SOMETHING thumped the underside of the hood, and then the air conditioner turned from cold to hot. I checked the rearview mirror and saw bits and pieces of my shredded compressor belt strewn across the road. I rolled down the windows, felt the heat blast my face, and missed my truck.

Bryce's place was immaculate and empty. The only signs of life were five crows that had lit atop the center screen and squawked at me when I emerged from the tree line. I walked through the trailer, across the deck, and back into the woods where the obstacle course had been extended. Somebody had brought in some heavy machinery and extended the run section down into the soggy lowlands. The wet, grassy ground ran beneath the oaks and around the bamboo for almost a mile

before it encountered the edge of the swamp, which fluctu-
ated with the rain.

By the time I reached the swamp, sweat trickled from every
pore in my body, sticking my shirt to me like a vacuum seal.
When I reached the edge of the water, I didn't feel like going
back, so I sat up on a hickory stump and tried to exhale my
anger. That's when I saw the rope.

It was new black nylon, looped around a tree and tied in a
hitching knot much like someone would use to tie up a
horse. One pull on the free end and it would pull itself loose.
The rope led me around the tree and about six feet away to
a fourteen-foot johnboat. It floated empty, dry, well used,
and complete with one hand-oiled oar. I looked off into the
water and saw that as recently as today, someone had paddled through the pollen. The trail had yet to erase itself in
the water.

I pulled the rope, pushed off, and dipped the oar in the
water, following the cracks in the pollen. They weren't too hard
to follow, and neither was the small canal that frequent use had
created between the trees. Nighttime would be another story,
but between fresh scars on the trees and places that were only
wide enough for the boat, the path was hard to miss in the daylight. A mile passed, then another, and finally another.

Three hours later, I tried to find the sun and realized I had
made a big mistake. I was about to spend the night in the
swamp. If I'd had any sense at all, I'd have looped myself to a
tree, lain down in the bottom of that boat, pulled my shirt
over my head to protect myself from mosquitoes, and tried to
get some sleep. Problem was, I wasn't feeling very sensible.

I poled another hour into the darkness until I could scarcely
see twenty feet in front of my face. I set down the oar, coasted
across the black water, and checked Papa's watch, which I

think told me it was after eight, and only then did I smell the smoke.

Trying not to bang the side of the boat, I poled and paddled closer. Finally I sat down in the back and inched toward a cluster of trees. High above me, maybe thirty feet in the air, I saw a single flame, flickering like a kerosene lantern. It shone through what looked like slats in a tree fort, except this fort was about the size of our bedroom at the house. The timbers supporting it were rough-cut beams that stretched across the cypress trees shooting up out of the swamp.

The light from the lantern shone down through the hole in the floor and illuminated a rope ladder. I tied up the boat, stepped quietly onto the ladder, and pulled myself up. Some thirty-five feet later, I poked my head through the trapdoor and looked around. What I saw amazed me.

The roof above was made of aluminum sheeting, supported with rough-cut trusses, making the inside watertight. The tongue-and-groove cypress floor had been swept clean and looked loosely octagonal in shape. The eight walls also were cypress plank, and each had been fitted with a window.

On two walls there was a kitchen of sorts. A large farmhouse sink had been sunk in the countertop; it was fed by a hand pump connected to a series of pipes that disappeared through the floor and evidently into the tannic black water of the Salkehatchie below. I worked the pump, and crystal-clear water flowed out, meaning someone had either dug a well or tapped into a spring. Maybe both.

Across the room was a built-in bunk, and on the bedside table sat a worn copy of Herodotus. Occupying the rest of the room were two chairs, a shelf with about a hundred Louis L'Amour books, and a large footlocker. Leaning in a rack along the last wall rested three rifles and as many shotguns. One of the rifles was fitted with a large telescopic sight, making it look like some sort of sniper rifle. Four handguns—two revolvers and two automatics—hung from nails driven into the wall. Each was oiled, and despite the fact that most had a matte black finish, each glistened slightly in the pulsating light behind me.

The idea had crossed my mind that Bryce had simply built himself a summer home, which was odd given that he could have owned a slope-sided chalet in Aspen. But my other idea said that someone had built a getaway shack, hidden in the middle of nowhere, that allowed him to keep an eye on his moonshine still, marijuana plants, or meth lab with little fear of intrusion.

My shadow stretched across the room like Peter Pan's, and my heart pounded like a war drum. I looked down into the water at the boat, around the room, and in search of fading shadows. All of that told me one thing: I could not make it out of this swamp tonight, and the best opportunity I had was to sleep right here. Yet I also knew that whoever had built this place and left that light on would be back, and based on the difficulty of finding this place, I wasn't sure he wanted to be found.

I stepped toward the wall and lifted one of the revolvers off the nail. A Smith & Wesson .357. I clicked open the cylinder and found it loaded. I stuffed it inside my pants and stretched out on the bed, where for two hours I kept my eyes pried wide open. Finally sleep set in, and I dozed off. Sometime later, I woke to the sound of someone standing at the sink.

I cracked open my eyes, but the lantern had been dimmed. I could see the form of a person standing some eight feet from me. I slipped the revolver from my belt and lay as still as I possibly could. From the smell in the room and the repetitive motion of the man's arms, I figured he was cleaning a fish.

Only when I sat up did the bunk creak. I slowly aimed the pistol at the broad dark frame in front of me and waited. It was useless to try to aim, because my hand was shaking like a leaf. When the person turned, and the lantern lit his face, I nearly lost my bladder again.

I lay back, shaking my head, and dropped the pistol on the floor. *"Bryce!* What the—!?"

Bryce clicked on a gas stove and threw the fish filets onto the skillet. He poured in a touch of oil, then reached out a window over the ledge and lifted the lid on a propane grill that seemed somehow built into the side of the tree house. He used some tongs to flip over whatever was on there and returned to the fish. He added seasoning and some pepper and popped the tab on a Chek soda. Then he pumped the hand pump in the sink, filling a glass of water, which he swigged down in three gulps.

While the fish sizzled and the grill cooked whatever it was cooking, Bryce set the table with two plates, two forks, and two glasses of water. He pulled plates from above his head, flipped the fish one last time, and then slid two filets each onto the plates. He reached across the ledge and pulled in what appeared to be two ears of corn and two baked potatoes, wrapped in aluminum foil.

While I worked to reinsert my jaw into its rightful place, Bryce sat down and turned his attention to his food. Beneath the light, I could see he was decked out in all black, his feet were bare, and his .45 was tucked in its shoulder holster on the left side of his chest. He looked at me and continued eating as if he were judging the food for its culinary details.

I sat at the table and looked at the breakfast before me while Bryce took small bites and paid me little mind.

"How long have you had this place?"

Bryce chewed, pushed his food around his plate. If he heard me, he didn't appear to care.

I tried again. "What do you do out here?"

Bryce looked around, scraped the last of his fish onto his fork, and filled his glass again. Conversations with Bryce were often one-sided. He'd talk when he felt like it.

I looked at my watch and knew that I'd been gone too long. "Bryce, I don't mean to be unkind, but I need to get going, and I need some help getting out of here."

Bryce finished off another glass of water, then walked to a bare wall and opened a shoulder-width door that led onto a balcony, four feet by four feet square and surrounded by a railing. On the balcony sat a wooden box fitted with a porcelain white toilet seat. With his back to me, Bryce lifted the seat and peed through the hole.

I listened as the stream fell thirty-five feet to the water below. I tried again. "Well, I need to get home to Maggie."

Bryce shut the door and spoke for the first time. "She's fine." He washed his hands in the sink, sat back down, picked up his corn, and started into it like a typewriter.

"Bryce." I set down my fork and wiped my mouth. I noticed that since being up here, I hadn't swatted at a single mosquito. "How long have you been watching my house?"

He shrugged.

"Why?"

He grew very still, and his eyes glazed over as if someone else had entered the room. He cleared his plate and then climbed down the ladder to the boat. Alongside it sat a small black-and-green two-man canoe.

We loaded into his boat, and with the two of us paddling and Bryce's sense of direction, we banked the canoe onto the grassy landing below the obstacle course before daylight. I stepped out and turned to thank him, but he had already backed up and was poling himself back into the swamp. When I tried to open my mouth, he just waved. For the first time since I'd met Bryce, I saw an expression of pain on his face— the kind that had sewn itself into the sinews of his person.

I turned down our drive at daylight and pulled around the house. Blue came trotting out to meet me. Maggie too. She was wrapped in a blanket, and her short hair was sticking up as if she hadn't slept.

She saw that I was okay and looked as though she wanted to say something, but the words didn't make it out of her mouth. She returned to the barn, her blanket dragging on the ground, climbed into the loft, and then shut the door and clicked on the AC unit.

Blue licked my fingers, and his quiet whining told me what Maggie's silence and my heart already had—that I'd been stupid to leave, selfish to go to Jake's, and that spending the night out was a dumb thing to do.

chapter thirty-six

FROM THE KITCHEN, I WATCHED MAGGIE WALK OUT of the barn and into her vegetable garden—a small forty-by-forty-foot patch where she experimented with growing vegetables. Ordinarily, it was overgrown with produce; now it sat overrun with weeds. Even the raccoons had quit coming around.

I poured her a cup of coffee and met her midway through what was once the tomato section. She took it and sipped beneath the broad rim of her hat. I tipped her hat back slightly and then leaned on a tomato stake. "You sleep any?"

She shook her head and sipped again. The caffeine did little to raise her eyelids.

I looked at the weeds around us. "You want some help?"

She smiled and let me off the hook. And while that was nice, it reminded me of how much Maggie had withdrawn.

A little later I drove to Walterboro, stopped by Dr. Frank's office, and then found a hat store that I'd heard about in the whispers around church. An elderly lady helped me find what I needed, wrapped it in a box, and sent me on my way with a remembering look in her eye.

Evening brought a blessed cool breeze, a warm shower, and some welcome cloud cover that blocked out the late afternoon sun, dropping the temperature into the upper seventies. Understanding that she was allowed to change her mind at a moment's notice and without reason, I was not surprised when Maggie told me she wanted to get out of the house. We cleaned up, dressed, and drove the four miles to the church property.

A blue circus tent had been erected above the cement foundation, which had been cleared of ash and rubble and new portions poured. Another tent stood alongside, and beneath it sat tables loaded with food.

Cars lined the roadside, and despite the impromptu service, women showed up wearing their favorite and newest hats. Amos had assigned a young deputy to direct traffic, and elsewhere young men in coats and ties were escorting ladies across the dirt parking lot to folding chairs beneath the tent.

Maggie stepped out of the van and looked both ways across the highway before I could get her attention from the rear of the van. "Honey?" She walked around the side, and I handed her the box. "Didn't want you to feel underdressed."

She accepted the box, untied the bow, and lifted the hat from inside. It was a blue sun hat with a broad white band and feathers on one side. Miraculously, it matched both her eyes and her dress.

I held the tail of the ribbon while she settled the brim on her brow, forcing tears out of the corners of her eyes. I pulled my white handkerchief from my pocket and gave it to her, and she dabbed her eyes. She kissed me on the cheek—which told me she was sorry—and hooked her arm inside mine—which told me that she loved me—and we crossed the street.

We took a seat near the back while those around us filled up. Amos looked spry in his coat and tie, which Amanda no doubt had matched because he hadn't displayed that much style in his entire life.

Amanda was busy with the flower arrangement and white tablecloth spread across the folding table up front. Her tummy had grown some more. She was now into the full-on pregnant woman waddle, and she glowed from head to toe. She saw us and hurried down the aisle to hug Maggie.

Maggie smiled, teared up, and placed her palm across Amanda's tummy as though feeling the ripeness of a melon. Amanda gawked at Maggie's hat while I marveled at my wife.

I watched her—the way her shoulders moved with the tilt of her head, the way her smile lit up the six people around her, the way her hair, tucked behind her ears, framed her face like baby's breath. I thought about the way her heartbeat sounded the rhythm for our dance atop the magnolia floor. I wanted to tell her all this but didn't know how. Just because something is broken doesn't mean it's no good. Doesn't mean you throw it away. It just means it's broken, and broken is okay. I wanted to tell her that broken is still beautiful, still works, still wakes me in the morning, and at the end of every day past and those to come, I can love broken.

The choir, a purple mass of matching robes and sweaty faces, appeared and started swaying and humming. The congregation stood, ladies fanned themselves with bulletins, and the choir began clapping and singing a responsive hymn, proving once again that they had more rhythm in five minutes than I'd had in my entire life. We swayed, sang, and clapped until fifteen minutes later when Pastor John stepped up and the choir lowered their voices to underscore his.

He stood several minutes, smiling and looking for an entrance. Finally he raised his hands, the choir dropped their voices even more, and he said, "If you're with the fire department, please raise your hand."

We did.

He laughed. "Well, if you needed a reason not to end up in hell, now you've got it."

The laughter spread like a wave. It felt good.

Pastor John tucked his Bible beneath his arm. When he looked up, his face was soaked, but it wasn't with sweat.

Up front, Li'l Dylan said, "Daddy! Daddy!" Amos picked him up and bounced him on his knee.

Maggie grabbed my hand and squeezed it.

Pastor John raised his chin and began, "I've been asking the Lord to forgive me for the things in my past that brought this upon all of you. I have asked before, and I will ask again, please forgive me."

The choir swayed and hummed a melody, and Pastor John placed his Bible on the altar. He palmed the sweat off his cheeks, dabbed his eyes, and returned his handkerchief to his pocket. Finally he picked up his Bible again, turned toward the back, and read, "And God will wipe away every tear from their eyes; there shall be no more death, nor sorrow, nor crying."

Maggie's fingers wrapped more tightly about mine.

"There shall be no more pain, for the former things have passed away."

Maggie dropped her head and fought back a sob, and I started looking for an exit.

"Behold, I make all things new."

Maggie dropped her head, stood, and hurried between the chairs and out the back of the tent. Pastor John waited while I followed her out. She ran across the parking lot toward the river, hit her knees, and buried her face in her hands. The moss hanging from the oak above looked like arms swaying in the wind, reaching down to sweep the riverbank.

I knelt next to her, and she fell against me. Finally she managed a breath deep enough, and I helped her to her feet. We made our way across the parking lot toward the van.

Midway through the cars, an SUV pulled up to the back of the tent, and the driver got out. He was tall and broad-shouldered, and his skin was dark as night. Although I couldn't see his face, his body posture told me that he wasn't here for church. Maggie, too, picked up on it and stopped walking.

The man walked up to the back of the tent and began striding confidently down the middle aisle toward Pastor John. I led Maggie to the side of the tent where we could see and hear inside.

Pastor John saw the man, stopped midsentence, and said, "Welcome, James."

The man called James stopped and laughed loudly. "Thought I'd stop in and see how the flock was doing, Preacher."

Amos, sitting in the front row and still holding L.D. on his knee, tensed like a dog before a fight.

Pastor John never skipped a beat. He pointed to a seat down front. "There's always room for one more."

James laughed. "No, no, I think I've given you enough of my money for one lifetime."

Amos's deputy slipped out the side and around the back. He stood at the rear of the tent, speaking into a radio clipped to his uniform shirt.

Pastor John addressed the congregation. "Friends, this is

James Whittaker. James and I were once partners, stealing everything we could get our hands on and even some things we couldn't."

Not a foot shuffled; not a person could be heard breathing. If Pastor John was afraid, he didn't show it.

James smiled. "You know, John, after twenty years in prison, I learned something very important." He twirled in the aisle, walked toward the front, and pointed at him. "In the end, we all get what we got coming!"

Pastor John nodded and stepped forward again, now just a few feet from Whittaker. He looked him in the eyes. "Yes, we do."

Whittaker looked down his left arm where Amos sat two feet away—ready to pounce. Had L.D. not been on his lap, I think he would have. Amanda sat next to him, her arm hooked inside his—both holding on to and holding down.

Whittaker looked at L.D., then at Amos. He leaned closer and said, "I don't think he has your eyes." Then he turned and walked sideways across the front of the altar and out the side of the church. He weaved among the ropes that held down the tent.

I don't know the cause—it had something to do with the smug look on his face. The look sparked something I hadn't felt in a long time. Somewhere inside me, deep down, something snapped. I stepped in front of him, started at my toes, and threw everything I had through my fist and into his face. It was the hardest I'd ever hit anyone in my life.

His head jerked sideways and blood trickled off his lip, and faster than a cat, he backhanded me four feet in the air, over a tent rope, and flat on my back, where the stars spun in circles above me.

I looked up, tried to balance on an elbow, thought I might vomit, and saw a black freight train flying sideways through the darkness.

Amos's body-tackle toppled Whittaker like a bowling pin. The collision sounded loud and painful—like two Mack trucks meeting head-on in an intersection. Amos landed on top, fended off a vicious right, and then landed his own squarely on Whittaker's chin. Two seconds later he had Whittaker facedown and hogtied. Little mud bubbles were circling around Whittaker's nose and popped every time he exhaled—which was often as he fought the thick zip ties that bound his hands and feet.

Amos's suit was smeared with mud and soaked with sweat, and the seams behind his shoulders were stretched taut. He squeezed the sides of Whittaker's cheeks so that they'd have a better chance of being cut by his teeth. He pointed Whittaker's face at me and leaned over him, whispering low enough that the folks sitting a few feet away in the folding chairs couldn't hear him. "That is my best friend on the planet. You ever do that again, and I'll finish this fight."

Whittaker outweighed Amos by maybe eighty pounds, but Amos's adrenaline seemed to be making up the difference. He pulled back my eyelid, studied my pupil, slapped me gently on the face, and then picked up Whittaker like a sack of potatoes, dragged him to his deputy's car, and flung him onto the backseat.

Amos and Amanda followed Maggie and me home and helped get me settled in the loft. My eye was turning black and puffy, but my jaw was still connected. And I still had all my teeth. Amanda gave me something for the pain, and while my arms and legs turned to noodles, the three of them stood over me and talked in whispers.

"You be all right?" Amos asked.

I tried to nod, but my words sounded as though I'd just come from a drill-happy dentist. "I've been hit harder."

Amos shook his head. "I doubt it." He pulled the door

behind him and whispered in hushed tones, "We can hold him tonight, until he makes bail, then . . ."

Amanda spoke up, louder. "Amos, this is not going to stop."

He poked his head back through the door and nodded at me. "Keep your guard up."

"You too."

They left, and I climbed right out of bed and watched their truck's taillights disappear. Then I fumbled my way down the steps, hobbled across the yard, and found Blue standing on the front porch, stretching. I walked into the house, using the hallway walls like curbs, unlocked my writing closet, and pulled out the Winchester. I slid a shell into the chamber, clicked the safety on, and walked back into the barn.

ABOUT MIDNIGHT MAGGIE GOT OUT OF BED AND STOOD A long time in the shower. Long after the hot water ran cold, she turned off the stream and stood dripping, eyes closed, leaning against the post that held the showerhead and shaking her head.

I watched from the loft and saw only what one eye and one slit allowed. Maggie's lips were trembling, goose bumps traveled up and down her arms, and her shoulders were tilted at an angle. I climbed down out of the loft and handed her a towel.

She wrapped it around herself, tucking it beneath her arms but not bothering to dry with it.

"You hungry? I could fix some—"

She looked at me as if I'd lost my mind. I turned to cross the yard and find something in the kitchen when she called, "D.S." It'd been a long time since she called me by that name.

Maybe it was time. Maybe I could come clean and tell her the stories I'd been hiding. I stepped closer, into the single bulb above the shower. "Maggie, I know how you—"

She stood straight, her back rigid, and pointed her finger at me. *"Don't* tell me you know how I feel!"

"Honey, I was just saying—"

"You don't know anything! You can't possibly!" She dropped her towel and stood clutching her stomach as if she'd been shot. "You don't know what it's like." She held out her fingers. "Three of your own!"

She clutched her stomach again, and I walked closer.

She held me off. "What kind of a woman am I!? What good is—" She pounded her stomach and chest and squeezed the taut skin. *"Why!?"*

She fell to her knees and beat the pallet that served as the shower floor. I picked up the towel and draped it over her shoulders. Blue hung his eyes over the loft, afraid to come down but troubled by the sound. Her crying quieted Pinky, who had started to complain about her lack of a midnight snack.

I turned around, kicked the stall, and told her to hush.

Maggie collected her towel, climbed naked up to the loft, and shut the door behind her.

I walked to the house and into the kitchen, where I percolated some coffee, threw some ice in a ziplock, and then walked back to the barn and nursed both my eye and my caffeine need at the base of the loft. I looked across the yard at our house, draped in a blue tarp, smelling like smoke, and by most definitions sitting in shambles. I looked up at the closed door, thought about Maggie tossing tearfully inside, and then considered the state of our lives, which was by most definitions much like our house.

I shook my head, spat, poured out the cold coffee, and wiped my eyes—loss is a painful thing.

chapter thirty-seven

AROUND 3:00 A.M.—SOME THREE HOURS AND FOUR cups of coffee later, I sat leaning against the barn door, downwind from Pinky, when Amos's voice crackled over the scanner. It took a second to recognize him because he was out of breath and nearly screaming.

"114 to 110, 114 to 110!"

"110 to 114, go ahead, 114."

"207 in progress. Suspect is 962. I've got a 998 and 999, NOW!"

"114, what's your 20?"

"Parking garage southeast of the hospital."

"10-4, 114. Do you know the name of the person who's been kidnapped?"

There was a pause, then a click from Amos's radio. His whisper was barely audible. "Amanda . . . 'Manda Carter."

I jumped off the steps, climbed the stairs, and burst through
the door. The sound woke Maggie, who jumped up angry and
cross. I grabbed the shotgun and jumped into my boots.

"Come on," I managed. "It's Amos. They took Amanda."

Maggie moved quickly, and we met at the van about the
same time. I placed the shotgun in the backseat and made
room for Blue while I dropped the gearshift into drive and
dug a trench spinning dirt out to the road.

Ten minutes later I slid to a stop in front of Pastor John's
house, which was lit up like a runway. Police cars and flashing
lights were everywhere. Standing on the front porch, Li'l Dylan
was crying and could not be consoled. Maggie jumped out of
the van, ran barefooted across the grass, and picked him up.

She wrapped her arms around him and pulled a pacifier
out of her pocket. She smiled at him and put the handle end
of the pacifier in her mouth, and he bit. He laid his head on
her shoulder, his crying quieted, and they disappeared inside.

Several deputies had gathered around the trunk of one car
as a SWAT truck pulled up and several men jumped out. Amos
stood in the middle, spouting orders like a man possessed. He
ripped the microphone off his shoulder and screamed, "And
tell the judge I need that warrant now!"

The dispatcher responded, and Amos swore. "I don't care
what his aide says; you get him out of bed now!"

Pastor John stood nearby in a white T-shirt, slacks, and
slippers.

I eased up next to him and asked, "What happened?"

He swallowed. "Amanda was on call. Her beeper went off
about two o'clock. Amos drove her to the hospital and dropped
her off. When she walked in the door, a truck pulled up, block-
ing Amos, and two men jumped out. They wrestled her into the
truck." He crossed his arms and walked back inside the house.

I edged closer to the circle of law enforcement men huddled in the street. I heard them say that the highways and streets leading out of town were covered, but the expression on their faces told me they were looking for a needle in a haystack. I wanted to help but knew I'd do well to stay out of their way.

I walked inside and helped Mrs. Lovett make coffee, then I found Maggie in the den. The lights were off, and L.D. was asleep in her arms. When I walked in, she held a finger to her lips. I offered coffee and she shook her head, pointing outside and waving me off.

I walked back outside just as the men loaded up and squealed off down the street. Jumping into the van, I followed them across town to what looked like a duplex. Three men in black with *POLICE* written across their backs in reflective white letters, carrying shotguns and pistols, ran to the door on the right, while three more ran around back. They waited five seconds, then kicked the door in and stormed inside the house. I sat in the front seat of the van a block down the road.

Within seconds, fifteen more police cars and a dozen undercover cars had parked in front and lit the house with both spotlights and headlights. Amos ran into the house, followed quickly by a team of thick-muscled men.

I stepped out of the van, leaned against a fence, and noticed a small boy looking out the window of a house next door. He waved at me, and I waved back. Five minutes later, he crawled out through a hole in his fence wearing Spider-Man pajamas and carrying a plastic squirt gun. He was a good-looking kid, might have been ten, and his eyes were as big as half-dollars. He started to wave the gun at me, and I quickly said, "Hey, let's not get confused with the bad guys."

He looked at his gun, then at the swarm of law enforcement

a block away, and nodded. He sat down on the curb and said, "They ain't there no more."

"Who's not?" I said, sitting down next to him.

"The fishermen."

"Who?"

He pointed at the house. "Two guys. Lots of tattoos. Said they liked to fish."

"They say what they were fishing for?"

He shook his head. "Nope. But they had a canoe."

I stood and started to walk away when the kid offered, "But I don't think they really liked to fish."

"Why's that?"

"'Cause," he said, "they didn't have no fishing poles."

I asked permission of one of Amos's deputies, and he escorted me inside the house where Amos and his men were huddled around a big table, poring over maps of the Salk and a printout of times—almost like a TV guide but without the stations or programs. Amos saw me, and his eyes returned to the printout. He studied it another minute, turned his attention to the map, then back to the printout. Finally his head tilted back and he sat down in the chair behind him.

I stepped up alongside, and he laid the printout on the table. "It's Amanda's on-call schedule," he whispered.

DAYLIGHT FOUND US AT THE POLICE STATION, WHICH HAD been transformed into a multi-agencied communications center. Law enforcement of all colors, sizes, and uniforms were busily manning phones and radios, hovering over maps, and bumping into one another.

Around 9:00 a.m. Amos disappeared into an office and shut the door. I followed. The room did not have windows, and the lights were off. Amos was kneeling on the floor, his head in his hands.

I sat next to him and said nothing.

After a minute he looked up, wiped his eyes, and shook his head. "They just released Whittaker. Made bail. Can't hold him." He wiped his eyes. "We've got most every agent in the state out looking for her. If they're in a car, on a road, at a rest area, or within a city limit, we've got a chance of finding them. The first forty-eight hours are the most critical."

About then the lightbulb clicked on. "What if they're not traveling by car?"

Amos looked at me suspiciously.

"I talked to a kid a block down from the house your team stormed. He said two guys with tattoos had a canoe, said they liked to fish but didn't have any fishing rods."

Amos scanned the floor, then jumped onto his feet and walked back out into the command center.

BY EVENING, THINGS HAD COOLED DOWN. ALL THINGS except Amos. I called the Lovetts' house, and Maggie picked up.

"Hey," I said.

"Hey," she whispered, as though someone was sleeping.

"You okay?"

"Yeah, you?"

I shut the door of the office I was in and sat in the chair. "Yeah, just standing around trying to figure out how to help. How's L.D.?"

"He misses his momma."

Just then an undercover officer ran into the room and tapped a superior on the shoulder.

"Hey, something's happening. I'll call you later."

"Be careful."

I walked out into the room where the superior was handing Amos a sheet of paper. He read the dispatch, and his face turned nearly white. He looked down at the ground, steadied himself with both hands, and said, "I'll go." He spoke to a man sitting behind a desk. "You're in charge. I'll be back in a few hours."

Amos walked to a water dispenser, filled a cup, and swigged it down. Half the water dribbled down his chest.

"Wherever you're going, I'm going."

He looked at me, his eyes a road map of red. He nodded, swallowed hard, and managed, "Thank you."

We loaded into his truck, and Amos drove through town and onto I-95 south toward Savannah. He flashed his lights, increased our speed, and drove without saying anything until we reached the outskirts of town. The AC was on high, and he was sweating. He spoke above the noise.

"Amanda has a birthmark about the size of a quarter on her left hip. You wouldn't ever see it unless you were married to her." He tried to laugh. "I kid her sometimes that it looks like a set of Mickey Mouse ears."

He fell silent then as we pulled into town and parked in front of the city morgue. Amos steadied himself on the front of the truck and took a deep breath. We walked through the swinging front doors and were met by a man in a white coat who looked like a doctor but did not smell like one.

"Sergeant Carter?"

Amos nodded.

"Follow me."

Another man in uniform stepped aside as Amos passed and then stepped in front of me and put his hand on my chest.

I looked at him and didn't blink. "I'm with him."

We walked down a long hall and into a sterile room where three black bags lay zipped up across three stainless steel tables. Two lay together on one side of the room; the third lay alone against the far wall. The white-coated man led Amos to the single bag and cleared his throat.

"She was found in an area of woods outside of town. We know that she's twentysomething, was wearing medical scrubs when we found her, in her third trimester, and—was decapitated after death." He looked from Amos to me and back to Amos. "We haven't found her head yet."

Amos steadied himself on the table, gritted his teeth, and placed his hand on the zipper. His hand trembled, he sucked in a deep breath, and one knee buckled. Finally he placed both hands on the table and shook his head.

I put a hand on his shoulder and looked at the bag. "Which hip?" I whispered.

Amos squinted and managed, "Right."

I stepped between Amos and the bag, grabbed the zipper, and pulled it toward the feet of the person. I pulled back on the bag, and at my nod, the doctor slid on a pair of gloves and rolled the body on its side. I studied the hip, turned toward Amos, and shook my head. "It's not her."

Amos turned and walked down the hall and out the front door. He turned into the grass along the front walk, fell to his knees, and vomited. His sobs and groans pierced the quiet Georgia night. It was the most painful sound I'd ever heard in my life, and I did not try to stop him.

We returned to the command center about daylight. I was pretty sure Amos had not eaten in thirty-six hours and was running on fumes. I asked a deputy to bring him some breakfast. An hour later, color-swatch Ira—wearing orange from head to toe—appeared carrying bags of steaming hot food. I helped her clear off the conference table and lay out the spread out for anyone who wanted it.

She saw Amos sitting alone in an office to one side, walked in, kissed him on his bald head, and walked out. I followed her to her car and tried to give her some money. She folded it, stuffed it into my shirt pocket, and drove off.

By the second evening the media had picked up the story, and most of South Carolina and the surrounding states were looking for Amanda Carter. I watched the news reports, the interviews with Pastor John, with Maggie, with other nurses, and the shots of L.D. playing in the front yard, asking, "When is my mommy coming home?" And finally the interview with me.

Deputies had set up cots in two of the offices where men and women could nap for an hour or so. By nighttime I was dead on my feet, so I slept for thirty minutes, then splashed my face and drank three more cups of coffee. My hands were shaking.

I found Amos sitting at a desk, listening to the radio reports. His eyes were heavy. "Hey," I whispered, "why don't you lie down for a few minutes. You're no good to us if you can't keep your head up."

He shook his head and kept listening, waiting.

At daylight, some fifty-five hours after Amanda had been taken, I stepped out of the command center and looked around. The sky was a brilliant blue, not a cloud anywhere. I loaded into the van and drove to the Lovetts' house, where I found Maggie asleep on the couch. L.D. lay on her chest, a pacifier in his mouth. Drool had spilled out the side of his mouth and trickled along her chest. Her eyes opened, and she reached out to grab my hand. I knelt by the sofa and watched L.D. nuzzle his nose against Maggie's bosom.

She kissed my fingers, and I brushed her cheek and said, "You're good at this."

She smiled and pulled the blanket above his shoulders.

"I'm going to take Blue for a while. I'll be back." I walked out the back door, grabbing Amanda's sweater—the one she often wore to work—off a hook and tucking it under my arm as I went.

Blue and I drove down roads with no names and no lines. Some had been paved with asphalt; most had not. I didn't know what I was looking for, but I couldn't sit in that station any longer. I thought about Felix and Antonio and what that kid had said about the canoe.

Blue and I drove to Mr. Carter's house, where he was looking every bit as helpless as I felt. I pointed at Badger and Gus and held Amanda's sweater out the window. I didn't have to say a word.

Mr. Carter, seventy-two years young, jumped off the porch and flipped the gates on the dogs' kennels, and we hopped in his truck. Blue sat up front with us, smelling the sweater and pointing his nose everywhere Mr. Carter turned.

We drove every road that crossed the Salk, and at every bridge or entry into the water, we stopped to let out the dogs. We waited, but the bark never came. Throughout the day, we kept up with reports on the scanner, but we could tell by the tone that the men had disappeared—completely. In midafternoon we heard a report that Whittaker had walked into a movie theater in Walterboro and shaken the tail that had been following him since he walked out of the courthouse. For some time after that, the radio was relatively quiet.

By dark we had scoured the south end of the swamp, but the Salk was huge, and we knew it was useless. Around midnight we drove back to the command center. Seventy hours had passed.

I found Amos leaning over the conference table, eyeing the map of the Salk. He was in a bad way. I knew he hadn't slept or eaten, but I also knew better than to say anything. His dad walked to the map and explained what we'd done.

While Amos thought, a commotion erupted just outside the doors. I heard somebody scream, "He's got a gun," and then a loud crash. I ran to the door and looked through the glass.

Bryce stood in the middle of the room, four agents piled at his feet on the floor. Three other agents knelt behind a desk, pointing their Glocks at him.

I shoved open the door and walked into the room.

One of the deputies screamed at me, "Get down! He's got a gun!"

Bryce's .45 lay untouched in his shoulder holster, but I knew if he so much as twitched a finger, he'd never clear the leather before thirty shots cleared his center mass. He was covered in mud from the waist down. His feet were bare, and he was chewing a wad of gum the size of a boiled egg. The room smelled of pungent swamp decay and spearmint. He was a picture of calm.

Bryce looked at me and at Amos, who stood, hand on his SIG. He spoke slowly, his eyes level and steady. "The girl's not with them."

Amos's eyes narrowed. Two of the agents on the floor moved slowly, both holding their heads.

Bryce looked at me, then at Amos. "You'd better come with me."

Three minutes later, eighteen police or federal vehicles followed Bryce and me to Willard's store, where Mr. Carter and his coon-hunting brigade had assembled en masse. It looked like a bad marriage between a coal miner convention and a SWAT exercise.

Mr. Carter stood in the bed of his truck and conferred with Bryce, who nodded and pointed at the map, lit by Mr. Carter's headlamp. Amos listened and spoke into the microphone on his shoulder, then addressed the sixty-some-odd men around him.

"Two men and a woman were spotted in a canoe making their way downriver. We believe that one of the men is injured. They are armed and dangerous, but nobody does *anything* without my order." Amos's eyes glared like rubies into the night.

As if shot out of a gun, forty vehicles ranging from muddy pickups to shiny Hummers cranked their engines and followed Bryce and me toward his place. We wound up the drive, around the back of his property, and up to the entrance of a logging road I never knew existed. I stopped the van, and Bryce jumped out. Without a word, he began walking into the trees. I shouldered the shotgun and followed.

The moon was high, the temperature was somewhere in the nineties, and there was no breeze to speak of. Two miles into the swamp, I was wheezing, and Bryce was barely breathing hard. We came to the water's edge, and somewhere in the distance an owl hooted. Bryce motioned to Mr. Carter, who walked up alongside.

Mr. Carter took Amanda's sweater and some clothing taken from the duplex, rubbed them in Badger's and Gus's faces, and unhooked their leashes. Badger and Gus disappeared like two ghosts in the darkness while we waited. Five minutes passed as we caught our breath. Badger sloshed off into the darkness, sending out periodic barks, which were occasionally answered by Gus.

Ten minutes passed. The whispers behind us grew. Most of them were directed at Bryce and sounded something like, "Who does this guy think he is?"

Mr. Carter looked off into the swamp, raised his chin, and then raised his hand toward the men behind him. Silence fell across us, and the smile on Mr. Carter's face spread. About the time that his teeth shone through the darkness because of his smile, Badger broke out into a full-blown howl.

Amos didn't hesitate, and neither did anyone else.

Except Bryce. He listened and looked somewhat confused, and when the entire hunting party ran off into the darkness— say toward twelve o'clock on a watch—Bryce ran off the dial toward three o'clock.

I watched the lights scour the darkness ahead of me, then turned and ran as hard as I could after Bryce. I caught up just as he stepped into the water. I stepped down into the cold, swirling blackness, raised the shotgun above my head, and tried to keep up. We partly waded, partly swam through deep water, up onto mushy earth.

Bryce ran through the darkness as if he were following streetlights. The vines and limbs tore at me, and I stumbled and fell, smashing my head against a stump and planting my face in the mud. When I stood, Bryce was waiting on me. We ran what seemed like two more miles, while the sound of Badger's howl faded off into the distance. When I could, I grabbed Bryce by the sleeve and said, "Bryce, are you sure?"

He held a finger to his lips and motioned me to follow. A few hundred yards later, I was neck-deep in muck and paddling. Bryce lifted me onto a log, said, "Wait here," then reached up and grabbed a rope. I looked up and saw his "summer home" directly above.

He disappeared through the trapdoor and reappeared a second later. He slid back down, the sniper rifle strapped over his shoulder, and stepped off into the water. Waist-deep and walking against the current, we waded through the swamp where the mosquitoes sucked a pint of blood out of my neck and flew constantly into and out of my ears.

Thirty minutes later, listening to the sounds of my own breathing and my heart pounding outside my chest, I saw Bryce turn and hold his finger to his lips again. He pointed. Maybe two hundred yards through the trees ahead, a light flickered. I checked the safety on the shotgun. We lay on a mound of fern. The sound of Badger's moaning came out of the distance maybe a mile beyond the house and started a commotion in the structure ahead of us.

"Poacher's cabin," said Bryce softly.

In the distance, I heard one man screaming at another. Then a door slammed, someone splashed into the water, and footsteps started coming at us fast.

Bryce's face was a picture of focus. He turned quickly, jumped up, and swung the butt of his rifle into the running man's face with pinpoint precision. The man's head rocked back, his feet flew out in front of him, and he fell two feet from where I lay. Bryce grabbed him by the belt and started dragging him through the swamp.

The other man was still hollering, frantically trying to load himself into a canoe. The dim lantern light from the shack shone down on him. He wasn't wearing a shirt, and he seemed to be limping. He put his bad leg into the canoe and tried to shove the canoe off the bank.

Bryce dropped the man he was carrying, slid the rifle off his shoulder, aimed, and squeezed. The shot rang out, and the man flew back, clutching his left knee. He lay on the ground, grasping for the paddle with one hand while holding a shotgun in the other and screaming at the top of his lungs.

Bryce picked up the first man again and crept through the stagnant water. We slithered through the mud, and at sixty yards, Bryce stopped. He knelt, breathing slightly, and said, "We met in Saigon. 1970."

"What?"

Bryce watched the man writhe in pain on the far shore. The river, some twenty yards wide at this point, separated us from him.

"She was not American."

The man grabbed the oar and pulled himself up on it like a crutch. Bryce aimed a second time. The man limped toward the canoe, Bryce squeezed, and the shotgun in the man's left hand exploded in the middle. Something must have blown into the man's face, because he fell again, clutching his face and hand.

The man at my feet was bleeding profusely from a huge gash in his face, and his nose was badly twisted out of place. He had yet to move.

Bryce whispered, "There was a chaplain in my unit. Had been an Episcopal priest before we drafted him."

The sound of Badger's moaning grew louder, but not yet closer.

"We got married in a hut, and I kept her a secret until my third tour of duty when they saw me coming out of her village."

We walked to the edge of the water where the man on the other bank lay screaming and clutching his face, his left leg twisted.

Bryce stepped into the water and began swimming across, bringing the first man with him. I stepped into the current, and it pushed me along after Bryce. He kept the man's head above water while I struggled to do the same.

When we reached the other bank, the man on the ground began yelling obscenities. Slowly the first man came to. He, too, clutched his face as Bryce threw the first man down on top of the second. They lay there, tangled, unable to move and cussing both each other and us.

Bryce chambered another round, slid the rifle over his shoulder, and squatted. His eyes were focused out over the swamp. The sounds of Badger and Gus grew closer, as did the sound of sloshing feet and the sight of flashing lights.

Bryce spat in the water. "They burned the village. Lined everyone up and shot them while I watched from the trees. When they shot my son, I . . ." Bryce trailed off. "My unit thought I'd been taken, thought I'd been pinned down. So they came in to get me, but the enemy was good. There were too many. The last one they shot was the bugler."

Bryce shook his head and cracked half a smile. "We used to talk about home, about Scotland—and at night, he'd been trying to teach me to play the pipes."

Badger cleared the trees, took three steps, and pounced on the first man. He opened his jaw, placed it over the man's throat, and stood there waiting. Like a ghost in the darkness, Gus bounded alongside him, clutched the other man's throat, and waited.

Bryce smelled the air and looked southward. "It took me nearly a month to find them all."

The memory of Bryce in my cornfield came flooding back. I pointed in the direction I thought my house sat. "The cornfield?"

Bryce nodded.

AMOS CHARGED OUT OF THE TREES. HIS SIG WAS UP, IN HIS hands, along with his SureFire light, and his eyes were scanning the dilapidated cabin. He saw us and the men at our feet, then jumped up onto the porch and kicked in the door. He shone his light inside, saw nothing, and then walked to the bank. He was breathing hard, but he was hardly out of breath.

He knelt next to the first man. "Antonio, where is she?"

Several of Antonio's teeth were missing, and he couldn't breathe through his nose. He cussed Amos while the remainder of the hunting brigade emerged from the swamp. Their lights lit the area around us like daylight.

Amos holstered his pistol and turned to the other man. "Felix—my wife."

Felix clutched his knee, laughed a sickly laugh, and said, "Yeah, that sweet young thing was so sweet, we just thought we'd come back for more."

Amos cocked his fist and was throwing it forward when Bryce caught it in midair. He shook his head and stooped over Felix. He pulled a knife out of a sheath that ran along the belt at his back, grabbed Felix's right hand, turned it backward in a direction it was not meant to go, placed the blade to the first digit on the man's finger, and pressed.

Felix writhed and screamed, and even the SWAT guys stood back.

Bryce looked at Antonio, but he was of little use because he was fading in and out of consciousness. Bryce leaned closer to Felix's face, raised his eyebrows, and waited.

Felix spat in his face and kicked the ground.

Bryce pressed harder.

Felix pointed his face downriver. "She ran that way!"

Amos leaned in closer and spoke through gritted teeth. "Define 'that way.'"

Felix tried to point with his other hand that had been shot while holding the gun. He began to cry. "She ran that way." He pointed downriver. "Two days ago. Little witch stabbed me in the leg and took off."

Amos looked downriver, then at his dad. Mr. Carter rubbed the sweater against the dogs' faces and pointed them that direction.

Amos looked to one of his men, then pointed at Felix and Antonio. "Handle this." Without hesitation, he ran into the darkness, followed by his team of men and their lights.

Bryce stood up, eyed the river, stepped in, and began swimming—upstream.

I watched Amos disappear, turned toward Bryce's wake in the water, and dove in. We swam against the current a couple of hundred yards until we came to a sandy bank.

Bryce climbed out by the roots of a pine tree that were exposed because of erosion. I extended my hand, and he lifted me up. He smelled the air and spoke without looking at me. "I don't like it when men lie to me."

He walked along the edge of the water. Behind us, Badger's bark faded into the night, and I followed the dark frame in front of me. Bryce studied the waterline, following God only knew what. We weaved for a mile through the brush until we came to a huge canopy of trees that must have been at least two hundred years old. If there was a heart to the Salk, we'd just found it. The ground was soft with moss and smelled of mint.

Bryce turned hard right, away from the water. He smelled the air repeatedly, weaving among the trees. We circled a huge oak tree, the top of which had been twisted off in a tornado, and he paused. He walked again in a circle around the tree, listened, then quietly thumped the side of the tree with the butt of his pistol.

From within the tree, I heard a woman's voice whimper.

I hit my knees and dug with both hands at the soft dirt mounded against the tree. Bryce dug too. We cleared roots, dirt, and sand, and soon I could hear her crying inside. When my hands broke through into the cavity inside the tree, she began kicking at me.

"Amanda! It's me. It's Dylan."

She kicked harder, screaming frantically.

I climbed through the hole while she backed up against the far side of the trunk. She was looking at me, but she had yet to see me. The inside of the tree was hollowed out and as big around as the interior space of our van—maybe five feet across. Moonlight shone directly above and threw a shadow on the ground.

"Amanda, honey." I crawled closer. "It's just me."

Despite the visible rounding of her stomach, she had tucked herself into a ball and shook her head. I sat up alongside her and gently took her hand. "Amanda, it's me, Dylan."

She blinked, looked at me, and could not speak. Her face was swollen from ten thousand mosquito bites, and one eye was shut, but she was breathing. I reached out, and she took my hands.

I carried her through the trees to the river, while Bryce followed. It was dark, the ground was uneven, and she was pregnant, but for some reason none of that really mattered. We reached the bank, and I set her gently down in the water. She drank like a man in the desert.

Bryce unholstered his .45 and pointed it into the air. Just before he squeezed the trigger, I held up a hand, and he waited. I wrapped my arms around Amanda's shoulders, pressed her head to my chest, and covered her other ear with my hand. She clutched me tightly.

I nodded, and Bryce fired three times; his shots were answered immediately by two shots downriver. Bryce fired three more, and I watched as the brass shell casings arced out across the river and disappeared into the water.

Ten minutes later I heard Amos screaming in the distance, "Amanda! Amanda!"

Amanda looked up, her hands shaking. "Take me to my husband, please."

I picked her up, and we walked along the bank through the shallow water. A hundred yards down the river, Badger and Gus emerged from the trees, followed quickly by Amos. He ran into the water, reached me, and looped his arms under mine.

Amanda let go of my neck, wrapped her arms around his, and said, "I want to go home now."

He heard her speak, and the cries of a man in anguish exited his chest. I knew what they sounded like because I'd heard them before. Amos fell to his knees, the water lapping up around his waist, and held Amanda. Finally he placed his hands on her tummy and whispered, "The baby?"

Amanda tried to smile. "Playing soccer right now."

Amos lifted her off the sandy bank and sloshed toward the trees, the sound of feet, and the sight of lights. When I turned around, Bryce was gone.

AT 3:00 A.M. MAGGIE AND I DROVE HOME. SHE HAD BABY-sat L.D. for the better part of three days. As we drove, a smell that I couldn't place filled the car. I wrinkled my nose and was sniffing the air like Bryce when Maggie noticed. She held her hand to my nose. "It's Desitin."

I nodded. A few minutes passed while I tried to figure out what that was. The look on my face betrayed me.

Maggie placed her heels on the dashboard and leaned back. "It's a cream for diaper rash."

"Oh." The adoption committee can say what they want, but my wife will make a great mom one day.

Emotionally we were about as strung out as two people could get. Physically we weren't much better. The events of the night, and of the last six weeks, had taken their toll. I knew that I was breathing and that sleep was only moments away. All I wanted to do, all we wanted to do, was lay our heads on a pillow, close our eyes, and wake up next week. We'd worry about tomorrow, tomorrow.

I parked, cut the ignition, and opened the door. Blue hopped out and began sniffing around the house. Maggie and I were inside the barn when a light in the kitchen caught my eye. I tried to ignore it, but I heard Papa whispering over my shoulder, *"Money doesn't grow on trees."* I turned to Maggie. "I'll be up in a minute."

I whistled for Blue, but he had disappeared. Probably down by the river or running down a corn row. I climbed up the porch steps, pushed open the door, and walked through the kitchen to the hall to flick off the light. That's when I saw the blood. Three spots of fresh blood led from the kitchen into the den.

"Blue?" I waited, followed the trail, and saw several more spots. Darker red. I called again, "Blue?"

The only noise was the sound of Maggie tossing corn out of a pail and into Pinky's stall. I turned the corner into the den, and there lay Blue. His eyes were half-open, and I couldn't tell if he was breathing. I knelt and reached out, but a huge hand flashed out of the darkness, grabbed me by the throat, and choked off any thought of screaming or breathing. The hand lifted me off my toes, pulled me toward a tormented face, and threw me into the fireplace, where my head hit soundly on the brick hearth.

The room spun. I heard a laugh and the muffled thud of someone kicking Blue's body. The sound told my ears what my heart already knew.

I pulled myself onto my hands and knees, felt a boot in my rib cage, then something hard came down over my head and everything went black. Somewhere between awake and not, I heard heavy footsteps fading down the hall and heard the screen door squeak. I stumbled to my feet, fell, and pulled myself up on the sofa as the blood blurred my vision. A few seconds later I heard the gunshot.

I pulled myself down the hallway, trying to get up but unable to steady my knees. The pressure in my head was growing, my eyes were blurry, and the sides of my vision were narrowing, like a tunnel. The floor felt as if it were moving, like the first step onto an escalator. I reached the kitchen, then the screen door, and finally I rolled down the porch steps, spilling blood all around me. I got to one knee, where the ground felt like a spinning merry-go-round, tried to yell for Maggie but muttered something inaudible instead. I fell again, then elbowed my way past the van.

Maggie stood in the barn doorway, holding Papa's Model 12 and pointing it in the face of Whittaker, who lay unmoving on the ground. She wasn't trembling, but her forehead was wrinkled, her finger was wrapped around the trigger, and her knuckles were white. It struck me that the barrel wasn't smoking. I steadied myself on one knee and saw a flash of gunmetal out of the corner of my left eye. I jerked, the blood spraying off my face, just in time to see Bryce stride out of the cornfield. He was carrying his rifle, and a thin line of smoke was trailing out of the barrel.

Pinky started kicking her stall, snorting and squealing.

Barefooted, Bryce approached slowly, his toes digging into the mud like fingers. He reached across Whittaker's body and gently placed his hand on the Model 12's barrel. He lifted it, and Maggie's eyes followed. When they made eye contact, Bryce hesitated, then shook his head. Maggie looked down, then at me, and finally let go. When she did, the darkness returned.

THE HEADACHE WOKE ME. I OPENED MY EYES, A WAVE OF nausea hit, and I arched over the side of the bed where two hands sat holding a bucket. I must have been doing this awhile, because I opened my mouth and nothing came. The sheets were white, the bed was hard, the air was smoke-blowing cold, and my left eye was completely swollen shut. I studied the room and knew that while it felt familiar, it wasn't mine.

Maggie set down the bucket, touched my arm, and kissed me. She looked three days past tired. Somewhere out of the left side of my bed, Amos came into view. Farther down, I recognized Pastor John. Somebody else I couldn't place, dressed in white, stood at the foot of my bed. I leaned back, braced my hand on the bed, and tried to stop the world from spinning. Somebody spoke, but the words just ricocheted around my head, eventually singing off into nowhere. Maggie said something about not going anywhere, but I felt as if I were breathing the air atop Everest and couldn't respond.

Sometime later I cracked my eyes slightly, looking through the psychedelic crisscross of my eyelashes. Daylight was coming in over my shoulder, my feet were cold, and I smelled Maggie's perfume, Eternity, wafting through the air, mixed with the scent of Pine Sol. My head felt thick, but my left eye was letting in some light, which meant progress.

I felt a hand on my left arm, tracing the lines of my scar. I turned slowly and saw Maggie looking back at me. She waited. All I could muster was a whisper. "I'm hungry."

She smiled, and her face flooded with tears. "What do you feel like?"

"Eggs. Toast. Grits. Some bacon. Biscuits. Maybe a few pancakes. Some—"

She kissed me above my eye, her tears wetting my face, then walked out the door. I heard someone speaking over the intercom outside the door and felt the blood pressure cuff inflate on my right arm.

A few minutes later Maggie returned, her running shoes squeaking on the waxed floor. She slid the rolling table over my lap and set down a tray. The eggs were steaming, had been scrambled with some sort of cheese, and tasted better than anything I'd ever eaten in my life. I tried to sit up, but the pain in my rib cage changed my mind. Maggie held a straw to my mouth, and I sipped orange juice, thick with pulp, which tasted almost as good as the eggs. I ate slowly—eggs, then a piece of bacon, a biscuit with butter and honey, two helpings of grits, more bacon, all the orange juice.

My stomach full, I sat back, breathed, and closed my eyes. "I could get used to this."

Maggie leaned in close, her breath brushing my face. She was smiling and crying at the same time. "Not me. I don't know how you did it. I'm about to lose my mind in this place."

I pulled back the covers, exposing my flowered gown, patted the bed, and lifted my arm. Maggie lay down beside me, gently laying her head on my shoulder.

I was dozing off again when the thought hit me. "How's Amanda?"

Maggie was almost asleep. "She went home two days ago."

The phrase ricocheted around my head and finally took root somewhere in my understanding. "Two days? How long have I been here?"

"Five days."

I thought about her sitting here at my bedside for five days. That meant that between Amanda's being taken and my time here, Maggie couldn't have really slept in almost a week. I replayed the events, those I could remember, in my head.

"Blue?" I asked.

Maggie took a deep breath, one of those that told me she'd not been looking forward to answering that question. She closed her eyes and shook her head.

chapter thirty-eight

THEY RELEASED ME FROM THE HOSPITAL A WEEK after Whittaker tried to beat my head in with the fire poker. He'd been moved to a hospital that specialized in spinal injuries, but even if he ever made it out of prison, which we doubted, he'd never walk again.

The doctor said my concussion was about as bad as it gets while still being considered a concussion. Given the fact that they couldn't wake me up, they were worried about the swelling causing permanent damage. Maggie said that when Amos heard that, he shook his head and kept telling them I was tough and I'd pull through. But that was little comfort, because every time I woke up, I promptly vomited and my eyes rolled back in my head. They didn't know about my ribs until day four in the hospital, when Maggie noticed the bruise while bathing me.

In the late afternoon, we left the hospital and drove by the vet to pick up Blue's body. I cradled the cardboard box that held my buddy and knew that Blue deserved better. As we drove out of town, I turned to Maggie. "I want to stop at the nursery."

When I told Merle what I was looking for, he nodded and helped me pick three young good ones. We loaded them into the van and headed home.

Near our son's grave I dug another hole, laid Blue's box in the ground, and tried to say something, but the words wouldn't come. Maggie stepped up alongside me and hooked her arm inside mine, and I felt a part of my heart crack off and float away downriver.

She wiped her tears and whispered over the hole in the ground, "Blue, thank you for taking care of Dylan when I couldn't."

I knelt, rubbed his cold muzzle one last time, and clenched my teeth so tightly I thought they'd crack. I closed the top of the box, shoveled the dirt down on top of him, and then stood there leaning on the handle. But something felt wrong. Really wrong.

I dropped to my knees, pawed away the dirt, and opened the lid of the box. "Hey, pal—since you'll get there before me, take care of my kids. All three of them. They'll need a buddy to run with." My tears fell into the hole, landed on his shoulder, and trickled down the side to his heart. I touched his muzzle one final time. "You're the best."

I closed the box again and covered the hole. The pain hurt. It hurt deep down where my soul lives. I walked to the van, pulled out the three weeping willow saplings, and began digging the holes down by the river. They were young, maybe three feet tall, but if I planted them closely enough, they'd sink their roots into the riverbank and in years to come shade both my son and my dog.

Maggie helped me pull back the sandy earth, set the root bolls in, and then cover them back up. We used the plastic pots to pour water over the roots. When I stood back, the sight satisfied me. The three young trees stood some ten feet apart and, when mature, would lean over the river, allowing their long limbs to dip in and drag along the tops like floating fishing lines or maybe a woman's hair when she washed it in the sink.

I think the sight comforted Maggie, too, because she stood alongside me, sweat rolling off her temples, the veins in her biceps throbbing beneath the skin. Her shoulders fell, relaxed, and her face showed signs of having come to terms with what is our life.

We climbed into the loft, turned the AC on "snow," and pulled the curtains across the single window. If there was any type of normalcy to our lives, I lay half-awake thinking we were pretty close to it.

THE NEXT DAY, MAGGIE SLEPT PAST LUNCH. SOMETIME after two o'clock, she appeared out of the barn and started across the lawn to me on the porch, where I'd been sitting and thinking. She shaded her eyes against the sun, walked barefooted across the grass in the 99-degree heat, and sat on the porch while I scrambled some eggs. When I handed her the plate, she set it beside her and rested her head on her arms across her knees. Even under the porch, the heat was oppressive and the humidity stuck like spray paint to my skin.

Maggie tried to whisper, but the emotions that had built over the last six weeks choked off her voice. She disappeared into the kitchen and came back with the calendar from off the wall. When she sat back down on the porch, she crossed off the last few days and whispered, "I'm sorry. It's not . . . It's not coming."

The marks showed that she was somewhere between twelve and seventeen days overdue.

I tried to hold her, to hug away the pain, but some pains must be shared before they can be carried. A hot breeze rattled through the corn and brushed across my face. She pressed her chest to mine; her face was wet, and her tears slid along my cheek. Her sobs shook her entire body.

Finally I just lay down on the porch, holding her. When I did, the dam burst, and I felt her soul crying.

She looked up at me. "How can you love a woman like me?"

There was no answer to the question she had just asked. Love is not a noun; it's a verb. I walked into the house and into my writing closet. Hands trembling, I pried open the floorboard where the truth lay wrapped in a plastic grocery bag.

I walked back out onto the porch. "Maggs, I lied to you. This is the story I could not tell you."

The look of confusion on her face grew when I placed the manuscript in her lap.

"I wrote two stories: one for you, one I thought you could handle. The other—this one, I wrote for me—the one I needed to write."

She registered the pain in my voice.

"This is the story of a man who loves his wife. Of a man who died for a time and then lived again. Of a man who felt pain unknown for what seemed like a thousand lifetimes and then joy untold. Maggs, it's the story of us. It's everything I've wanted to tell you but didn't know how for fear of letting you know how far down I fell."

She held the pages, then sat up and handed them back. Her voice cracked, her fear apparent, as she said, "Read to me."

"Honey, I—"

"Shhh . . . Read."

We took the phone off the hook and spent the day on the front porch. Maggie lay on the swing, swaying, while I sat on the steps or walked back and forth.

My story started with the pink line that announced that she was pregnant and went through my ride in the back of the truck when I held my son's casket between my legs. I took her through the painful weeks that followed, and when I read about my walk through the cornfield where I tried to peel the skin off my arm, Maggie slid off the bench, knelt, and ran her fingers along the scar.

"Why, Dylan?"

"Because I couldn't get clean."

She patted the page, and I continued. I took her to church, communion, the baptism. I brought her back to the bed she slept in, my longing, my tears, the wrinkle on her forehead, the doctors' dire predictions, and the first time she squeezed my hand. Somewhere in there, she realized that walking into her room every day was killing me. She also realized that no matter how many times I died, I'd keep walking in. Forever.

Around dusk my story brought us into Pinky's stall, to her snorting and slamming me into the fence rail. I told Maggie how I jumped into the truck and pegged the accelerator till it leveled out somewhere over a hundred, and then tripped up the stairs where a mass of people were standing outside her hospital room. We reached the part where I walked into her room, covered in pig smear, and I set the book down. I didn't need to read anymore. I knew that story by heart.

"When I walked into your room and saw those beautiful

brown eyes looking at me, I didn't know who to be; I didn't know who we were. I needed you to tell me."

Maggie slid off the swing and lay down beside me on the porch. We lay on the wooden boards, both out of tears, while the manuscript surrounded us like a blanket. Her chest rose and fell, and her breathing told me that the healing had started. She placed a hand across my chest, hooked one leg around mine, and dug her head into my shoulder.

chapter thirty-nine

BY SUNDAY AFTERNOON, WE WERE BOTH DREADING
Monday morning. We had slept through church, eaten a late
lunch, and spoken hardly a word throughout the day. We had
a pretty good idea what they were going to tell us. Talking
about it wouldn't make it any better.

A vehicle turned into the drive, crunching gravel, so we
stepped off the porch and craned our necks around the corner. In front of me was what might have been one of the most
beautiful things I'd ever seen—next to my wife's open eyes. A
1972 Chevrolet C-10 pickup, the spitting image of my first truck,
except this one had been restored to its original condition.

Bryce sat behind the wheel. The truck's paint matched his
hair—classic orange—and it shone like the sun. The engine
sounded like a dream, and if you listened closely, you could

hear the lope of the cam in the big block. That's engine-talk for "It sounded wonderful."

Bryce stepped out, pulled a rag out of his pocket, and started shining the hood. He was wearing shorts—or cutoff BDUs—a T-shirt, boots, and his shoulder holster. Absent the pistol, he looked rather normal.

The truck bed had been sprayed with a padded black liner, all the metal trim had been dipped and re-chromed, the windows looked like new glass, the tires were oversized Michelins. Bryce popped the hood. Somebody had put his tender loving touch under the hood as well as everywhere else. Most of the engine had been chromed, the tubes were made of a shiny metal material, the spark plug wires matched the truck, and there wasn't a speck of dirt or grease anywhere to be found.

Bryce was really beaming. Because he's not one to start conversations, I walked up alongside him and was about to open my mouth when he walked back to the driver's side, pulled the keys from the ignition, and placed them in my hand. I heard Maggie suck in a breath of air as if it would be her last on earth.

He held the keys there for a minute while his mouth and mind searched to find each other, then connect. He nodded and said, "I always did like this truck."

I looked at the truck again, and my eyes grew as round as half-dollars. "That's my old truck?"

Bryce nodded and wiped his hands with the rag. "What time is it?"

I pulled Papa's watch and said, "Almost seven."

He eyed the sky, tilted his head, and said, "Movie starts in about thirty minutes. We'd better get going."

Maggie looked at me. "What movie?"

Bryce looked at us as if we should know. "*The* movie." His eyes twinkled, and he tried to conceal his smile. He had really pulled out all the stops, and even though I had no idea what movie he was talking about, if it meant I got to drive my truck to his place, I'd have watched just about anything.

Maggie ran inside to grab her bag and a couple of blankets, then threw everything into the back of the truck and slid across the seat. Bryce sat in the passenger seat and clicked the door shut, and both waited on me. I slid onto the driver's seat, pulled the door shut, and turned the key.

When I get to heaven, I hope God lets me drive a truck like that.

I dropped the gearshift into drive, and we idled around the back of the house, down the drive, and out onto the hard road. At sixty miles an hour, I almost started crying.

We pulled into the drive-in, where Bryce hopped out and ran into the projector house. I heard him shuffling pans in what used to be the concession stand, and pretty soon I smelled popcorn. I parked the truck in the middle of the lot in front of the biggest screen, next to one of the hundreds of iron poles topped with microphones. I let down the tailgate and spread Maggie's blanket across the back.

Bryce soon appeared carrying three large bowls of popcorn and a six-pack of Old Milwaukee. Then he returned to the projector house and started flipping switches.

I looked at Maggie and said, "Do you have any idea what movie we're about to watch?"

Maggie put her hands on her hips and looked at me over one shoulder. "Why, Rhett Butler—"

"You've got to be kidding. Please don't tell me." I looked at the screen as the first of the credits began rolling.

Maggie flipped a piece of popcorn at me and said, "Yup."

I scanned the property and saw that Bryce had made a few more changes. To our right, beyond the film house, he had laid out a long-range target with eight rifle targets some eight hundred yards away. Like a golf range, every hundred yards was marked with a large white sign. I pointed and asked, "You doing some shooting?"

Bryce nodded. "When your buddy saw my trophy, he asked me to teach his team some of what I know." He looked at me, and his eyes grew quizzical. "You think that's okay?"

It was the first time Bryce had ever asked me a question that required us to swim below the surface.

I studied the target, then Bryce's face. "Yes, I do."

I thought about what he said. In the years that I'd known him, Bryce had never shown me a trophy of any sort whatsoever. "What trophy was that?"

He pointed to a glass case just above the old concession stand. Inside was a four-foot silver trophy polished to a reflective shine. Evidently it'd been there for years, and I'd walked by it a dozen times, but I'd never seen it. "What's it for?"

"The Wimbledon Cup. 1970."

"You played tennis?"

Bryce shook his head. "It's given to the winner of the Marine sniper competition."

"How many other marines did you beat out?"

Bryce considered that. "All of them, I guess."

"How far away was the target?"

Bryce looked downrange, his eyes coming to rest beyond the farthest target. "Thousand yards."

I started putting the pieces together. I thought about Antonio, Felix, Whittaker. "Bryce?"

"Yes."

"Were you *trying* to hit Antonio in the hand?"

He nodded.

"And were you *trying* to hit Whittaker in the spine?"

Bryce looked at Maggie, then at me. He nodded.

"Why?"

Bryce pulled a pack of gum from his pants, popped all twelve pieces into his mouth, and walked toward the film house.

FOUR HOURS LATER, THE END OF THE TAPE STARTED FLIP-ping in the projector house and woke me. I looked up and saw Bryce crashed out alongside me, sleeping as quietly as a church mouse. On my other side was Maggie, who'd eaten almost all of our popcorn and was now sniffling and drying her eyes.

I stretched and yawned. "Wow, I just love that movie."

She elbowed me and dumped the rest of her popcorn in my lap.

"Come on," I said, hopping out and then helping her down out of the truck. "Big day tomorrow."

Bryce lifted an eyebrow. "What about tomorrow?"

I brushed him off. "We've just got a meeting with the, um, the folks down at the adoption agency."

Bryce's eyes narrowed. He pulled a fresh pack of gum from his leg cargo pocket and started popping all twelve pieces into his mouth. "'Bout what?"

"Well, it's the appeal board."

The smell of wintergreen was overwhelming. Bryce moved the mass to the other side of his mouth. "What're you appealing?"

"Their decision." I looked at Maggie. I didn't want to make it any harder on her.

She looked at Bryce. "They rejected our application."

Bryce looked all of a sudden angry. He chewed harder, and it looked as if his lips and cheeks were pulling his face in two different directions.

I shrugged, thinking more about Maggie than Bryce. "It

doesn't mean we can't go to other agencies, but we'll have to disclose that they refused us."

Bryce scratched his head and looked confused. "Oh." Without so much as a good night, he stood up, disappeared into his trailer, and started banging around inside.

We cleaned up, cut the lights in the projector house, and hollered good night across the parking lot. If he heard us, he made no response.

chapter forty

WANTING TO PUT OUR BEST FOOT FORWARD, MAGGIE asked me to wear a coat and tie. I did, but I couldn't hold a candle to my wife. I descended the stairs out of the loft and found her standing in the middle of the barn, where the sunlight had broken through the slits in the walls and lit her from calf to halo. She stood heel to arch, hands in white gloves. I'd missed a belt loop and cut my face shaving, and my tie was crooked and too short. She was the canvas on which God had painted all the wonder and beauty of summer. I stood openmouthed. She touched my chin, closing my mouth, and smirked. "Well, say something."

I gulped. "Will you marry me?"

She straightened my tie and peeled the toilet paper off my cheek. "That'll do."

It'd been nearly a month and a half since the white flower of the cotton plant had bloomed, turned pink, faded into red, then grew deep purple and fell to the earth below. By rough calculation, time was drawing near, but how near was anybody's guess. While some farmers have attempted to make farming a predictable science, it is not. Never will be. You can beg, cuss, dance, even manipulate conditions, but she will grow, blossom, and produce only when she's ready. Nothing short of the hand of God can change that.

Evidently God thought it was time.

We walked out of the barn and were met by a hallelujah chorus of white. As if sprayed from heaven, the fields had exploded into a seamless sea of fluffy white. Hundreds of thousands of cottony white hands rose up out of the earth and reaching to heaven blanketed the landscape with texture, tenderness, and promise.

We eyed the cotton, Maggie's dress flapping gently in the warm breeze. She stepped into the field, snapped off a fist-sized boll like a rose, and raised it to her nose.

Indomitable.

I held out my elbow, she slipped her hand inside, and we drove the back roads to Charleston.

ALTHOUGH WE ARRIVED EARLY, MR. SAWYER AND MS. Tungston were waiting on us. Kayla, the receptionist, led us into the conference room, where Mr. Sawyer pointed us to our seats and then rested his hand on his notebook, which had grown thicker. He tapped the vinyl cover. "We've received several letters in support of you. Many of them quite complimentary."

I nodded. "Yes, sir. Like your letter suggested, we asked a few of our friends."

Maggie sat listening, watching the proceedings, but I could tell she didn't like being under the microscope.

He was opening his mouth to speak again when the door behind us opened, and John Caglestock walked in. He was carrying a tape recorder under one arm and several folders under another.

Mr. Sawyer stood up. "Excuse me, sir, but these proceedings are closed."

John nodded and set his things down on a side table. He straightened his bow tie and extended his hand. "I'm John Caglestock. And that's part of the problem."

Maggie smirked.

John spoke softly to us. "Hi, you two, hope you don't mind." He addressed the committee. "Dylan called me a couple of weeks ago and asked me to write a letter in support of them. I said I would, only to find out that I could not. I'm good with numbers, not letters, and what I have to say, well, I can't make it fit in a letter."

Mr. Sawyer sat back down and waved his hand. "While unprecedented, please continue."

"I manage an investment firm. I met Dr. Styles here when our best client marched him into my office and told me that I was to do whatever he said. Needless to say, I wasn't too happy to have met him." John paced the room and looked at me. "I had a few questions. Like, just what did a farmer from the sticks know about investments and managing money? But when your best client, who's worth"—John looked at the ceiling and calculated in his head—"somewhere north of three hundred million dollars, speaks, you do what he says."

"You mean to tell me that Dr. Styles is a member at your firm helping to manage that amount of money?"

John waved his hand. "Not technically."

"You're not making much sense," said Sawyer.

John nodded. "Think I'm bad? You ought to meet my client. Let me explain: my client trusted Dylan, placed faith in his common sense. He instructed me to run every decision by him. In a sense, he tied my hands, and I could not move a penny without first consulting the man in cowboy boots at the table here."

John continued pacing. "I have an MBA from Harvard Business and a Ph.D. from Stanford, but I quickly learned that Dr. Styles knows a good bit more than his cowboy boots and farmer's tan suggest. I wasn't the only one who studied in school. Nor was I the only one worth listening to." He looked at me. "I've learned a lot from him. And I and my client have made a lot of money as a result. At last count, Dr. Styles has helped make my client somewhere around a hundred million dollars."

Maggie gulped. "You never told me that," she whispered.

Sawyer tapped the notebook beneath his elbow. "Dr. Styles, why did you elect not to include this? Obviously its omission was purposeful on your part."

I shrugged. "Well, sir, I'm not officially an employee for either John or Br—his client."

"Then just how do you get paid?"

"I don't."

"You mean to tell me that you helped a man increase his portfolio by some 30-plus percent over—"

He looked at John, who interjected, "Five years."

"Five years, and you've never been paid?"

I nodded. "Yes, sir."

Sawyer paused and looked at Ms. Tungston, then back at us. "Why?"

"Well, sir, " I said with a shrug, "I never figured it any other way."

Sawyer sipped from the mug in front of him and considered.

John plugged in his tape recorder and said, "I wonder if you'd allow me about two more minutes."

"Please."

"When this process began several months ago, Dylan called me, and this is a recording of our conversation."

Sawyer broke in. "Did you tell Dr. Styles that you were recording him?"

John shook his head. "Not directly, but if you call our 1-800 number, the answering voice tells you that all calls are recorded for quality assurance." John paused. "And to keep us out of trouble with our auditors."

Maggie grabbed my hand as John pushed *play*. We all listened as John offered me a one-day employment opportunity and I declined. When the conversation concluded, Caglestock clicked off the machine and rolled the cord around it.

Sawyer looked at me. "Dr. Styles, I don't understand. Why didn't you accept the offer?"

"I couldn't."

"Why not?"

"Because, sir." I looked at Maggie, at John, and back at Sawyer. "I gave my word."

Sawyer whispered with Ms. Tungston briefly, then said, "Thank you, Mr. Caglestock, for your input. You have confirmed that Dr. Styles is a principled man. But you haven't offered insight into the character of Mrs. Styles."

Maggie twitched uncomfortably.

A Scottish brogue barked behind us, "I can."

I turned and saw Bryce, clothed in all his military-dress glory, standing at ease in the rear of the room. Evidently he'd been there awhile. His chest was gleaming with medals, his saber clanked at his waist, his beret tilted down over his left eye, his boots were glistening, and his white dress shirt was starched and creased. Last of all, his kilt hung to his knees.

He approached the table, clicked his heels together, and quickly placed his beret under his left arm. Tied with twine around his neck, carried almost like a bugle, hung the worn rifle scope. He nodded. "Good morning to you."

Sawyer and Tungston sat back, eyeing the growing spectacle in front of them.

"Sir, my name is Bryce Kai McGregor. I understand the point of this hearing is to determine whether or not these people will make good parents."

Sawyer crossed his arms and said, "Yes, but for their sake, we don't usually make these hearings public." He pointed at us. "For *their* sake."

Bryce pointed at Caglestock, who was leaning against the desk and smiling. "I'm the client. And I'm here for two reasons."

Sawyer's face told me that a lightbulb had just clicked on.

Bryce cut to the chase. "Is money the issue here?"

Ms. Tungston raised a finger, but Sawyer spoke first. "No, not really. Dr. and Mrs. Styles have satisfied this committee in that regard."

"Then what is?"

Ms. Tungston finally got a word in edgewise. "Frankly, Mr. McGregor, the issue concerning this committee is Mrs. Styles and her medical and mental history over the last twenty-four months."

I turned to Maggie and watched her bite her lip as she uncrossed and then recrossed her legs.

Bryce raised an eyebrow and scratched his head. "Are you talking about that lady right there?"

Tungston nodded.

Bryce walked over and put his hand on Maggie's shoulder. "This one?"

Maggie patted his hand and then folded her own in her lap.

Bryce walked behind us. "You two feel that she—Maggie— is not capable of loving someone, like a child?"

Tungston didn't respond. If she intended to speak, Bryce didn't give her much time.

"Ma'am, I am one of the most unlovable people I know. I have more issues than you've ever thought about. I've seen more death, more hatred, more acts of evil than any one hundred people put together, and I've committed most of them. I know issues."

Maggie grasped my hand. She had tucked a tissue in the palm of her right glove.

"I also know love and what it looks like, how it feels, and I know it when it's freely given." Bryce stood behind Maggie. "There was a time in my life when I knew what love looked like and how it felt. Then there was a long period of time when I forgot I ever knew it. When all the evil stuff covered up the good. When even the smell of it escaped me.

"Then I met these two people, and they reminded me. Both in how they love each other and in how they have loved me. I will stake my life, these medals hanging on my chest, and my honor that the finest two people I've ever met in this life are sitting in these two chairs right here.

"I watched my son, my wife, and our unborn daughter die in another country at the hands of very angry people. I held my son in my arms as he took his last breath, so I know loss. Please . . ." Bryce choked. "Please don't give that to these two people here. Give it to me, but not them." A single tear fell off Bryce's face and splattered across the mirror toe of his boot.

Ms. Tungston opened her mouth to speak, but Bryce zeroed in on her and approached the table. "When an angel flies too close to the ground and clips her wings, she needs time to heal. But this one—" Bryce pointed at Maggie. "She'll fly again."

Maggie's bottom lip was quivering, but her eyes were sparkling.

Bryce brushed his stomach against the table, used both hands to place his beret on his head, nodded at the committee, and turned to leave.

Mr. Sawyer sat up and spoke softly. "Mr. McGregor?"

Bryce turned.

"You said there were two reasons?"

Bryce stopped, breathed deeply—his chest round as a barrel and his stomach flat—and looked at me. "As my friend John Wayne once said, 'Words are what men live by.' And he kept his."

Without warning, Bryce clapped his heels to attention and saluted me. Standing wrought-iron straight, his hand shading the eye that had puddled with tears, Bryce blinked, and the corners of both eyes broke loose at once, sending long trickles down the sides of his freckled nose. After a moment he slowly released his salute, straightened his saber, and then lifted the twine around his neck that held the rifle scope. He eyed it several seconds, laid it on the desk in front of me, and strode out the back door.

I watched him leave, amazed at the complexity that was and is Bryce. Maggie patted my leg and kissed my shoulder. She was sniffling, so I reached in my pocket for my handkerchief, but a hand appeared over my right shoulder and beat me to it. I turned and found Amos, Amanda, and Pastor John sitting quietly behind us.

Caglestock collected his things, nodded at me, and then

turned toward Mr. Sawyer. "Thank you again for your time and for allowing me a few minutes."

Tungston leaned in toward Sawyer and attempted to whisper something, but he waved her off.

"Sometimes we fail to get a complete picture. This may be the case here today. The committee—we had decided prior to your coming in here that we would not approve your application."

Maggie let out a deep breath, and her shoulders dropped slightly.

"But I wonder if we don't have an alternative." Sawyer pointed over our shoulders and said, "Sir, are you Pastor John Lovett?"

Pastor John, wearing a black suit and his clerical collar, nodded. "I am."

"In his letter here, Pastor Lovett offers to provide counseling. Mrs. Styles, would you agree to this over the next several months, and upon completion allow us to return here and reconsider this?" Sawyer looked at Tungston, then back at Maggs. "At such time, I think we'd look more favorably upon your application."

Maggie looked at Mr. Sawyer. "Yes, sir, I would."

He set his pen down on top of his notebook. "Let's put a hold on this for six months, at which time I'll confer with Pastor Lovett. Does that suit you?"

We nodded, and I spoke. "Yes, sir."

THE FIVE OF US WALKED OUT INTO THE BRILLIANT SUNSHINE, where Amos slid on his sunglasses and smiled at me.

Amanda looped her arm inside his and said, "He's such a baby. Don't let the biceps fool you." She put her hand on her stomach. "How's everybody feel about some lunch? My baby needs some of Ira's biscuits."

We drove a glorious hour in my new-old truck back to Walterboro. Amos was so impressed that once we hit the city limits, he flashed his lights and gave us an escort. Having noticed the commotion, along with most of the rest of town, Ira met us at the door of her café. Today she was lime green, including her lipstick, eyeliner, and the scarf holding back her bushy, long red hair. If I hadn't known her, she'd have scared me half to death.

She kissed me on the cheek. "Hey, sugar, ya'll come in here, and I'll have the food out in a minute."

About ten minutes later, she delivered plates filled with steaming eggs, biscuits, bacon, grits, and pancakes.

While we talked, I watched Maggie change like a chameleon before my eyes. The wrinkle was mostly gone, some color had returned, and if hope really does spring eternal, then a trickle was coming up through her eyes. Under the table, she hooked her heel around my leg and pulled my foot a little toward her.

We walked out into the sunlight, where Amos's dad waved to us. He was sitting on his tailgate and holding something little. Its feet were too big for its body, its ears were long and floppy, and its wrinkly body seemed to follow its nose like a slinky. It lay half-asleep and looked like a chocolate chip cookie.

We stepped off the curb, and Mr. Carter walked over to me. He extended his hands and placed the puppy in my arms. "Ten weeks old. Badger's son." He sucked through his teeth. "He's certified bluetick hound. I haven't named him. Thought I'd let you do that."

I looked down, held the puppy to my face, and felt his wet tongue lick my cheek. "I'll call him Tick."

Mr. Carter nodded and pulled a red handkerchief from his back pocket. "It's a good name."

chapter forty-one

IT WAS WEDNESDAY NIGHT, AND WE'D BEEN PAINTING the better part of three days. We'd started in the kitchen and then moved down the back hall and into our bedroom. When we got to the door of the nursery, holding a paintbrush and a roller, we looked at each other and scratched our heads. Neither one of us wanted to tackle the real issue—guest room or nursery. Amplifying our dilemma was today's date—a fact that was not lost on us.

I looked at Maggie, who was staring blankly into the room, and said, "I'm tired of painting."

She dropped her brush in the bucket. "Me too."

The sun was disappearing, the tree frogs were tuning up down at the river, the wood ducks were jetting like F-16s overhead, and daylight was almost gone. Maggie and I watched in amazement as an enormous moon, as big as Christmas, rose directly in front of us and popped its glowing head over the treetops.

We sat on the porch teaching Tick how to eat the last of Old Man McCutcheon's produce. Maggie sat on the top step, feet spread, watermelon between her knees, and her face, hands, and cutoff jeans covered in red juice. When the wind blew, the frayed edges of her shorts flittered like tiny fingers. She took a bite, chewed, leaned back, funneled her lips, and then blew like Shamu out across the front yard. Messy but effective.

The shiny seed spun like a football some fifteen feet across the yard and into the grass where about fifteen other seeds lay. In the process she'd pretty well covered the porch steps, and me—sitting downwind—in spit spray. I looked at the yard and knew in about three months we could quit stealing from McCutcheon, because we'd have watermelon growing right here at the base of the steps.

Given everything that had happened, Dr. Frank had held off starting Maggs on a low dose of oral hormone therapy. But now that life had returned to mostly normal, he'd scheduled an office visit. Tomorrow. Maggs didn't like the idea, and neither did I, but she'd been moody lately. Knowing this, and seeing its effect on me, she agreed to try it a month and see what happened.

Because eating watermelon makes me have to pee a lot, I walked inside. When I came back out, Maggie was staring out across the cotton, looking at the river, white paint caked on her forehead and red watermelon juice smeared across both corners of her mouth. Resting at her feet were two clean, folded towels. She looked at me, the river, then back at me. "You want to go swimming?"

With all the pregnancy stuff the last few weeks, I hadn't really pressured Maggie to be with me. I just figured that was not what she needed. I looked from the river back to her. "Do you mean swimming or . . . swimming?"

She smirked ever so slightly, waved her head back and forth as if she were weighing the options, and said thoughtfully, "Swimming."

I scooped Tick into my arms, and we raced barefoot through the grass—corn on one side and cotton on the other. Midway down, we spooked two deer that were feeding through the corn, and then Pinky spooked us. She was rooting along the edges of the corn rows and looked up as we passed by. Her massive jowls, caked with mud, shook like jelly rolls as her lower jaw ground the kernels of corn against the top.

We reached the river, and I climbed the gently sloping bluff and Peter Panned off into the moonlight while the Milky Way showered down about me. The black water covered me, and the gentle current pulled against me. Few things in life were sweeter. I surfaced, swam toward the bank, and dug my toes into the sandy river bottom.

Maggie stood on the bank, pulling her tank top over her shoulders. She slipped off her jeans, waded in, and wrapped herself around me, her short hair sticking up and out. Chill bumps ran up and down her arms, but she pressed her warm chest to mine. The river moved around us, carrying away old memories and filling the empty places left behind.

Because that's what rivers do: they do life.

From downriver, the sound approached slowly. It filtered up through the trees, then across and around us like fireflies dancing on the daylight. Moments later, Bryce appeared. Butt-naked but for the boots, he stood, his face beet-red, blowing through the pipes. He stood, his soul spilling out through his fingers and the tips of the pipes. He played for several minutes. If I'd ever worried about Bryce, and I had, my fears disappeared with those fading notes. Moments later, having said what he came to say, he stepped into the water and faded away downriver, carrying his song with him.

When he had disappeared, Maggie nodded toward the bank and tugged on my arm. Fingers locked, we waded through the current and climbed up the bank. While the moon lit the water droplets cascading down her back, I handed her a towel and spread the blanket across the sand. She toweled off, knelt beside me, and ran her fingers through my hair.

She was just about to kiss me when something out of the corner of her eye grabbed her attention. She tilted her head and stared. Leaning closer, she squinted and held the towel up to the moonlight, and that's when the wrinkle reappeared between her eyes.

Seeing the change, my voice cracked. "Are you okay?" Maybe I had pressured her too soon. Maybe something reminded her of something she wanted to forget.

Without a word, she jumped up, grabbed her clothes, and started a fast jog back to the house. By the time I got into my jeans, she was out of sight. I slipped on my shirt, picked up Tick, and walked back to the house, kicking the dirt and wondering where I had just messed up.

I reached the barn and climbed the steps into the loft, where the light in the bathroom was shining through the crack at the floor. I laid Tick on the bed and tapped lightly. "Maggs?"

"Yes."

"You okay?"

She didn't answer, so I took a cold shower, climbed into bed, and counted to a million. Maggie finally stepped out of the bathroom, wearing sweats, and quickly got in bed. Her feet were cold, and she pulled the covers up around her shoulders. She scooted over next to me and placed her arm around my stomach.

I didn't know much, but I did know that if I opened my mouth, I'd only get in trouble, so I started doing my times tables, and when I got tired of that, I started trying to think of the largest prime number I could find.

Finally Maggie whispered, "I don't really want to go see Dr. Frank tomorrow."

He had told me she'd be moody without the hormones and would probably protest right up to our appointment.

"Okay." I figured we could talk about it tomorrow when she had gotten over whatever was bugging her.

A few minutes passed, then she tapped me on the shoulder.

I was getting a bit exasperated. "Honey. What?"

Tick heard my change in tone and dug his muzzle under a fold in the sheet.

She laid her head on my chest and placed her palm flat across my heart as Tick climbed up our legs and plopped himself in a cavity created by the sheets and shapes of our bodies. "I don't want to go because I don't need to."

Dr. Frank had predicted that too. She'd argue that she didn't need any hormones, and it would take me to convince her that she did.

"Well, okay, but Dr. Frank said it might help."

She patted my chest. "No, you don't understand."

I was getting a bit angry, so I sat up straight in bed. "You're right. I don't. Why don't you—"

Maggie shoved me backward onto the pillow. She hooked her right leg over both of mine, wrapped her right arm around and under me, and then tent-pegged it into the bed.

She raised her head, the moonlight shining in her eyes and revealing the tears and the smile painted there. "I don't need them because my body is making its own."

I squinted one eye while trying to translate what she was saying.

She pulled up the covers, closed her eyes, and said, "Don't worry. I'll take you swimming again in about a week."

Tick had rolled over on his back, paws in the air. He was out cold.

LYING ON AN OLD LUMPY MATTRESS IN THE LOFT OF OUR barn, beneath all the star-filled wonder of the Milky Way, God spread his blanket over us, and when I studied it, the frayed edges and seams had been hemmed. Faint stitching meandered across the quilt like country roads on a state map. I shook my head. *What makes the broken whole? How does deep-down pain, interwoven like sinew, come untangled?*

I looked at my wife, her breathing easy, her spiky hair growing out, her fingernails scratching my chest. Then I looked at us—two chipped and cracked cups, and yet despite the fact that we were leaking like a spaghetti colander, we could still pour water. Still laugh. Still hope. Still cry. Still dream. Still take a swan dive into the moonlight where the mystery of the river would meet us, bathe us, and make us whole.

I wrapped my arm around my wife, pulled her toward me, and felt her heart pounding powerfully inside her. My drumbeat. Our rhythm. It resonated, filtered back down within me, and came to rest somewhere alongside my soul where I'm most alive, where I am me and we are us, where I know pleasure and pain, heartbreak and rage, where I hope, dream, and begin again—down where my love lives.

Brimming with relief, maybe some fear but all excitement, I pulled the blanket up around our shoulders and slid my fingers inside hers. She hooked her leg around mine like a wisteria vine spiraling up a fence post, and we slept.

acknowledgments

SUMMER 2000.

I was sitting in my office, paying bills, shaking my head at the numbers looking back at me. It was over. My pipedream had come to an end.

I had shut my door because I didn't want Christy to see me hanging my head in my hands. *Maybe I should've taken that job.* In my file cabinet next to me, hung the folder where I kept all the rejection letters. Currently, there were 85.

For eight months the letters had been returning. Slowly at first, then almost one a day, now maybe one a week. I had quit going to the mailbox months ago. Broken man.

I looked at the yellow note stuck to my computer screen that read, "126"—my reminder of the number of times that F. Scott Fitzgerald's *This Side of Paradise* had been rejected. It was little consolation.

Early in 1997, Christy and I had returned to Jacksonville. Thinking I'd continue working as a teacher, I applied everywhere from college to high school. When the phone didn't ring, my brother-in-law took mercy on me and gave me a job working at his insurance agency. Fast forward to 1999. After two years of hard work, we had taken his agency from a rather small one to a very successful one. That had everything to do with Tommy's ability to sell and, to a much lesser extent, my ability to help him put legs on his promises.

Because of this, I had caught the eye of the corporate officer of the insurance company we represented. Friday afternoon came and, with Tommy's blessing, I found myself sitting in the President's office. He was offering me a job—asking me, in short, to do on a much larger scale what I'd been doing the last few years for Tommy.

Did you ever see that scene in the movie, *The Firm,* when Tom Cruise was brought in to meet the Memphis attorneys? Remember the feeling in that room? How they laid the envelope on the table? My experience reminds me of that scene. The red carpet, the leather couch, the view out the windows stretched for miles. So did the opportunity—six-figure money, benefits, signing bonus, yearly bonus. Life on a silver platter.

There were just three problems. The first was travel and lots of it. I'd be living on planes and in hotels. The second was the job itself. I just didn't enjoy the insurance business. I needed it, still do—I'd just rather someone else sell it. The third was that little voice inside my head—and he was screaming at the top of his lungs.

Before I left the President's office, he paused and looked me in the eye. Dick Morehead had risen to the top because he worked harder than anyone else, was pretty close to brilliant, and because he was good at reading people. In that instant, he was reading my emotional pulse. He said, "Charles, life's too d—n short to not do what you love."

I nodded, "Yes sir."

He paused again, this time longer, "Charles . . . life's too d—n short to not do what you love."

I knew my decision before I left his office.

He asked for an answer by Monday, so I shook his hand, stepped into the elevator, and asked myself not what new car I was about to buy or what new white-picket-fence-neighborhood we were moving into, but how was I going to explain this to my wife.

Word spread quickly, and before I got home the phone started ringing with congratulations. "Vice President? Wow!" I found it difficult to talk with my stomach in my throat.

After a few hours at home, I'd made little progress with Christy. She was already painting our new house.

I didn't sleep much. Somewhere around three in the morning, Christy tapped me on the shoulder and whispered, "That's a lot of money." I watched the ceiling fan spin and knew it was going to be a long weekend.

My argument was simple. I could survive the travel, could work at the job and maybe even excel, but no matter what I did or how I tried to appease him, I could not quiet that little voice inside my head.

Christy's argument was also simple—take the money. Write in the morning. Late at night. Do both. Do whatever you've got to do, but take the money.

We argued most of the weekend. Not finger-pointing, shouting, or ugly stuff, but gut-wrenching, who-are-you-and-what-do-you-want-to-be-when-you-grow-up stuff. Our son, Charlie, was almost two, John T. would be here in a few months, and we had outgrown our house. The only thing I had working for me was that Christy knew my heart—she had read my novel (what is now *The Dead Don't Dance*), and she believed it was good. Maybe even good enough.

Saturday afternoon, I went for an aimless drive trying to find the words to explain to my wife and family that I really didn't want the job. That I was sorry if I'd failed them. That I was grateful for the opportunity, but I wanted to follow my heart. I knew they'd think I'd lost my mind. Especially the older generation who had lived through the 1930's. To them, this was a once-in-a-lifetime deal. My ship had just come in. All aboard.

Sunday morning came, and I found myself facedown, clinging to the railing after communion. It was the first time all weekend I could hear above the racket in my head. I don't remember what all I said, but I think it sounded something like, *Please help.* When I opened my eyes, Christy was there too.

By Sunday afternoon, we were both cooked. I sat on the couch, dreading Monday morning, nauseous from the knot in my stomach. I couldn't throw up because I hadn't eaten in three days.

I don't know what happened or how, probably never will, but Christy walked in, her big brown eyes puddling with tears. She stood at a distance, took a deep breath, and said, "We're going to do this one time. Nothing held back. If we fail . . ." She shrugged and took another deep breath. She waved her finger like a windshield wiper across the air in front of me, "But, I don't want you to turn forty, look back, and wonder *what if . . .*" She blinked and the tears fell, "I don't want to take that from you."

Those words still echo in my heart.

For the next year I worked briefly for a non-profit, then started my own Mr. Fix-it business—if you can call it that—and begun pressure washing, building docks, decks, cabinets, you name it. Whatever would put money on the table. Hitched to my truck was a trailer full of hoses and machinery—my cell phone number prominently printed across the back in billboard-sized letters. My family was not impressed. We had lasted almost a year.

Christy cracked the door of my office and walked in with a single piece of mail. I couldn't even look at it. *Please, not one more.* She laid it on the desk, kissed me, and shook her head, "You're not a reject to me." I dropped the letter in with the others and cried like a baby.

That was six years ago.

Today, I've published more than a half a million words, and this morning I received a fax showing where *Southern Living* has picked *When Crickets Cry* as their 'Read of the Month.' If you could see me as I sit now, I'm scratching my head.

When people hear this story, they often respond, "That's incredible." Or "Wow, you really stuck with it." While that does wonders for my ego, I know the truth.

Neither my talent nor perseverance got this book in your hands. I'm neither that good nor that strong. The miracle of our story is not me. It's a girl who, with a single kiss and six words, reached down beyond my fear and doubt, down where my love lives, and gave me a gift—she stood beside me and believed.

Maggie: THE SEQUEL TO THE DEAD DON'T DANCE

1. In *The Dead Don't Dance,* Maggie Styles spent four months in a coma after she and her husband Dylan lost their first son. In *Maggie,* she's awake, and her desire to have a child is as strong as ever. How does motherhood define Maggie in this novel? Do you think she is obsessed with having children, or does the novel simply show the honest feelings of many women? Have you or someone you know ever struggled with fertility? If so, how does that experience relate to Maggie's?

2. Gardening could act as a metaphor for Maggie in the novel. What does her love of plants represent at the beginning of the book? Does this change by the end of the novel?

3. Maggie and Dylan deal with grief and loss in different ways. Describe these differences. In the midst of her emotional struggles and hormonal changes, does Maggie's behavior ever cross the line, or would any woman who has experienced such loss act similarly? How does Maggie's character change over the course of the novel?

4. The deep relationship between Dylan and Maggie is the central force of the novel. When asked if Maggie could hear him while she was in the coma, Dylan says, "Of course she could. Love has its own communication. . . . It is written on our souls, scripted by the finger of God." How is this godly love displayed in the novel? Are you, or have you ever been, in a relationship of this kind?

5. Adoption seems like a good solution for Maggie and Dylan, but the adoption agency sees things differently. Why did the

agency turn them down at first? Why did they change their minds during the appeal? After reading about the couple's experience, what impression do you have about adoption? How does that impression illuminate Maggie and Dylan's situation in particular?

6. Pastor John Lovett's former life of crime involved three other men. Two of them—Anton and Felix—are covered in tattoos, which reminds Pastor John of Queequeg in *Moby Dick*. The last names of these twin brothers are never given. The third convict, James Whittaker III, is a former Hollywood pyrotechnics expert who earned the nickname Ghost in prison. What do these descriptions tell you about the men?

7. John Wayne is mentioned more than once in the novel. As kids, Amos and Dylan play cowboys and act "like John Wayne in *True Grit*." In the present time of the story, Dylan watches *The Shootist* as The Duke, who has terminal cancer in real life, plays a famed gunfighter with terminal cancer. Why is *The Shootist* particularly relevant? How does The Duke's death reflect Dylan's emotions at this point? What values does John Wayne represent, and how do those relate to the story?

8. At one point, Dylan says about Maggie: "Just because something is broken doesn't mean it's no good. Doesn't mean you throw it away. . . . I can love broken." In what ways is Maggie "broken"? When Pastor John reads from the Bible "Behold, I make all things new," why does Maggie leave the church? In what ways does the couple try to make a whole from the broken pieces? Are they successful?

9. Dylan writes two stories about what happened during Maggie's hospitalization and coma. Describe the differences between the two. Why does Dylan decide to give Maggie the "watered-down, G-rated version"? Do you agree with his decision? Why or why not?

10. When Maggie loses the twins, she isolates herself more and

more. At one point, she tells Dylan that he can't know how she feels and throws a bedside table across the room. Do you think Dylan is unsupportive of Maggie? Does he grow more or less supportive over the course of the novel? Is there any way he could have shared the stress of her experiences more fully, or can he, as a man, never really understand?

11. *Maggie* is a distinctly southern novel. In what ways does the southern setting propel this story? How does the small town of Digger and the mythical Salkehatchie act as characters in and of themselves? How do food, church, dogs, guns, clothing, and automobiles signify the south in this novel?

12. The river plays an important role in this story, as it did in *The Dead Don't Dance*. Before Maggie's coma, she and Dylan floated down the river on the raft and discovered a rare iris that can only grow in a particular spot—where the tannic swamp water meets fresh spring water. What was their journey into the heart of the swamp like? What does this location represent in the story? Why did the author choose an iris rather than some other flower?

13. What impact does the past have in this novel? Dylan's grandfather said that farmers "cut the soil and get rid of what remains of the old. . . . The past fertilizes the future." How does this relate to Maggie and Dylan's present situation? To what extent do characters in this story seem able—or unable—to break free of their past?

14. Through Bryce, the novel takes a hard look at the role of human sacrifice and the loss of life in war. As part of the Marine's elite Delta Force in the Vietnam War, he was a "one-man killing machine" who became "a highly-decorated veteran." Bryce tells Dylan about the loss of his Vietnamese wife and son during the war. What are your thoughts about Bryce's military experience? Ultimately, how do you view Bryce—as a killer, a hero, or something else?

15. *Maggie* tackles the nature of loss. In chapter twenty-nine, Dylan notices the utter emptiness in Maggie's eyes: "Something had severed. . . . When she looked at me, she was looking at the world beyond me where her dreams once lived." He then asks, "What can heal the human soul?" Have you ever experienced loss this deep? What do you think can heal the human soul? Do Maggie and Dylan ever heal?

16. Discuss the theme of forgiveness in the novel. Who forgives whom? What does Pastor John say about forgiveness in particular?

17. Children and childhood are themes in *Maggie*. What particular meaning does the novel ascribe to them? Why is it significant that a boy in Spiderman pajamas with a plastic squirt gun tells Dylan that the convicts left with a canoe?

18. Integrity—keeping your word and telling the truth—are important character traits to Dylan. How are these traits exhibited—or not exhibited—in the novel? What significance do the following words from Dylan's grandfather have in the story: "There's just one problem with pulling the wool over someone's eyes. And it surfaces whenever they take it off."

19. The novel mentions the "fight of good versus evil." What does this battle look like in the story, and what meaning does it have?

20. Dylan and Amos discuss the need to protect their wives from the former convicts, and Dylan is troubled that he cannot protect his wife from the emotional pain that "threatened to kill her." Which threat do you think affects Dylan the most, and why? What do these suggest about the differences between men and women, if anything?

21. Just as in *The Dead Don't Dance*, blood is a recurring motif in *Maggie*. Name the references to blood and discuss their relevance. The concluding reference occurs when Maggie begins her cycle. What kind of future do you envision for Maggie and Dylan? For Amos, Amanda, Little Dylan, and their coming baby?